ASSASSINATIONS THAT SHAPED THE ANCIENT WORLD

ASSASSINATIONS THAT SHAPED THE ANCIENT WORLD

PHIL CARRADICE

PEN & SWORD HISTORY

AN IMPRINT OF PEN & SWORD BOOKS LTD.
YORKSHIRE - PHILADELPHIA

First published in Great Britain in 2025 by
PEN AND SWORD HISTORY
An imprint of
Pen & Sword Books Ltd
Yorkshire – Philadelphia

Copyright © Phil Carradice, 2025

ISBN 978 1 39905 399 0

The right of Phil Carradice to be identified as Author of this work has been asserted by her in accordance with the Copyright, Designs and Patents Act 1988.

A CIP catalogue record for this book is available from the British Library.

All rights reserved. No part of this book may be reproduced, transmitted, downloaded, decompiled or reverse engineered in any form or by any means, electronic or mechanical including photocopying, recording or by any information storage and retrieval system, without permission from the Publisher in writing. No part of this book may be used or reproduced in any manner for the purpose of training artificial intelligence technologies or systems.

Typeset in Times New Roman 11/14 by
SJmagic DESIGN SERVICES, India.
Printed and bound in the UK by CPI Group (UK) Ltd.

The Publisher's authorised representative in the EU for product safety is Authorised Rep Compliance Ltd., Ground Floor, 71 Lower Baggot Street, Dublin D02 P593, Ireland.
www.arccompliance.com

For a complete list of Pen & Sword titles please contact
PEN & SWORD BOOKS LIMITED
George House, Units 12 & 13, Beevor Street, Off Pontefract Road, Barnsley, South Yorkshire, S71 1HN, England
E-mail: enquiries@pen-and-sword.co.uk
Website: www.pen-and-sword.co.uk

or

PEN AND SWORD BOOKS
1950 Lawrence Rd, Havertown, PA 19083, USA
E-mail: uspen-and-sword@casematepublishers.com
Website: www.penandswordbooks.com

Contents

Introduction	vi
Acknowledgements	ix

Chapter One	Assassination, Did It Ever Really Work?	1
Chapter Two	Ancient Egypt, Early Assassination Plots	16
Chapter Three	Assassination in Persia and the Middle East	29
Chapter Four	Far Away Places, Strange Sounding Names	41
Chapter Five	In the Shadow of Alexander the Great	52
Chapter Six	Brutality in All Things	63
Chapter Seven	A Biblical Interlude	74
Chapter Eight	Women, More Deadly Than the Male?	89
Chapter Nine	The Death of Julius Caesar	97
Chapter Ten	Early Assassinations In and Around Rome	108
Chapter Eleven	Assassinations in the Empire of Rome	119
Chapter Twelve	The Madness That Was Rome	130
Chapter Thirteen	Eastward Ho, the Byzantine Empire	145
Chapter Fourteen	The Dark Ages	155
Chapter Fifteen	Mass Assassination	168
Chapter Sixteen	A Conclusion (of sorts)	182

Notes/References	184
Bibliography	188
Index	191

Introduction

I am very conscious that this volume does not include every assassination ever planned or carried out in the ancient world. The book was never intended to be that specific.

It would have been a relatively simple task to compile long lists of rulers, high officials, politicians and other notables who fell before the assassins knife, spear or poison jar but that was not what I wanted to achieve. Such an exercise would be a list, no more, no less. Useful, no doubt, to the researcher or writer but not exactly the most interesting of books for the general reader.

Assassinations That Shaped the Ancient World was always intended to be a work of interest, something to catch the imagination and the concern of not just the historian but also the casual browser. It is meant to be read in the same way as a novel would be read and in order to achieve that I have deliberately omitted several of the ancient world assassinations, not because they are uninteresting but also because space and time are limited. You may never have heard of some of the assassinations I have included but they are, in my opinion, the most interesting as well as the most significant and far reaching from a wide range of options.

Apart from anything else, to include every assassination that ever took place in the ancient world and add descriptions and comments would require a book that is ten, twenty, thirty times the size of this one. You would be struggling to hold it, let alone read what can at times, even in the form used here, be a stultifying regurgitation of facts and figures.

What is presented here is a gathering of fascinating, even engaging, assassinations, if such a description can ever be applied to the considered death of another individual. They are presented in this book as events that brought people up sharply, made them think about their lives, always within the remit that, in one way or another, they helped shape the ancient world.

Assassination has long been a part of political manoeuvring. In *The Art of War*, one of the earliest known books on military tactics, the Chinese General Sun Tzu was clear about its value:

Introduction

> 'Raising a host of a hundred thousand men and marching them great distances entails heavy loss on the people and a drain on the resources of the State.'[1]

Assassination was much cheaper and just as effective. Justification, perhaps, but it remains true in every respect.

And yet, attempting to count the number of assassinations carried out over a period of many years, hundreds or thousands of years perhaps, has always been an act of gigantic proportions and never simple. The act of trying to count and list the number of deaths, many of which went unrecorded or were put down as suicide or accidental demise, would take a scribe or secretary an aeon to complete.

The writer Aiton Birnbaum has commented on the large numbers of assassinations in the ancient world and has made his point without overplaying his hand:

> 'It is virtually impossible to ascertain the precise number of rulers of nation states and empires in antiquity whose demise was the result of assassination, but their numbers were clearly large.'[2]

'Clearly large?' I can accept that as a fact. There are many assassinations that stand out because of their interest, their bloodiness, the style of execution, the characters involved. And they are an equally large number. So, not a list, not an academic tome. This book is meant to be read and enjoyed – as much as I enjoyed researching and writing it. At this point you might like to skip on from this Introduction and read the story. If not, there is more to declare.

The nature of this book lends itself to a basic, chronological format. Not always, however. Many of the ancient world assassinations were unique in their style and magnitude, others were made different simply by the makeup of the assassination group and their motives. In order to achieve fuller understanding and comparison, one or two of the killings are presented out of direct chronological position.

I make no apologies for doing this, in order to make such incidents as effective and entertaining as possible – the old art of the storyteller is still there, lingering in the background. Consequently some of the assassinations are presented as stand-alone chapters rather than being included in sections covering, say, the Roman Empire and other more global issues.

What that means, of course, is that in addition to expected chapters on the Egyptian, Roman, and Persian assassinations you will find here chapters on female assassins, Biblical events, mass assassinations and so on.

As I said, I make no apologies for this. As far as I am concerned it is that variety of presentation and approach that makes the topic interesting and the theories more plausible.

Acknowledgements

Grateful thanks to the people who helped, by talking or offering sources, in the writing of this book. In particular:

Thanks to poet and writer Taz Rahman for his invaluable help on the Byzantine Empire, its problems and successes, and the Muslim conquests of the seventh century.

Kath Giblin, owner of Bardic Books, for her intrepid tracking down of books and sources.

My darling Trudy, always watching at my elbow. I can't believe it's now eight years since you left us. God bless you, girl.

My son Douglas whose efforts to save 60,000 words when I threw the computer at my office window were much appreciated. It's a story worth telling – one day.

Chapter One

Assassination, Did It Ever Really Work?

Assassination. A simple word but one that is sure to cause an immediate shiver of fear, a flutter of trepidation, to run up and down the spines of many thinking people. However, that emotion or reaction is surely more to do with our own pre-conceptions, our own involuntary use of latent imagination, than it is to any form of real life experience. At least for most of us.

Regardless of how objective we may normally feel about things such as murder and mayhem in the distant past, the thought of assassination invariably changes everything. The deliberate and cold-blooded act of killing renowned figures, be they known to us or seen only from a distance, perhaps through books or films, forces its way into the forefront of our minds.

Each century since the dawn of time has been marked or marred by the assassins knife, sword or bullet. Some of those killings have been quickly forgotten, even ignored. Others like the demise of Julius Caesar or the brutal end of Emperor Caligula, the sudden and unexpected shooting of JFK in 1963 and of the Archduke Franz Ferdinand of Austria in 1914, remain fixed in human memory and in our history.

As a tool - political, social and military - assassination has haunted the regimes of many rulers and generals, all of them aware of the possibility or perhaps even the inevitability of sudden death and disaster. Assassination has been employed both on a national scale and on a local one but whether it is used against kings or presidents, gangland leaders or local rabble-rousing politicians there remains a single unifying definition behind all effective assassinations.

Many writers have attempted to define assassination but the explanation that appears to best capture the act is one that sums up the commonality of the process. According to this explanation or interpretation, the act of assassinating another person or persons is, in the main, relatively specific, forcing it to stand apart from murder for personal profit and from state-employed execution:

> '(It is) the murder of an opponent or well-known public figure, one of the oldest tools of power struggles, as well as the expression of certain psychopathic disorders. It dates back to the earliest governments and tribal structures of the world.'[1]

Assassination has little or nothing to do with the explosion of emotion which often accompanies the bar room brawl or the protest march that brings together two opposing beliefs in a clash of idealism. It is not even close to the post-pub street fights that, after closing time, bedevil our towns and cities. Equally, it has no connection with the dark back-alley knifings which are more the adjunct of gang warfare, robbery and theft than they are a planned and deliberate strike against any particular individual or group.

Assassination is invariably a considered act, something that has been thought through by the perpetrator, even if only for a few days or hours. It is rarely, if ever, a spur of the moment action when the behaviour of the victim triggers an emotion in the brain of the killer. Seizing a sudden opportunity might be spontaneous but the need and decision to proceed when opportunity presents itself has usually been already made. And, as the above quotation shows, it is an act that normally has a distinctly political purpose. Political, that is, with a small p.

It remains difficult to judge the effectiveness of any assassination, modern or ancient. Once the crime has been committed there is no way back. It is an act of such finality that no-one can really assess what might or might not have happened had the assassination not taken place. At best that is mere star gazing, at worst another example of the 'what if' school of historical analysis.

It might be stating the obvious but the act of assassination and the people who carry it out can be divided into three distinct groups.

First comes the lone assassin, the man or woman with, perhaps, a grudge against another member of society or maybe with a score to be settled. Many such assassins hold a deep-seated belief that they and they alone have the answer to significant problems. Such people harbour their pain, their obsessions, plan to act at some stage and then strike when opportunity presents itself. Joab's murder of Absalom, Cain's killing of Abel, the anonymous soldier who killed Socrates, the examples are plentiful.

The second group is comprised of the assassination clique. Mostly these groups of killers date from the Roman period and present as a well organised professional body who hire out or offer their services on a regular basis. Groups such as the Jewish Sicarii who preyed on Roman interlopers and whoever they perceived to be Judean turncoats is an obvious example.

There are also assassination groups brought together by a specific need. Once the killing has been completed there is no purpose behind staying together and so the group normally disbands. The conspiracy hatched by Brutus, Cassius and the other Roman plotters against Julius Caesar gives an indication of the strength such gatherings can create.

The third group is made up almost entirely of soldiers or palace guards. Ordered to assassinate by their leaders, these are the men who commit large scale murders or massacres. No individual stands out but examples range from the killing of the Druids on Anglesey in 61 CE to Charlemagne's order to assassinate somewhere in the region of 4000 Germanic tribesmen on one day in 782 CE.

Most assassins were quickly identified by those in authority and while they may not all have faced retribution or judgement, most accounts of the slaying of kings and dictators appear to resonate with more than a little self-satisfaction or pleasure. That is hardly surprising in societies where assassins often occupied positions of some repute and status:

> 'An assassin who could effectively kill discretely was in high demand in an age where challenging political factions and alliances was dangerous and could get you killed if found out.'[2]

As a result, secret societies or groups of professional assassins were relatively commonplace in the ancient world. There were always men who had contacts with these killers and were able to bring them into the service of powerful potentates – for a price, of course.

Most of the assassin bands were standard enough, small groups of killers, highly skilled in their chosen profession and with little or no conscience to trouble them. There were exceptions, of course.

In ancient Japan there existed a special order of ninjas, quite apart from the normal and renowned secret brotherhood of assassins. These were the Kunoichi, a formidable collection of women assassins whose success was based on the hypothesis that in the market place or in crowded town or city streets women would be less noticeable or suspicious than men and were therefore considered to be harmless. That, inevitably, meant they could get closer to their targets, without attracting alarm or distrust.

Although not technically an assassination squad, the bands of Thuggees from ancient India 'took out' many influential businessmen and state officials. It is not known when or where the Thugs came into existence but it was almost certainly long before the first recorded incident of their activity in the thirteenth century. Whenever they began, the term 'thug,' from the Sanskrit word meaning 'concealment,' has gone down in English folklore and descriptive prose.

Thug attacks were dictated by chance rather than by design, each band operating independently for profit and driven by reverence for and worship of the goddess Kali. In many respects they were the ancient world's equivalent of the mafia, instituting a reign of terror across India, preying on travellers who grouped themselves together for protection and therefore laid themselves open for attack by gangs rather than individual robbers.

It is estimated that, over a span of many years – the exact length of time they were operating is not known - more than a million unsuspecting travellers fell to the Thuggee method of killing. This was a specific method which was almost ritualistic. A scarf, weighted at one end, was swung and then slung as a ligature around the victim's neck, his head forced to the side so that he died either from strangulation or a broken neck. The word 'he' is deliberately used as the Thuggee did not normally assassinate women and children.

Incessant travel, usually on foot or perhaps on the back of a slow-moving bullock cart, along jungle paths and badly maintained roads, was partly to blame. Such constant travelling was alien to most western minds but in *The Deceivers* the novelist John Masters caught with consummate ease the atmosphere of the time and country:

> 'It struck him that India was always moving, always going somewhere. Between Kashmir and Cape Comorin, how many hundreds of thousands of people daily faced the dangers, known and guessed and unguessed, of the road ... How many had failed to reach the place they were going? How many died on the way and were not missed?'[3]

Ancient India was also home to the Vishkanyas, an assassination sect that specialised in the use of poison rather than the sword or dagger. Their techniques were different from the Thugees but equally as ingenious.

Their standard mode of operation involved administering small and regular amounts of poison to young girls, effectively making them immune to the poison that was being used. The young women would then be introduced into the palace or home of the victim, as serving girls, cooks and, occasionally, as mistresses.

The young girls would eat and drink the same food and fluid as everyone else but, being immune, they would survive while the target, his buffet suitably laced with poison, quickly died. The same technique was also used to pass on infectious diseases.

There is another important assassination group, technically working just outside the timescale of this book but still worth mentioning as they became one of the most significant murder groups of the late Dark Ages. They were The Assassins, a radical Isma'ili Order founded in 1090 in the mountainous regions of Persia and the Levant.

Their primary weapons were the dagger and nerve poison but they were also one of the few assassination orders to regularly use the bow and arrow. They existed until 1257 when they were attacked and destroyed by troops from the Mongol Empire.

Apart from trading links, the powers of the ancient world, grouped as they were around the Mediterranean, had little to do with far off empires like India and Japan. Countries such as Egypt, Greece and Roman Italy each, in turn, became the centre of the known world. They retained their positions for a period but then, usually quite gradually, slipped out of premier dominance.

It is perhaps a simplistic way of looking at ancient history but what happened, in turn, to each of the great powers was an accurate reflection of the microcosm existing in their internal society. Dynasties and families, even individuals, were dominant for a while before losing power and influence. And so it was with the countries themselves.

Nobody could remain in control for ever although most of the empires tried their damndest to do exactly that. Inevitably, it was a hopeless enterprise. Like falling dominoes, toppling one after the other, each of the western empires were replaced by stronger, more dominant powers, each of them eager for their turn in the sun.

If there was one constant in the ancient world it came in the shape of the brutality that accompanied high levels of culture and learning – albeit culture for the privileged few. True democracy was rare, death and devastation were common.

During the life of the Roman Empire, for example, there were seventy-one emperors, most of them tyrannical, many of them quite insane. Thirty-one of the emperors were assassinated, a dozen more luckily escaping fatal injury from the assassins blades and coming out of the clash with only minor wounds. About half of them died in their beds but only one emperor ever abdicated and settled down to a fulfilling retirement.

One of history's best known and most effective assassination gangs was the Sacred Band of Thebes. More than just a band of killers, in the fourth century BCE they operated as an elite force within the Theban army. Led by General Pelopidas, they filled a necessary role as a front-line fighting unit for forty years from 378 until 338 BCE.

It was a time of chaos and confusion in Greece, city states such as Sparta trying to establish their superiority, smaller and less notable cities like Thebes attempting to retain their independence. What made the Band of Thebes special was that it was comprised of just 300 men, 150 pairs of gay lovers, one of the pairing being older and more experienced, one younger and desperate to learn.

The belief was that loving couples would scheme and fight more fiercely than pairs who were not emotionally involved with each other. Their service, apparently, ended at the age of thirty when they were retired with dignity and fame. The Band of Thebes was an essential part of the Theban army, playing a leading role in the defeat of the Spartan forces at the Battle of Tegyra in 375 BCE.

Their reputation as assassins came, not from any surreptitious murder plots against opposition leaders but from their declared tactic of deliberately identifying and targeting the best and most able of the enemy generals and soldiers. Having got them in their sights the members of the Sacred Band would then attack this specific group and kill them, leaving the rest of the Theban army to take on the remnants of the enemy force.

Their special skills were raiding and hand to hand combat although they were not afraid to stand in the front row of battle as they did at Leuctra when they finally helped defeat the Spartan force and freed Thebes from Spartan control. Vicious and dynamic, they were a markedly different and unusual assassination group.

The strength of Thebes and the Sacred Band were finally broken in 335 BCE when Philip of Macedon and his son Alexander the Great defeated their army in battle. Alexander went on to annihilate and destroy the city of Thebes. It was the end of an era but the style of operation meant that the assassinations of the Band of Thebes had certainly been successful.

The Tyrannicides were an Athenian assassination group led by the gay lovers Harmodius and Aristogeiton. In 514 BCE they, along with several other conspirators, laid plans to kill the Athenian tyrant Hippias. At that time the term 'tyrant' did not necessarily denote a malevolent ruler, but was applied to someone who operated outside the state laws and conventions. Even in the earlier stages of his reign Hippias, aided by his brother, certainly did that.

However, as Cicero later said, assassination was a permitted and acceptable action if the tyrant or ruler began to commit atrocities against his people. This was a judgement with which Harmodius and Aristogeiton firmly believed so that when Hippias and his brother Hipparchus began to demonstrate undue abusive measures towards their citizens the two lovers resolved to rid Athens of their influence.

The planned assassination was carefully prepared. Daggers would be concealed inside ceremonial wreaths carried on the occasion of the Panathenaic Games. The festival was apparently the only time that Athenians could openly carry weapons, ideal cover for what the assassins had in mind. With all the conspirators suitably armed, the arrival of the king and his brother was the signal to attack and slay them both.

The plan began to go wrong, however, when one of the co-conspirators was seen greeting Hippias in an overly friendly manner. The two main assassins panicked, thought they had been betrayed and charged. Hipparchus, brother of the king, was immediately struck down but Hippias, the main target, escaped assassination when Harmodius was killed, run through by an Athenian spearman. In the resulting chaos, Aristogeiton was knocked down and dragged off to prison.

Once in custody, Aristogeiton was tortured, apparently by Hippias himself. He agreed to tell everything, including the names of his fellow conspirators, if the tyrant would only shake his hand. This was agreed, whereupon Aristogeiton shouted that Hippias should be ashamed of himself, shaking the hand of the man who had just killed his brother. Hippias immediately swung around and, in a fury, stabbed Aristogeiton to death.

In death Hipparchus and Aristogeiton managed to achieve what they had failed to do in life. They became heroes to the Athenian public, acclaimed as martyrs and consigned to posterity as the Tyrannicides. King Hippias was soon defeated by the Spartans and sent into exile. A degree of democracy was subsequently established in Athens.

In the eyes of many historians the Hashashins who operated in Syria and Persia in the later years of the ancient world were the perfect assassination sect. They would kill if it was absolutely necessary but often left 'a calling card' instead. This was a message intended to frighten their victims into obedience. It normally took the form of a note advising the victim to leave well alone and was invariably accompanied by a plate of scones or cakes shaped in what became known as a singularly Hashashin way.

The great Saladin, the Muslim leader who defied the Crusader armies and foiled their intention to retake Jerusalem, once received a note from the Hashashins, warning him to withdraw from their territory. While he was asleep, a Hashashin operative had crept into his bedroom and pinned the note by a poisoned dagger to a table by his bed side. It was accompanied by a plate of the unmissable scones. Saladin promptly withdrew his forces.

The Hashashins had their base in a huge and opulent castle at Alamut in modern-day Iran. From there they conducted their affairs and followed an opulent life style, a semi-religious and structured existence that had people queuing up to join the order.

The Sicarii were a renowned band of Jewish assassins, taking their name from the vicious curved dagger which was their primary weapon. Small and easily hidden, the daggers were sharp and the ideal secret killing weapon.

Formed in Jerusalem in the year 6 CE, the primary purpose of the Sicarii was to free Judea from Roman overlordship, using assassination as their main tool. They were a splinter group of the Zealots, one of the more extreme factions in the Jewish hierarchy of the time.

Concealing their daggers, sicas as they were called, beneath their cloaks, the sicarii assassins would approach their victims in a crowd, in the market place or even the Temple. When they were ready, perhaps when the hubbub of noise was at the greatest or the victim's attention drawn elsewhere, the sicarii would stab them in the back and then take part in the hue and cry which always followed the assassination.

Viewing any Jew who submitted to the occupying Romans as a traitor and a coward, no-one was above the vengeance of the sicarii. Killing the High Priest Jonathan in 57 CE was probably the highest point in their reign of political terror. Assassination like that would have been frightening enough on its own but the sicarii also operated as a bandit group, raiding opposing sects, taking bribes and killing without compunction.

Eventually the populace of Jerusalem along with their Roman occupiers and overlords drew a line in the sand. They had put up with more than enough violence and murder and by 67 CE the Sicarii had been driven out of Jerusalem. The assassins sat out the rest of the Great Rebellion, as the revolt against Roman control was known, on the heights of Masada in the southern part of Judea.[4]

The general consensus of opinion indicates that daggers, or short stabbing knives like the sicas, were the most popular choice of weapon for the various assassins. With single or double edged blades, they were lethal and certainly well used.

There is no doubt that if a publicly witnessed demise, such as the killing of Hipparchus or Julius Caesar, was required then the dagger was the favoured choice of the assassins. There were, however, several other weapons that could also be employed. Some automatically excluded themselves as inappropriate.

Swords were not used that often, being too long and unwieldy to be hidden and then brought out at the crucial moment. The assassins invariably carried them but they were sidearms and expected accoutrements rather than stealthy killing weapons. With spears and bows it was much the same story. They were employed but were more fitting for use on the battlefield than the forum.

Japanese Ninja weapons, notably the caltrops, were used regularly by many assassins and also by armies as a weapon of war. Caltrops were pieces of metal, small enough to fit into the palm of a man's hand, designed so that the sharp points were always facing upwards when the obstacle was thrown to the ground. Men and horses could be quickly and easily disabled by the weapon which was also sometimes thrown at the faces of opponents.

Throwing stars were a more usual form of killing from a distance although the multi-bladed Kusarigama, a vicious knife attached to a long line of durable steel cable, was deadly accurate in the hands of an experienced assassin. Most assassins, however, were content with the stiletto, a thin-bladed knife that was easily concealed beneath clothing and sharp enough to pierce heavy leather jerkins. The stiletto would also cause less bleeding than other weapons.

And then, of course, there was poison. Never a weapon of anger or for use when the assassin was in a raging temper, poison was something that needed consideration and time if it was going to be used effectively. Over the years, the use of poison became a fine art:

> 'Throughout the course of history poison has proven an extremely valuable item for the assassin's toolkit. What it lacks in reliability it makes up for in silence.'[5]

Knowledge of toxic substances has been commonplace since humankind took its first faltering steps with the result that poison has probably been the most ancient method of killing another person. In the days before DNA and other scientific methods of probing bodies for causes of death the use of poison was virtually untraceable. In legend, in fiction and in fact, poison has ended many a life.

Homer, in *The Odyssey*, related how Odysseus tipped his arrows with poison when he came to wreak his terrible revenge on the suitors who had desecrated his house while he was away fighting in the Trojan War. Hercules, a classic figure from Greek legend, apparently covered his arrow tips with poison from the Hydra. Neither of them could fail, it seems. If the arrows didn't get you, the poison certainly would.

The philosopher Socrates died from huge doses of hemlock while Cleopatra ended her life by graciously allowing her chest to be bitten by an Egyptian asp. It has never been proven but a long-running rumour still circulates stating that Alexander the Great was poisoned, while in 19 CE Germanicus Caesar, father of the Emperor Caligula and the 'glamour boy' of early Roman politics, almost certainly met his end as a victim of the poisoner's art. The name of the man or woman responsible is another matter.[6]

Weapons now are sophisticated, ranging from high powered revolvers and rifles to ricin-firing umbrellas. But assassins in the ancient world ran an altogether more dangerous path, usually operating from a position of close proximity to their victims. They did not expect to die themselves but it was a decided possibility and the assassins needed to be well-prepared and trained.

Assassination, Did It Ever Really Work?

Apart from anything else, assassins needed to be physically fit. Assassination groups such as the Hashashins set rigorous training schedules and divided new members into a wide range of class or rank. The lowest of these was the *Frida 'yin*, a rank that everyone wanted to pass quickly through. Other assassination groups such as the Japanese Ninjas, set similar standards.

Assassins needed to be physically strong and subtle, able to work with weapons of all styles and types. They also needed to be articulate and well educated, able to understand and appreciate the viewpoints of opposition figures. Above all they needed to have an acute sense of danger and a natural propensity to work stealthily – and, if necessary, alone.

Character assassination is a predominantly modern trend or invention but it was also sometimes used in the ancient world. Deliberate efforts to damage the reputation of enemies were a means of destroying an opponent's ability to defend himself by making him unsure and confused about reality. The use of misinformation was therefore an important tool for the assassins, an early form of gaslighting that confused supporters, crowds and the individual victims themselves.

Mark Antony and the future emperor Augustus (Octavian as he originally was) had a difficult relationship, each of them trying to score points off the other by using character assassination. At one stage Antony claimed that Augustus/Octavian had wormed his way into Caesar's affections by providing him with sexual favours. Antony knew that rumours such as this would lower his opponent's standing with the people of Rome. And, for a while at least, the whispering worked in Antony's favour.

Shakespeare's *Julius Caesar* offers a perfect example of character assassination. Written several hundred years after the actual event, Shakespeare's version of the assassination might not be historically accurate but as a piece of drama, capturing the mood of the city and of its fickle inhabitants before and after a significant event, it cannot be bettered.

After Caesar has been struck down by Brutus, Cassius and the rest of the assassins (the Liberators as they termed themselves), Brutus ascends the platform to address the potentially violent crowd. He justifies his actions and gains support of the plebs, conjuring an imaginary friend of Caesar to ask hypothetical questions:

> 'If, then, that friend demands why Brutus rose against Caesar,
> this is my answer: not that I loved Caesar less, but that I loved

Rome more. Had you rather Caesar were living and die all as slaves, than that Caesar were dead, to live all free men? As Caesar loved me, I weep for him; as he was fortunate I rejoice at it; as he was valiant, I honour him; but as he was ambitious, I slew him.'[7]

With the dangerous Roman crowd now firmly on the side of the assassins, Brutus makes way for Caesar's supporters, confident that his position is unchallengeable. Yet when Mark Antony addresses the crowd he manages to turn their feelings and ignite their anger by performing a skilful character assassination on Brutus. By constantly repeating the line 'he is an honourable man' and by appealing to their sentimentality Antony raises the wrath of the crowd against Brutus and the other conspirators – 'If you have tears, prepare to shed them now.'[8]

Assassination provided the citizens of the ancient world with moments of shock and disbelief. The demise of significant politicians and leaders such as Julius Caesar and Pompey the Great, the death of revered scientists and philosophers like Archimedes and Socrates, were stunning events that brought people up short, stopping them in their tracks. For the ordinary Roman, Greek or Egyptian citizen the unexpected killing of political and social leaders turned life upside down, smashing away the known, however hard or unpleasant that might have been, and replacing it with new notions, new ways of life and new ideals.

Change might have been advocated or spoken about for some time but once in place these new concepts would still have taken a long time to accept. Whatever the changes were about – leadership, military campaigns, tax increases and so on - quite how they would appeal to the public taste remained, perhaps for months, maybe even years, an unknown quantity. Talking about change was one thing; working with it was very different.

Assassination was, therefore, not something to be taken lightly. For those in control or with their hands on a degree of power, it was an accepted part of political life in the ancient world. But no matter who they were, would-be 'movers and shakers' still needed to think twice, several times perhaps, before employing assassination to help them achieve their aims.

Concern about the consequences of what can be best described as political murder was sometimes ignored by fanatics. No change there, then! However, for rationally minded people, that emotion or fear was something that laid down an unofficial check and limited the use of assassination.

And yet when people had been pushed too far, when assassination did actually take place, the causes of the killings were many and varied. At the risk of falling into the trap of weighing good assassination against bad assassination it remains important to note that good and bad were two very different beginnings to the same event.

The reasons for falling back on assassination were many and varied. They ranged from religious fervour to simple greed on behalf of those about to commit the murder. There were, obviously, genuine political concerns, fears that might have been very real. But genuine concerns were sometimes offset by fear or apprehension about the future and by the belief that the assassins, whoever they might be, could do things better. Sometimes it was just sheer affront that pushed people over the edge.

There is an argument that assassination is really an act of war, a declaration of conflict without ever bringing troops into line of battle. Certainly it often had, and usually still has, the same effect as war between nations. These include the toppling of regimes, the conquest of enemy territories, the settling of old scores, old arguments. However, what they do not have is the wide sweep of death and glory that invariably accompanies outright warfare.

Tyrants or absolute monarchs were an obvious target for assassins but only when they went too far or 'got it wrong,' as so many of them seemed to do:

> 'Whatever latitude an absolute monarch may assume in his own conduct, whatever indulgence he may claim for his own passions, it is undoubtedly in his interest that all his subjects should respect the natural and civil obligations of society.'[9]

One thing remains abundantly clear. Successful or unsuccessful, in the ancient world the effects of assassination did not always turn out to be what the killers had intended or wanted. The obvious example, yet again, is the assassination of Julius Caesar, this time based on the facts about his death rather than on the rather dubious historical tenor of Shakespeare's play.

Brutus and Cassius hatched their plot to kill Caesar because they saw him as a threat to Republican Rome. They believed that Caesar, a single, powerful figure who, despite being three times offered and three times refusing the throne of the city and the burgeoning Empire, still had ambitions to rule and run things in his own fashion.

The assassination took place with the conspirators firmly believing that the Roman citizens, the plebs as they were known, would accept and agree with their actions. After all, the democratic creation of the Roman Republic was the envy of the known world. Wasn't it?

In fact the opposite happened. Impassioned speeches at the reading of Caesar's Will turned the Roman citizens against the assassins and Brutus and Cassius were forced to flee from the capital. They headed for Greece and despite a somewhat uneasy relationship between Antony and Octavian, Caesar's nephew and adopted son, pressures on the two main conspirators remained intense. Soon they were facing a numerically superior and better trained army led by Mark Antony and Octavian. The conspirators lost two battles and felt they had no option other than commit suicide, to 'play the Roman fool' as Shakespeare later described it.

Over the next dozen or so years Octavian and Antony vied for power, the war reaching a conclusion with Antony's defeat at the Battle of Actium in 31 BCE. Octavian was promptly declared First Citizen of Rome, then Emperor, taking the throne name Augustus.

With more power than Julius Caesar ever dreamed of, Augustus, the first Emperor of Rome, set about ending the Roman Republic forever. As a result, within a handful of years the creation of one person rule had come to Rome, the very opposite to what Brutus had intended when he first considered assassination.[10]

There are many more examples of assassinations leading everywhere apart from where the assassins had planned, so many in fact that the question has to be asked – were assassinations ever really successful?

If we are to believe the Biblical story of The Massacre of the Innocents, far from destroying Herod's potential rival monarch, the mindless slaughter of innocent children simply reinforced opposition to the tyrant and, regardless of whether the story is fact or fiction, helped in the growth of Christianity.

The assassination of Philip of Macedon succeeded only in bringing his son, Alexander the Great, to the throne. And Alexander was a much greater general and ruler than Philip could ever be.

Killing the clearly disturbed Emperor Caligula was never meant to result in the rise of another emperor or sole ruler but members of the Praetorian Guard, who had carried out the assassination, felt that they needed a leader. The Praetorians had become exceptionally powerful during the reign of Tiberius and now they took the matter into their own hands.

They discovered, literally almost at their feet, the most innocuous candidate they could, the hapless 'Uncle Claudius.' It was as much a gesture of indifference to the position of emperor as anything else but the Republicans in Rome were simply too weak to stop them and Emperor Claudius duly ascended to the throne.

From the beginning of recorded history assassination has been employed as a political tool. It may have been dangerous, both for the victim and for the assassin, but it was a popular method of removing enemies and opponents. Indeed, sometimes it appeared to be more normal, more acceptable, than waiting for the natural line of succession to take effect.

Dozens of assassinations took place in the ancient world, all of them justifiable in the eyes and minds of the killers and in the writings of some of the philosophers of the time.

Some assassinations changed the course of ancient history, others gradually faded in the memory of those who were there at the time, some slipped slowly but untroubled under the radar and were never heard of again.

Whichever way they are viewed, they are all well worth examining. And, by and large, in the eyes of the perpetrators at least, most of them can be considered as relatively successful.

Chapter Two

Ancient Egypt, Early Assassination Plots

There is no proof, at least no written proof, but it is reasonable to assume that the act of assassination has been used by men and women for many thousands of years. From the dawn of 'organised society,' the twin evils of greed and resentment, as displayed or made public in personal temptation and the means to kill off political and military opponents, have always been there. They have always been available to anyone who has sufficient nerve, determination and skill to use them.

Life in the prehistoric period was violent. That is a simple statement but one that is very true and it applies whether the location was the warm, sun-soaked deserts of Egypt or the rain-strewn wilds of Britain and Northern Europe.

Reasoned argument within prehistoric societies was virtually unknown and debate was sorely limited. It was all too easy to find the solution to any problem in the bunches of sticks and rocks that littered the sands of the desert. The beaches, coastal mud flats and the cave floors of ancient dwellings might have provided weapons but they did not offer anything like reasoned argument.

As if to back up this view, recent archaeological evidence has shown that many prehistoric deaths were caused by blows from blunt but heavy implements such as clubs or mallets. They produced blows that shattered the victim's skull and caused instant death. Other skeletons from areas like the western states of the USA showed that death often occurred from the victim being stabbed in the back using sharp rocks as daggers or knives.

Imagine yourself in a cave or rocky grove sometime in the Prehistoric Era. You disagree with your clan leader over some petty decision such as when or where to hunt. The answer is very simple – a club or stone over the back of his head and no more disagreements.[1]

That, of course, is an assumption, but a perfectly reasonable one given the nature and the way of life in ancient civilisations. It is only with the advent of written records, usually produced in hindsight by objective historians and writers, that we can begin making reasonably accurate judgements about life in that distant period.

And that, to begin with at least, leads us to Ancient Egypt, the setting for what was undoubtedly one of the world's first relatively modern civilisations. In keeping with that sentiment, the advent of Ancient Egypt marked a time of change for all of human kind.

Ancient Egypt

Ancient Egypt is the name applied to the period immediately following the Prehistoric Era in Egypt, a period developing and coalescing around 3100 BCE. It began with the unification of the two halves of the country, Lower and Upper Egypt, areas that had spent much of the previous few thousand years clawing at each other's collective throats.

The period which covers Ancient Egypt can be broken into three separate eras. These are the Old Kingdom, beginning about 2000 BCE, the Middle Kingdom, circa 1800 BCE, and the New Kingdom, 1000 BCE onwards. Egypt reached its pinnacle of power and influence during the New Kingdom, thereafter moving into a slow decline.

Increasingly, the Nile became the lifeblood of the country as conditions in the flanking deserts had grown particularly unpleasant and unproductive. From about 12000 BCE, at the height of the Prehistoric Period, the old hunters and gatherers who had populated Prehistoric Egypt began to move in from the deserts and settle along the River Nile. There they built crude houses and began cultivating the land.

Slowly, over many years, the people began to enjoy the comfort and security that marked the beginning of civilisation. Decent food and working conditions that were beneficial both to them and to the culture of the growing nation slowly became the norm. It was no longer good enough to live in caves and not know where the next meal was coming from. It did not happen overnight but religion and learning, often discovered through the auspices of what we might now term as magic, began to grow and develop.

Egypt was a perfect location to allow, even to encourage, the growth of a socially advanced civilisation. The climate along the Nile was warm but not oppressive and the soil of the river valley was exceptionally fertile. Almost every year overflows from the river brought water and a rich covering of mud to fertilise the agricultural lands that lay on either side of the Nile. Small wonder, then, that people began to see the river as a means of helping them to enjoy a better life.

Assassinations in Ancient Egypt seem to have been relatively rare or, at least, they seem to have been seldom recorded. The almost total absence of written testimony has left researchers and historians in the dark about much of Egypt's early history but such a lack might not be down to ineptitude. It could easily be due to the Egyptian belief in the afterlife. This belief was a degree of faith which saw death not as an ending but as the start of the long journey to paradise. And who would want that for any foe or enemy?

The Life and Death of Pharoah Teti

There were undoubtedly many politically motivated murders long before the demise of King Teti but the killing of this Pharaoh seems to have been the world's first recorded account of an assassination. Sometimes known as Othoes or Tata, Pharoah Teti was murdered in 2333 BCE.

According to the early Egyptian historian Manetho, writing some 2000 years after Teti's death, the Pharaoh was knifed to death as part of a harem plot. It is thought that his last wife may have been involved in the planning of the murder but he was actually killed by members of his own bodyguard. The motives for the killing have never been made clear.

As Manetho's writings and some of the official records, originally registered on the Turin King's List, have since been lost or destroyed it is best to view Manetho's claims with a degree of caution. There is some evidence to support his beliefs, however, evidence which might be circumstantial but which still appears to be significant:

> 'A number of senior officials including a vizier, the chief physician and the overseer of weapons had their memorials defaced. Some had their names erased, their images chiselled away or their remains removed. This was a dreadful fate usually meted out to hated criminals because it meant that in the afterlife they would be homeless and condemned to endless wandering.'[2]

The obvious assumption is that such significant destruction and condemnation of high officials has to have been the result of very serious betrayal. That would have had to mean something like a palace conspiracy and coup leading to the assassination of the Pharaoh, discovered perhaps in the wake of the killing. Teti's claim to the throne was thin, based upon his wife's family and lineage, rather than his own credentials. A conspiracy like this might therefore have a degree of credibility.

Teti was the first monarch of the Sixth Egyptian Dynasty. He came to the throne in 2323 BCE and ruled for somewhere between ten and thirty years. He was already middle aged when he came to power, taking the throne name Seheteptawy as his royal designation. It translates as 'he who pacifies two lands,' which seems to indicate that it was a time of unrest in Egypt. A physician and a learned scholar, Teti was the first Pharaoh to be associated with the cult of Hathor in Dendera, a few miles upriver from Thebes, Luxor and Karnak.

Teti's immediate predecessor was Unas, the last monarch of the Fifth Dynasty but he had died without siring an heir. With a clear eye for his own future and perhaps for the security of Egypt, Teti married Unas' daughter Iput in order to claim the throne. Wisely - or probably not as it turned out - he retained several of the officials who had worked effectively under the previous Pharaoh, men who knew how to wield the reins of control. In particular he retained the services of the two most powerful men in the kingdom. These were Mereruka and Kagemni who served the new monarch as his Viziers and advisors.

As Pharaoh, Teti had the luxury of taking several wives, as was the custom in Egypt. Consequently he did not have the same problem as Unas, he and his various wives between them producing three sons and ten daughters.

Teti improved safety in the royal household, employing more guards to ensure the comfort of his family and the general security of his palace, the royal necropolis at Saqqara. Employing more guards was an unsuccessful and somewhat empty gesture, given the way he died, but during his reign Teti did manage to draw much power and control back to the central government, pulling it away from the semi-autonomous system that had been installed and operating for some years. Another reason for his assassination, perhaps?

The period showed a marked interest in the cult of Osiris, the Egyptian god of the dead. There was also an increased interest in funerary arrangements, seen in the sudden escalation of pyramid building. Teti, however, exempted priests from paying taxes. The priests were ecstatic but it was not something that went down well with the Egyptian people.

Many funerary monuments were built during Teti's reign, including a five-storied pyramid for his mother Seshesdet and other impressive monuments for several of the more important noblemen. Included in these buildings, the first examples of pyramids for nobles, was a particularly fine tomb for the Vizier Mereruka.

In contrast, Teti's own pyramid remains a relatively modest affair which stands at Saqqara in Lower Egypt. For countless decades the tomb was a 'missing monument' until it was discovered by French Egyptologists in 1894.

One of the reasons for the failure to locate Teti's resting place is that, unlike so many other funerary monuments along the Nile, the pyramid is smooth sided. With a height of just over 52 metres and a breadth of 78 metres at its base, decay and sand have caused it to degenerate. For many years, it appeared to passers-by and historians more like a small hill than an Egyptian pyramid.

When the pyramid was finally excavated, a sarcophagus was found but it contained no mummy. All that remained were the remnants of an arm and part of a shoulder, the presumption being that these items came from Teti's body. There were also a number of Pyramid Texts which waxed lyrical about the re-birth of the Pharaoh.

Teti was succeeded by a relatively unknown figure, a man by the name of Userkare who seized the throne and ruled for somewhere between one and five years. There is no tomb for Userkare, suggesting that his reign and usurpation of the throne were not looked on favourably. It also indicates, potentially, a short reign with work on the pyramid incomplete at the time of his death.

Unfortunately, the absence of a tomb has also meant that there is no information about the ruler's life and times. Normally, details and dates in office of chief ministers and so on were carved into the stonework of a Pharoah's pyramid but not in this case. Similarly Userkare's name does not feature on any of the tombs of Egyptian officials of the time.[3]

Userkare's name is present, however, on the Abydos King List, a roll call that was compiled and written during the reign of Seti 1, between 1290 and 1279 BCE. On this List his cartouche is found as the 35th entry, sitting between Teti and his son Pepi and thus making him the second Pharaoh of the Sixth Dynasty.

Lack of information about Userkare might also mean that he was a stop gap ruler, a regent who held the reins of power during Pepi's childhood. As with Teti, we are left making 'educated guesses' about the man and his period in power.

The usurper Userkare was succeeded by Teti's son Pepi who reigned for over fifty years from 2323 until approximately 2291 BCE. Pepi continued his father's exploitation of the mineral wealth of the Nile valley, fought battles with potential invaders and died after a successful and well-lived reign.

Pharaoh Ramesses II

Possibly the best-known of the Egyptian Pharaohs, after Cleopatra and Tutankhamun, is Ramesses II. Also known as Ramesses the Great, he led no fewer than fifteen military campaigns, all of which ended in victory. Included in these campaigns is the Battle of Kadesh which took place in 1274 BCE and is recorded as a combat that pitched 5000 Egyptian chariots against 6000 from the Hittites. It was the largest chariot battle in antiquity.

Ramesses died in 1213 BCE at the age of ninety. He died peacefully, although wracked by dental problems. Not assassinated, his death did mark the beginning of the end of the great Egyptian Empire. His campaigns and wars had caused an irrevocable weakening of the resources available to the Empire so that he was able to pass on to his successor only a political and military power that was already on the way down.

It was no assassination as we would normally view it but by his relentless military campaigns – along with huge amounts of money spent on building temples, monuments, even the new capital city of Pi-Ramesses – he effectively killed off the Egyptian Empire. That was assassination of the highest order.

Pharaoh Ramesses III

The name Ramesses was well-used and popular as far as royal figures in Ancient Egypt were concerned. No fewer than eleven Pharaohs were christened with or, on succession, took the throne name Ramesses. Several more princes and would-be kings also claimed the name. Most of the Ramesses Pharoah's were famous for their enlargement of the Egyptian Empire and for the building of magnificent memorials and temples like the one built by Ramesses II, now standing in splendid isolation in the desert at Abu Simbel.

Ramesses III, however, was renowned for different reasons. He was particularly interested in architecture and built a magnificent mortuary temple at Thebes, He also oversaw the extension of both Luxor and Karnak temples. His chief claim to fame, however, was that he became the victim of one of the most brutal assassinations to take place in the ancient world.

As the second Pharoah of the Twentieth Dynasty in Ancient Egypt, the reign of Ramesses III began in 1186 and lasted until 15 April 1155 BCE. He was the last great monarch of the New Kingdom, the power of Egypt having already begun a slow but steady decline during the reigns of his predecessors. Now, under Ramesses III, internal problems, together with a number of significant invasions by foreign enemies, saw Egypt regress in military, economic and cultural standing.

Ramesses did his best to halt this decline and in some spheres or aspects of his duty, such as waging war, he was particularly successful. He defeated the infamous Sea Peoples in two bloody battles and earned himself the acronym of 'The Warrior Pharoah.'

The Battle of the Delta was perhaps the Pharoah Ramesses' greatest victory when he lured the ships of the Sea Peoples into the mouth of the River Nile where they were destroyed by the Egyptian navy and by archers on the river banks. Brutal hand to hand fighting finally finished the raiders from the sea who had also launched a second assault on Ramesses and his command, this time as a land force.

The Sea Peoples were a seafaring confederation operating in the eastern Mediterranean and coming from a number of different locations in Asia Minor. They were not just sea raiders, however, and there was more than a simple desire for plunder and war behind their actions:

> 'It should be stressed that the invasions were not merely military operations, but involved the movement of large populations, by land and sea, seeking new lands to settle.'[4]

Defeating invaders like the Sea Peoples, and the Libyans who also launched raids at this time, did not come cheaply for Ramesses. Quite apart from the high casualty list, the cost of waging war, even of a defensive nature, was enormous. The Treasury was under constant pressure, the situation made worse by soaring grain prices and a steady increase in the cost of living.

The reign of Ramesses III was troubled in many ways, not least by the human problems that beset the country. It saw the first known industrial strike in history, an action that showed the disgruntled and desperate need of the Egyptian people. Ramesses had been on the throne for nearly thirty years when failure to provide expected food rations, along with a two-month delay in paying out wages, saw the elite tomb builders and artisans working on the Royal Necropolis at Deir el-Medina lay down their tools and refuse to continue with the job.

Something had to give and the assassination of Ramesses III was the final stab in the back for a Pharoah who had done his best to help his people in a difficult period of Egyptian history.

The assassination plot was the result of yet another so-called Harem Conspiracy, this time organised and led by the Pharoah's secondary wife Tiye and by her son Pentawere:

> 'Ramesses III met his end in 1155, after thirty years on the throne, and thanks to the survival of 3000 year old papyrus court records, we know that more than thirty 'great criminals' from his court were put on trial over their part in the conspiracy against him.'[5]

Along with the general unhappiness in the nation, Ramesses had other significant problems. He had a number of wives but none of them had been designated as his chief or first wife. This meant that he had no acknowledged heir with the result that Tiye and two of the Pharoah's other wives were at loggerheads over who his successor would be. Ramesses himself favoured another of his sons who would go on to survive the assassination of his father and become Ramesses IV.

Sensing this potential outcome, Tiye and Pentawere began to plot. A large number of palace staff became involved, ranging from the royal butler and a number of harem officials to the overseer of the royal herds and three royal scribes. The overseer of the royal herds provided wax figurines that were supposedly cursed and would be used to disable the palace guards.

The assassination took place in the Spring of 1155 BCE during the Festival of the Valley at Medinet Habu outside Luxor. The cursed effigies or figurines did not work and the guards were not eliminated. Despite that failure Ramesses was duly despatched but, unfortunately for them, Tiye and the other plotters were soon arrested.

Although Ramesses was dead, justice could still be done and after three trials thirty-eight of the accused were sentenced to death. Tiye and Pentawere were among the condemned, their tombs robbed and their names erased. Pentawere was strangled, his body buried in an impure goatskin and Ramesses IV duly came to the throne.

It was the early twenty-first century before the cause of the Pharoah Ramesses' death was finally discovered. CT scans on the mummy of Ramesses III showed that underneath extensive bandaging around the neck, presumably done to mask the wounds, the Pharoah had a deep and long knife wound across his throat.

The cut in Ramesses' neck was so deep it had reached the vertebrae, destroyed the oesophagus and blood vessels. Infliction of the wound would have been incredibly painful but it was effective and probably killed Ramesses instantly.

There were many other wounds to the body, indicating that several people had taken part in the killing and inflicted injuries in a frenzy of dislike. The most bizarre of these was the amputation of the left big toe which had been chopped off by a weapon like an axe. The bones had not healed so the wound, along with several other scars on the body, must have been done before death. That would seem to indicate torture of some kind.

The assassination of Ramesses III effectively marks the end of Egypt's true years of glory. The country's slow slide continued for many years, only really coming to an end in 30 BCE when Ptolemy and his sister Cleopatra gave up their independence to the expanding Roman Empire.

After his death, the body of Ramesses III, heavily bandaged and mummified, was taken and buried in the Valley of the Kings. It remains one of the largest tombs in the valley and would, at the time of his entombment, been filled with valuable ornaments and pictures.

Pharoah Seqenenre Tao II

Seqenenre Tao 11 remains one of the least known of all Egyptian Pharoahs but during his reign he was renowned as a warrior and was called 'Seqenenre the Brave' by his subjects. The name Seqenenre means 'He who strikes like Re (the sun god).'

Pharaoh Seqenenre was killed or assassinated - the jury is still out on that one - in 1550 BCE after being captured in battle against the Hyksos. The Hyksos dynasty was a warlike tribe of West Asian origin, a fierce fighting force that had recently invaded and taken control of the Nile Delta and much of Lower Egypt.

The war began when a deliberately provocative comment was received from Apophis, one of the last rulers of the Hyksos Dynasty. Noises from the Egyptian herd of royal hippopotamus at Thebes, Apophis declared, were keeping him awake at night. Seqenenre must do something about it, he informed the Egyptians. As Apophis was based at his capital in the Delta, over 400 miles away, such a comment was ridiculous, perilously close to an insult and could only act as a spur to war.

For many years it was thought that Seqenenre had actually been killed in a battle, although nobody could say which one, as he strove to deal with the insulting attitude of Apophis and to regain the lost territory of Lower Egypt. There is no record of the engagement, not even its site and location, but Seqenenre's battered corpse was found and inspected after the action.

There were five terrible wounds on his head. One of them was a crushing blow from an unidentified blunt weapon alongside three axe-inflicted injuries. There was also evidence of a spear or sword thrust to the neck, running up into the lower part of the head. Death in battle, it was decided, had undoubtedly finished the Egyptian Pharaoh.

It was a hasty judgement. The corpse of the Pharoah had been lying in the dust, untouched, for several days and was already showing signs of decomposition. Examination of the body, in the field so to speak, was insubstantial but it had to be carried out before mummification could begin. So, Seqenenre received a quick examination, then the corpse was carried back to Thebes.

Opinion gradually changed however and, before the body was committed to its tomb, the wounds to Seqenenre's head were examined in more detail. Now, without fear of enemy intrusion, the examination was conducted at the leisure of the physicians and embalmers.

The death wounds were all on the top of Seqenenre's head or at the base of the skull but were all on the left side of the body. This seemed to indicate that he had been killed while lying down on his right side, possibly when he was asleep. That, it was decided, did not mean death in battle but murder, execution or assassination. It was a logical enough argument, one that was unanimously accepted for many years.

The first and most likely suspects for the assassination were Seqenenre's household staff who, it was claimed, murdered him after a battle against the Hyksos had been lost. It was an accusation that nobody could prove and was accepted as the truth for some time.

A revised opinion later declared that Seqenenre had been assassinated but not in his camp and not by his servants. He had been killed while he was being held captive. He was, the new theory now declared, assassinated on the orders of Apophis, the Hyksos king. It had been done while he was a captive of the Hyksos army and then his corpse discarded like so much rubbish. That was another insult to the men from Thebes.

For the moment the story rested there. Then, in the twentieth century, modern examination of the mummified corpse discovered a number of small cuts or wounds on the Pharaoh's right hand side. These could have been inflicted in battle or in a struggle of some kind.

The small cuts, along with other more serious wounds, had somehow been missed by the embalmers. It was soon discovered that he had also been stabbed behind his ear and his cheek and nose smashed-in by a mace. How such damage escaped the embalmers and physician remains mystifyingly unknown.

More significantly, X-Ray images taken in 1980 showed that there was serious mutilation to the Pharaoh's wrists and arms, suggesting that his hands had been tied behind his back at the time of his death.

The blows to his head had clearly been delivered from above, executioners or assassins smashing down with their weapons onto his defenceless body when Seqenenre was kneeling on the ground. His hands being tied behind his back meant that he could not use his arms to defend himself or deflect the blows.

The deep wounds on Seqenenre's head and neck were matched with Hyksos weapons held in the Egyptian Museum in Cairo. It was decided that similar weapons from the period could easily have been used to inflict the injuries.

The major head wounds had been cleverly concealed by the embalmers who filled the cuts with a liquid which worked like modern filler. There seems to have been no reason why the embalmers should do this but it was certainly effective in preserving the actual body. Whatever the reason, the 'filling in' of the wounds has enabled detailed examination with the result that it is now believed Seqenenre was not killed in battle. He was, in fact, assassinated in a rare and unusual execution ceremony held in the wake of his defeat at the hands of the Hyksos warriors.

After the death of Seqenenre the war against Apophis and his minions raged on, waged on the Egyptian side by the dead Pharaoh's wife, who also happened to be his sister. It was a mammoth task for the Queen but it was enough to keep the invaders at bay.

She pushed them back, driving them from one part of Upper Egypt to another and keeping them at bay until her son Kamose came of age. Victory was finally achieved when Seqenenre's second son, Ahmose, succeeded to the throne and drove the Hyksos out of Egypt.

Berenice III

Although she is little mentioned or written about these days, Queen Berenice - also known, confusingly, as Cleopatra - had been co-ruler of Egypt for some time in the last century BCE. She began by co-commanding the country alongside her father, Ptolemy IX, then with her first husband Ptolemy X, who also happened to be her uncle.

When Ptolemy X died in December 81 BCE Berenice, who had been declared co-regent that August, automatically became Queen of Egypt in her own right. She was at last ruling without a consort. Sole rule suited Berenice perfectly, she had always wanted to wield power, but her time at the helm was limited. In fact it lasted only a few months.

She soon came under pressure, particularly from the Roman dictator Sulla, to take a husband. By then Egypt had become something of a vassal state to the Roman Empire and the idea of a woman ruler in one of their important trade centres reminded the Romans a bit too much of the chaos that women in positions of power might cause.

Consequently, after just six months of sole rule Berenice found herself married to her stepson, who duly became King Ptolemy XI. The marriage and his sudden elevation to kingship was under the condition of joint rule.

Ptolemy, however, saw no need to share the kingdom and after just nineteen days of marriage he arranged to have Berenice assassinated.

What Ptolemy had not foreseen was Berenice's popularity with the people of Egypt. She had been their monarch, alone or in partnership, for some time. There was a public outcry at her assassination, followed by an uprising with the intention of avenging her. Taking out their anger and avenging her, that was something the Egyptian people certainly did. Blazing buildings, broken windows, riots and long instances of disturbance became the order of the day. What the crowds really wanted, however, was to get their hands on Ptolemy.

Ptolemy was apprehended hiding in a gymnasium and lynched by the angry mob. Moral? Make sure you know whose side the crowd is on and use, rather than abuse, their opinions.

Chapter Three

Assassination in Persia and the Middle East

Like all great empires, the decline and fall of Egypt as a 'world power' was inevitable, the country being finally conquered by Persia in 525 BCE. No great power lasts for ever and Egypt was no exception. Somebody was always going to conquer the declining country.

Long before that conquest it had taken a number of centuries for the decline to work itself out with an unhappy Egypt increasingly being seen as 'the sick man of the ancient world.'

Persia can be viewed as the most significant nation to even attempt to pick up the reins of achievement and control after the gradual demise of Egypt.

If the throwaway line was true and Egypt was, indeed, the sick nation of the world, Persia undoubtedly became the next great 'super power' of that same ancient community.

In one of the greatest land grabs seen in the ancient world, the Persians also eventually took over the Assyrian Empire which, like Egypt, was in gradual decline. The Persian Empire itself eventually submitted to the Babylonians where significant leaders like Philip of Macedonia and Alexander the Great were waiting in the wings to take control.

Also known as the Achaemenid Empire after the great dynasty that ruled the country and its dominions, Persia's control of the Middle East was supreme between approximately 550 and 331 BCE. It was a relatively short span of years for such a significant colossus but in that brief period the achievements of the Persian Empire were truly momentous.

Probably for the first time in the ancient world, the Persians created a hugely efficient centralised bureaucratic system of administration which, in its turn, led to effective infrastructures such as creating effective road networks, a working civil service and even a postal system.

At its zenith the Persian Empire, mainly through conquest, extended widely to encompass most of modern day Iran, a large portion of Egypt and Turkey, and significant parts of both Afghanistan and Pakistan. It was at that time, territorially at least, the largest empire or control base that the world had yet seen. Its acquisition of conquered land covered, in total, a land mass of just over two million square miles.

Originally a nomadic people from the western plateau of Iran, the Persians were not great cultivators or farmers and never really settled in one place or area. However, they were constantly striving to increase their territory and the inevitably greater power base that went with it.

Founded by Cyrus the Great in 550 BCE, the Persian Empire surged into prime position as the new imperial power in the world. It was young and it was vibrant and, at that time, nobody had ever seen anything like it.

The Persian Empire lasted until approximately 330 BCE when the all-conquering Alexander the Great rode roughshod over their territories. The previous 200 or so years had been a time of victory and defeat in equal measure, battles like Marathon and Salamis finally proving that the Persians had rather over reached themselves.

The nature of a dictatorial regime such as the Persian Empire meant that those 200 years were also a time of almost perpetual assassinations.

These assassinations were so significant that, at times, it appeared as if killing off the incumbent of the throne was the most successful way of ensuring a seamless succession. It was certainly a great deal less cumbersome and time consuming.

Sennacherib and a Pair of Wolves on the Fold

The Persian Empire succeeded in taking over much of the land and territory of the warlike Assyrians who had created their own empire in the 14th century BCE. Renowned as the Assyrians might have been, the Persians proved to be stronger and more warlike.

Under monarchs like Sennacherib, however, the Assyrians had operated as a collection of federated city states between approximately 900 and 600 BCE. Their power and their fame was legendary in the ancient world.

Sennacherib became King of the Assyrian Empire in 705 BCE, on the death of his father Sargon. He ruled until his own death in 681 BCE. Sennacherib is now best remembered as the central figure in the haunting first lines to Lord Byron's poem *The Destruction of Sennacherib*:

'The Assyrian came down like a wolf on the fold,
And his cohorts were gleaming in purple and gold,
And the sheen on their spears were like stars on the sea
When the blue wave rolls nightly on deep Galilee.'[1]

At the height of his fame, however, Sennacherib was a brutal but highly successful ruler who, in 681 BCE, was assassinated by two of his sons. His eldest son Ashur-Nadin-Shumi had been captured and executed by Babylonian and Elamite forces during the Levantine War of 701 BCE. Sennacherib extracted his revenge by beating both enemies and then levelling their cities.

The problem of his successor remained. Sennacherib appointed one of his two remaining sons as that successor, then replaced him with the other one. No reason was ever given but both boys were resentful and both of them had clear designs on their father's throne.

Neither of Sennacherib's sons was prepared to wait for him to die naturally. Not only that, Sennacherib had already shown that he could easily change his mind again, giving the crown to the other son or even bringing in someone totally new. There was, the sons thought, only one way to go. Assassination.

According to one legend Sennacherib was crushed beneath the heavy falling statue of a winged bull pushed by compatriots of his sons. It is a great story but there is no proof! However he died, Sennacherib should have expected it. He had assassinated his own father in order to seize the throne. Why should his own offspring be any different? Patricide and regicide were something of an occupational hazard, particularly for rulers of mighty empires.

The Assyrian World

Based largely on Mesopotamia, that fertile stretch of rolling hills, valleys and plains between the twin rivers of Tigris and Euphrates, the Assyrian days of power and glory can be divided into four distinct periods - the Ancient, the Old, the Middle and finally the Neo or New. The Assyrian conquests eventually melded together to become part of the Persian and Neo-Babylonian Empires.

The Assyrians, warlike and demanding, were the significant force in the Middle East before their decline in the Neo-Assyrian period. This decline was perhaps inevitable as their Empire had become too large and unwieldy to maintain and manage effectively.

During the heyday of their Empire, operating from their city bases like Nineveh and Nimrud, there were several Assyrian invasions of Judah and Egypt. These incursions created a huge Empire for the Assyrians and due largely to their belief in new technology like war chariots and iron swords they maintained their highly important position, far ahead of other nations.

Only when other powers such as Persia began to re-organise their fighting forces along Assyrian lines did the Assyrian Empire begin to crack and fall apart.

Phalaris and the Brazen Bull

One of the most fascinating stories from this period is the legend of Phalaris, the Tyrant Ruler of Acragos on modern day Sicily who reigned from 570 to 554 BCE. Commissioned to create and build the Temple of Zeus in Acragos, Phalaris seized power once the building was complete by the simple process of arming and organising his work force in military fashion

He commissioned the Greek builder Perilaus (sometimes spelled Perillos) to create one of the most horrendous torture devices of ancient history. The Bronze or Brazen Bull was a hollow bronze machine, the shape and size of a real bull, into which victims would be thrown. Then a fire would be lit beneath the bull and the unfortunate man inside would be slowly, painfully roasted to death.

The bull was fitted with tubes and stops that converted the dying person's screams to what sounded like a bellowing bull. Smoke wafted out like clouds of incense. The Greek poet Pindar later described the device as 'a copper bellowing bull.' According to legend the first victim of the bull was Perilaus himself but other versions of the story say he was pulled out at the last moment, then taken to a high cliff and thrown off.

The bones of the executed person were scraped out once the heat had died. Then they were fashioned into bracelets, a strange not to say hideous form of memento collecting. The significance of the bull as a semi-religious object should not be ignored. To the Greeks bulls symbolised power and were associated with several of their deities.

More legend, but one of the best-known Greek stories tells of a Queen of Crete who mated with a white bull. The result was the Minotaur which was eventually hunted down and killed by Greek hero Theseus.

Reality was different – or was it? The Brazen Bull might lack the ability to move and hunt but, in reality, it was not all that different. During the reign of Phalaris the Bull was used for executions, for murder and for assassination and it's last known victim was certainly someone in dire need of assassination!

Phalaris was eventually overthrown in 554 BCE and his Brazen Bull disappeared. However, it was not before Telemachus, leader of the rebellion, fed it one last time. Phalaris died inside his bull. The legend of the Brazen Bull is now part of Greek mythology but how much of it is genuine, how much is legend remains something of a mystery.

What is known is that, at its height, the strength of the Persian Empire was huge. Inheriting much of the Assyrian technology and skill base proved to be the root of that Persian success and power.

There was a fatal weakness in the military might of Persia, however. The wide range of their conquests meant that their army was made up of men of many different nationalities. These ranged from native Persians and Phoenicians to Babylonians, from Greeks and Egyptians to men of the Jewish race, in total nearly one hundred different nationalities.

Even the elite Immortals, a strong palace guard and heavy infantry unit, was forced to take in men of other nationalities. Controlling a fighting force of such dichotomy was virtually impossible, as King Xerxes I was to discover.

Xerxes I

Xerxes I was the fourth King of the Persian Achaemenid Dynasty, coming to the throne in 486 BCE. The son of Darius the Great, Xerxes was 32 years old when he became king and almost immediately found himself pitched into the warlike politics of Persia.

In a violent rejection of their overlords, the once-powerful Egyptian nation had begun a rebellion and now, in Persian eyes, needed pacifying.

Xerxes obliged in 484 CE but his campaigns, successful as they were, saw an erosion of the Persian Army. Battles against determined enemies had caused serious casualties and further unrest in Babylon did not help.

Xerxes was forced to rebuild his forces, centring them around his elite unit, the Immortals. They were intended to have exactly 10,000 men, no more, no less, every dead or wounded Immortal being immediately replaced by waiting newcomers. There were just not enough Persian soldiers available, however, and the result was that empty places in the fighting line were now being filled with men from all types of ethnicity and background.

More serious problems began when several of the Greek city states, unhappy with the tyrants imposed upon them by Persia, also rose in rebellion.

It was decided to punish Athens for that city's part in what became known as the Ionian Revolt. Consequently, in 480 BCE Xerxes crossed the Hellespont, constructing a long bridge of boats moored together across the water and, supremely confident of victory, entered Europe.

At the Pass of Thermopylae the Persians encountered a small force of 300 Spartans gathered together under the command of their King Leonidas. The Spartans, totally outnumbered, held Xerxes at bay for three days before a traitor from the immediate area showed the Persians an unknown path that took them to the rear of Leonidas' force.

Attacked on two flanks the Spartans fought to the last man, a courageous effort from men who were significantly outnumbered. Even so, they had done their job, managing to delay Xerxes and his army for several days and giving the Greek city states time to prepare for a fight to the death.

The battle has gone down in history as a heroic but ultimately fruitless sacrifice by the Spartans although the support the Spartans received from several thousand other Greek forces seems to have been conveniently forgotten. It clearly did not fit into the picture of heroic sacrifice.

Xerxes went on to conquer much of mainland Greece, particularly the area north of the Isthmus of Corinth. He also razed Athens to the ground but then came up short in a campaign he should never have undertaken.

The sea battle of Salamis was a resounding victory for the Greeks. Xerxes, wary of being trapped in a foreign country if the enemy should go on to destroy his bridge of boats across the Hellespont, headed back to Asia. He left a small army under General Mardonius in southern Greece but this was soon wiped out, thus ending the Persian invasion.

Once back in his capital of Persepolis, Xerxes threw himself into large-scale construction projects such as completing the Gate of Nations and the Palace of Darius at Susa. They were superb examples of architecture but extremely expensive to build, with the result that tensions in the country began to rise. The next step was confusing but inevitable.

Artabanus, commander of the royal bodyguards and a man with some pretensions to the ultimate prize of Kingship, had been plotting for some time how to remove Xerxes. By the middle of 465 BCE he had his seven sons appointed to positions of power in the government and finally felt ready to strike out at Xerxes.

The playing out of the assassinations which then followed is a little confusing. Firstly, there is the view that Artabanus killed Xerxes and then either assassinated his son, the Crown Prince Darius, or accused him of killing the king with the result that Darius was arrested and executed by Persian authorities.

Whichever version is correct, Artabanus then usurped the throne, firstly for himself and then, deciding it would be better to be the power behind the throne, installed another of Xerxes' sons, young Artaxerxes, as monarch. If that is true it was a grave mistake. Within a few months Artabanus was dead, assassinated by the sword of Artaxerxes.

There is another version of the events. This states that Artaxerxes killed both Xerxes and Darius before moving on to rid Persia of Artabanus. A third slightly different version states that Artabanus was betrayed by his fellow plotters before he could put plans into action and that Artaxerxes carried out the assassinations before seizing the throne.

The choice of which assassination version you prefer remains with you. However, Artaxerxes went on to rule the Persian Empire for forty years. He had 17 sons by various wives and on his death in 425 BCE was succeeded by Xerxes II.

The Battle of Salamis

The Battle of Salamis, 480 BCE, cannot be regarded as an assassination – or can it? Arguably, victory for the Greek alliance in one of the greatest sea battles of the ancient world, was nothing more, nothing less than the assassination of an entire fleet of Persian warships.

It was a deliberate and well-considered operation, one that changed the course of Greek and Persian history. For that reason alone the battle is an important element in the life and death of King Xerxes, indeed of the whole Persian Empire, and requires more than just a brief footnote.

The battle took place in the late summer of 480 BCE. It was fought in the straits between mainland Greece and the island of Salamis, a narrow and congested channel that the Greeks used to their advantage. They also used subterfuge and trickery.

Letters to King Xerxes, supposedly from an unknown source but actually penned by Themistocles, the Athenian General in command of the combined Greek fleets, recommended an immediate attack by the full Persian force. None of the Persians had any idea of what awaited them.

Xerxes, keen to exploit his invasion of Greece, fell eagerly into the trap. He immediately ordered his ships to be rowed into the strait, intending to block both entrances and thereby trap the Greeks. They would, he decided, have no place to run. It was exactly what Themistocles had hoped for and planned.

The greater number of Persian vessels was their undoing, causing confusion and chaos in their ranks. They were unable to manoeuvre effectively in the narrow and congested channel, in complete contrast to the smaller and totally out-numbered Greek vessels which maintained their line of battle and smashed into the enemy with frightening intensity.

The result was a complete and humiliating defeat for Xerxes. Hundreds of lives were lost, along with many fine ships and whatever credibility he had once held disappeared as his vessels sank to the bottom of the sea. The assassination of a fleet!

In the wake of the battle, the Persian forces withdrew, leaving only a small rearguard in southern Greece. When this unit was defeated at Plataea, the invasion and the war ended. Xerxes retired to his capital where, in due course, the defeat gave his opponents the ideal motive to remove him from power. The assassination of an individual ruler!

The Greek victory meant that never again would any of the city states have cause to fear other foreign nations, at least not until the Roman Empire intruded on their existence:

> 'Before Salamis most of the Greek city states were agrarian, parochial and isolated, intimidated by 70 million subjects of the Persian Empire to the east, and overshadowed by millions more in the Near East and Egypt ... After Salamis, for the next

three hundred and a half centuries, murderous Greek-speaking armies possessed superior technology and were bankrolled by shrewd financiers.[2]

After the ignominious retreat of Xerxes and his invasion force Persia went into a gradual decline. Persian warriors did not return to Greece and their empire faded as a world power, The Battle of Salamis marked the end of one empire and the growth of another. The days of Greek glory arrived.

Xerxes II

Artaxerxes, successor to Xerxes I, might have ruled for nearly forty years but his son, Xerxes II, managed to remain on the Persian throne for a mere forty five days. Even in the turmoil of post-Salamis Persian politics that was an amazingly short tenure.

Like so many of his predecessors and successors, he was assassinated but even if he had survived the attack it is unlikely that he would have achieved a great deal. Lazy, self-indulgent, Xerxes II was hardly the man to take on the running of the declining Persian Empire.

The only legitimate son of Artaxerxes – there were many more illegitimate children - Xerxes had spent most of his father's long reign just kicking his heels and enjoying the luxury of life in the royal palace. Wine, women and song appeared to be his general attitude and view of life. It is hard not to be too critical but Xerxes had been given much and very little had been asked back in return.

Given his character, it was difficult for him not to lie back and wallow in the richness of it all. He had served as the Crown Prince but that was a largely honorary position and did not intrude on his lifestyle. Time enough to start work when he succeeded his father. However, when he did become king, Xerxes saw no reason to change either his attitude or his behaviour.

A sensible man would have realised the precariousness of his position and taken steps to keep himself safe. Not Xerxes.

Two of the illegitimate sons of Artaxerxes, the new King's half-brothers Sogdianus and Ochus, had also made public their claims to the throne. Consequently, Xerxes was recognised as king only in Persia. It was a difficult, not to say deadly situation given the country's propensity for assassination, that clearly could not last for long.

Drunk, unconscious and incapable of defending himself, Xerxes was soon killed while lying in his normal inebriated stupor on his bed. Two assassins by the names of Phamacyas and Menostanes, paid for by Xerxes' half-brother Sogdianus, carried out the actual killing.

Installed as king, a few months later Sogdianus was himself assassinated on the orders of his half-brother, Ochus, who felt that he had a better claim to the throne. It was a presumption he would prove in combat.

The death of Sogdianus came after Ochus defeated him in battle and took him prisoner. At the request of his brother, Ochus promised Sogdianus that he would not be killed by sword, by poison or by starvation or by any of the traditional assassination methods. Thinking he had covered all bases, Sogdianus relaxed. It was a fatal mistake.

True to his word, Ochus used none of the usual methods of assassination but had Sogdianus smothered to death in ashes. Under the name and rank of Emperor Darius II, Ochus went on to rule for the next nineteen years. He was succeeded by Darius III.

Darius III

Darius III came to the throne of Persia in 380 BCE, the last monarch of the Persian Empire's Achaemenid Dynasty. He was unfortunate in that he soon found himself up against the power of Alexander the Great but his route to the throne had been unexpected as well as both difficult and dangerous and so, initially at least, Darius took the challenge in his stride.

An obscure and little known member of the Achaemenid Dynasty, Darius had performed well on the field of battle, so well in fact that he was rewarded by being given the task of controlling the Persian Postal Service.

The connection between war and the Empire's post might seem a little strange but running the Postal Service was a high ranking position in the Empire, one that carried much acclaim and prestige. At this stage he had no intention of making a play for the throne, being quite content with his position and status.

In the murky world of Persian politics, Darius was still something of an outsider who watched from a distance as the scramble for power increased. The most significant figure at this time was the eunuch Bagoas, vizier or chief minister to Emperor Artaxerxes III and a man determined to gain as much wealth and power as he could get his hands on.

It took time but Bagoas was hugely successful in realising his ambitions, gradually clawing more and more control away from Emperor Artaxerxes. What was taken from Artaxerxes was quickly bestowed onto the shoulders of Bagoas.

And then, when he was ready, Bagoas made his ultimate move. He poisoned the King and, in order to prevent them claiming the throne, took out most of the dead monarch's family as well. Bagoas then installed Artaxerxes' sole remaining son Arses as monarch. Arses was given the title Artaxerxes IV.

The new King was really only a puppet ruler, virtually all of the power remaining with the wily poisoner and eunuch Bagoas.

After two years of being manipulated and controlled, Arses finally grasped what was happening and decided on a case of poetic justice. He would remove his controller by poisoning him.

However, Bagoas was nothing if not alert to danger. His informants in the royal palace told him what Arses had in mind and, perhaps inevitably, the eunuch struck first. He used poison, the same poison that had been intended for him, to finish off Arses and remain in control.

The next stage of his plan involved the elevation of the unsuspecting Darius who duly became Darius III. As a distant and obscure figure in the lineage of the royal family Darius did have a claim to the throne, slight as it might be, and now Bagoas installed him as the new monarch. It was a far cry from the Persian Postal Service.

Darius, however, was more than a match for the eunuch and soon realised that Bagoas was not yet finished. What he had in mind for Darius was exactly the same fate that had finished off both Artaxerxes and Arses.

Darius was only too aware that it was time to act - and act quickly! He had Bagoas arrested and, with his bodyguards hovering, Darius personally forced him to drink the poison that had been intended for himself.

Everything seemed to be going well for Darius but, at that point, enter Alexander the Great. The long feared Macedonian invasion finally took place and war clouds loomed over the Persian capital.

At the Battle of Gaugamela, although his forces greatly outnumbered Alexander, Darius was soundly beaten and fled the battlefield. He was soon caught up with and apprehended by his general Bassus, a man with distinctly royal ambitions himself.

Bassus was clear that Darius had neither the skill nor the willingness to deal with Alexander. It is hardly surprising but his suggestion that Darius should hand over control of the empire and the army to him – he would give power back after Alexander was defeated, he claimed – was rejected out of hand.

Realising he had only one card left to play, Bassus had the unfortunate Darius bound hand and foot and thrown into the back of an ox cart. A captive emperor, he clearly thought, might still be a valuable asset in negotiations with the invading Greeks.

Hearing that Alexander was close, however, Bassus was thrown into a panic. He immediately stabbed Darius who was left to die in the back of the cart. Alexander was unimpressed by the act of regicide, had Bassus executed and sent the body of the dead emperor back to the Persian capital.

In due course, Alexander married the daughter of Darius in 324 BCE, thereby unifying Persia and Macedonia and making the machinations of Darius, Bassus and Arses irrelevant.[3]

A Strange Sort of Killing

Perhaps not an assassination in the true sense of the word, unless eagles in the ancient world harboured some secret knowledge that humankind did not then know and still do not, but even now, the death of Aeschylus, the so-called father of Greek tragedy, remains a remarkable event. As such it deserves to be noted here.

Aeschylus, now in his dotage, was sitting outside in the open air, as was his habit. He was killed when a passing eagle dropped a captive tortoise onto his head. The eagle may have lost his dinner, Aeschylus lost his life.

It has been suggested that the eagle mistook the writer's bald head for a rock, intending to use it to smash open the shell of the tortoise. It seems a rather curious explanation.

All birds of prey would be familiar with rocks and the landscape. The eagle in question would have been unlikely to mistake the head of an old man for a rock or boulder.

Pliny the Elder later wrote that Aeschylus had been given a prophesy that he would be killed by something heavy dropping onto his head. Aeschylus therefore took to spending as much time as possible out of doors where, he believed, he would be free of falling objects like books and ornaments. Wrong choice, Aeschylus.

You are left wondering. Was it all as the legend declares or was there some mysterious and hidden motive behind the death? At this distance in time the question is unanswerable and the legend is best left alone.

Chapter Four

Far Away Places, Strange Sounding Names

However intrepid the warriors of the ancient world might have been, they still remained part of a limited and relatively localised environment. Their world was located and remained fixed around the confines of the Mediterranean, give or take a hinterland of a few hundred miles.

Inevitably, this limited range of conquest and control meant that distant regions and countries like China, Japan and India were more or less unknown environments. Very few intrepid explorers ever attempted to discover and enjoy them.

Alexander the Great ventured to the borderlands of India but even he did not make it further east so that China and Japan remained unknown to the western politicians and generals. In time, trade routes were established between the empires around the Mediterranean and the vast regions of China but that lay some years in the future.

And yet, despite their distance, despite their alien cultures, many of these faraway places still managed to exert an influence on the western world. In the design and in the methodology of assassinations it can be argued that they were actually way ahead of the so-called civilised nations and empires of the west.

One fact, more than any other, stands out in so many of these eastern assassinations - the willingness of the killers and, in some cases, the victims as well, to self-sacrifice. Benefits in the next world and family prestige or status only partly explain this willingness to suffer and perhaps die in the exercising of what the perpetrators clearly thought of as the assassins art.

Amongst all of the many successful and perhaps unremarkable assassinations that were carried out, a whole range of self-inflicted pain and sacrificial efforts were displayed in the stories of killers and murderers from the ancient world of the east.

There were assassins who killed knowing that they too would probably be cut down; there were assassins who deliberately mutilated themselves before or after the killing; and there were victims who quietly and in a dignified manner accepted their fate. Amazingly, they are all to be found in those far away countries with very strange sounding names.

Brihadratha Maurya

The ninth and last monarch of the Mauryan Empire who held sway in north western India (covering much of the area now known as Afghanistan and Pakistan) was Brihadratha Maurya. He ruled for barely three years before being assassinated by Pushyamitra Shunga, one of his leading generals.

Brihadratha Maurya had come to the throne of the Mauryan Empire in 187 BCE, a positive relationship with the burgeoning Greek Empire of Alexander the Great and his successors on his western flank giving him hope of a peaceful reign. It was not to be.

There were many groups and individuals in India who were adamantly opposed to any sort of link with the Macedonian-Greeks who they had seen conquering country after country, almost under their noses. Pushyamitra Shunga was just one of the wary generals but, significantly, he was someone who was prepared to do something about it.

Pushyamitra Shunga also had ambitions that stretched far beyond commanding just a part of the army. He wanted to be ruler of the region and, indeed, went on to found the Shunga Empire after the death of Brihadratha with himself as the first Shunga Emperor.

Pushyamitra was well aware of the political situation in his country. Since Brihadratha had come to the throne much of the Empire had been lost. Dimetrius, one of the 'successors' to Alexander the Great had established himself in the Kabul Valley and had also taken over parts of the Punjab. Brihadratha seemed to be unwilling or unable to do anything about it.

Conscious that he was seizing power – and knowing that, one day, the same fate might await him – Pushyamitra Shunga knew that he had to make an impression. Shock and surprise were his weapons.

He did not just assassinate Brihadratha, he actually killed him in front of the entire Mauryan Army. He had ordered them to assemble, fully armed, and show their force to the emperor. Killing Brihadratha in front of them was a powerful and dramatic gesture, leaving no-one in any doubt about who was now in control. It was a message understood by everyone in the ranks of shocked but accepting soldiers.

There have been doubts cast upon this version of the assassination of Brihadratha but they have not, so far, been clarified by explanations of what the alternative ending might have been. What we do know is that Pushyamitra ruled from 185 until 149 BCE, successfully protecting India from the all-conquering armies of the Greek/Macedonian Empire.

Anula of Anuradhapura

The closest thing the Indian sub-continent – on the island state of Sri Lanka to be precise – ever got to the poison-happy Borgia family of Italy came in the shape of Anula of Anuradhapura who reigned for a brief period between 47 and 42 BCE.

Married to four different monarchs, Anula poisoned her way out of each of them until in 47 BCE she became the first Queen Regent in the history of Sri Lanka. That was the position she really wanted.

Dynamic and resourceful, even when she was married she remained the controlling influence behind the throne. She enjoyed wielding power and was quick to dispense with any of her partners who did not match up to her own levels of involvement in the politics of the state. She invariably did it by poisoning them.

Never one to worry too much about protocol and family connections, at one stage Anula became enamoured of a palace guard and had him manoeuvred into the position of control. He, too, was poisoned off when Anula became bored with him.

She met her match, however, when she was deposed as Regent by Kutakanna Tissa in 42 BCE. He had no time for the gentler assassins tools like the poison jar. He simply had Anula burned alive on a funeral pyre.

The Art of War

In his book *The Art of War* Chinese general Sun Tza made several interesting suggestions regarding the validity and use of assassination.

Amongst these suggestions was one idea that several ancient world emperors might well have taken on board and used to their own benefit. It would, at least, have made their lives easier and, for all we know, some of the ideas might well have been put into operation. The Indian philosopher, teacher and writer Chanakya certainly understood Sun Tza's views and, several years later, reinforced them for his own readership and patrons.

All nations, Sun Tza and Chanakya said, should employ groups of well-paid spies who would double as assassins. The spies/assassins could be brought into use as and when the occasion demanded it. The spies would either carry out the assassination themselves or, preferably, bribe close attendants like the victim's aide-de-camp, his door keepers, close servants or anyone who had regular contact and commitment with the target.

Such a force, Sun Tza believed, would be invaluable and also a great deal cheaper than keeping armies in the field. The 'ethics' of such a process were never discussed.

Prince Guang of Wu

In 515 BCE the Chinese Prince Guang of Wu, later King Helu of Wu, claimed that he had been cheated out of his full inheritance by the reigning monarch of the province, his uncle King Liau. He received little official response to his claim, something that was only to be expected but which annoyed Guang.

He would have to take matters into his own hands, Guang decided. Assassination was the only way forward but Liau was always well protected by his soldiers and personal bodyguards.

Perhaps more significantly, when out in public or sitting in state he always wore armour comprised of three separate layers in order to protect him from sudden knife or sword attacks. It seemed as if Guang's claims were going nowhere.

Then Guang was recommended the services of an assassin named Zhuan Zhu, a highly successful killer who had begun life, and sometimes still doubled, as a butcher.

The killing, Zhuan quickly realised, could be done but it was likely to be at the cost of his own life. Inordinately attached to his mother, Zhuan announced that he would be prepared to carry out the assassination on the proviso that his beloved mother would be cared for afterwards. She would, Guang agreed, be treated like a queen for the rest of her life.

At that point tragedy struck. Shortly before the date of the proposed assassination Zhuan's mother killed herself. She did it so that her son would not be distracted in his mission. Almost overcome with grief and now consumed with what he regarded as righteous anger, Zhuan insisted he would go ahead with his task.

Tapping on the skills picked up in his second profession, Zhuan managed to land a job as chef in Liau's kitchens. Once installed in his post he began to prepare a delicious fish dish for the king. The smell wafted over everything, making everyone's mouth water at the prospect of what was to come. As was customary and in great state Zhuan carried the dish into the dining room.

He was searched by the guards but no weapon was found. King Liau was mesmerised by the sight and smell of the fish, his eyes popping, mouth drooling and fingers clenched tightly together. He could hardly wait.

At that moment Zhuan Zhu thrust his arm into the belly of the fish, pulled out a hidden knife and slammed it into the chest of the unsuspecting king. The blade, sharp as a needle, went through all three layers of clothing and Liau died instantly. If the knife thrust had not killed him the poison that Zhuan had smeared onto the blade certainly would have ended his life.

As Zhuan had expected, he had no chance of escape. The guards pounced on the assassin and literally chopped him to pieces.

It was, of course, far too late to save their king but Zhuan was probably content to join his mother in the afterlife. He and his weapon went down in history, the dagger being known for ever afterwards as 'the fish intestine.'

Zhuan, his mother and Liau might all be dead but Prince Guang had achieved his aim. In the wake of his uncle's death he became king, fulfilling many of the tips in General Tzu's book – it had been a cheap but highly effective killing.

Nie Zheng, Assassin

Like Zhuan Zhu, the assassin Nie Zheng was also a butcher. When Yan Zhongli, an old friend approached him, asking Nie to kill Xia Lei, the Prime Minister of Korea, he refused. He needed to look after his sickly mother, he said, and turned down the rather hefty offer of one hundred golden Jin.

A number of months passed and Nie's mother died. At that point, the offer still remaining open, Nie Zheng agreed to assassinate Xia Lei. It was now 397 BCE.

His approach was simple. He smashed his way into Xia Lei's house and began striking out at anyone he encountered in his path. He apparently slaughtered over a dozen men, including his chief target Xia Lei.

With the job almost complete, Nie Zheng then slashed his face until it was unrecognisable, gouged out his eyes and killed himself. The self-mutilation had rendered the corpse virtually unrecognisable but Nie's body was laid out in the market place, gold being offered to anyone who might be able to identify the dead assassin.

Nie's sister, aware of Nie's intentions, went to view the body. She immediately guessed it was her brother and told the authorities, her intention being to give Nie a place in history. Then, stricken with grief, she collapsed and died.

Two Japanese Emperors

Assassinations in Japan during the ancient world period were rare, most people generally accepting the sovereignty and historical formation of society and its structure, always with an emperor at the head. Where the rare assassination did take place it was usually as a result of personal grievance or individual complaints.

The Japanese Emperor Anko, for example, was assassinated in 453 CE after a reign that lasted only three years. Little is known about him but he came to power after a bloody and destructive war between various members of his family. During his reign as the twentieth Japanese emperor the capital was moved to Isonkumi in Yamoto.[1]

Again, very little is known about his assassination but the deed was carried out by Mayura no Okima, Prince Mayoura as he was titled. It was apparently a revenge attack for the execution of his father but details of the assassination do not seem to exist. Anko was 56 years old at the time of his death.

We know a little more about the activities of Emperor Umako, the leader of the Soya family, the man credited with establishing Buddhism in Japan.

Umako was the driving force behind the destruction of the Mononobe clan. He was also the man behind the ascendence of the Soya clan, helping them to climb to the position of the premier family in Japan. Having been given permission by the emperor to build a small Buddhist chapel he, like many others, was astounded when an epidemic that killed thousands was blamed on a likeness of the Buddha that held a position of prominence in the chapel. A religious war soon erupted.

Things were made still more dangerous when the Emperor died. The Mononobe clan immediately put up their claimant for the throne; the Soya backed Sushan from their own ranks. Religious war melded into civil war but in 587 BCE the Soya clan under the command of Umako totally destroyed and annihilated the Mononobe threat and installed Sushan as Emperor.

Peace did not last very long as Umako and Sushan soon fell out. Rather than begin another war Umako simply ordered the assassination of his prodigy. The lesson to be learned was never argue or fall out with more significant comrades, especially the ones who had guided you to power in the first place.

Sushan was succeeded by Umako's niece Suiko. By installing her as empress rather than finding a suitable male candidate, Umako was breaking with tradition. It did not bother him as he turned his attention to developing the Buddhist religion in Japan.

He brought in Chinese monks and scholars, craftsmen and artists and with the support of Empress Suiko the religion was soon flourishing.

The Remorseful Assassin

In China in the second century BCE the diminutive assassin Yao Li had a reputation for vicious and effective killings that totally belied his size. Well under five feet in height, he was nevertheless a powerfully built individual who was determined and, as it turned out, selfless in carrying out his allotted or chosen tasks.

He was commissioned by King Helu of Wu to assassinate Prince Qingji who was hiding out in the state of Wei. Yao Li was nothing if not meticulous and went about preparing carefully for his mission. He decided that he would pass himself off as a criminal and gain acceptance into Qingji's inner circle as a murderer, thief and as a villain.

In order to create and manage the right effect Yao Li felt he needed to look and feel the part. What he did in order to achieve this was almost unbelievable.

Amazingly, he began by killing his wife and mother; next he persuaded King Helu to cut off his hand, the loss of a hand for thieving being a traditional punishment for many criminals. Then, preparations made, the assassin approached his target. The exact dates are unclear but it was circa 520 BCE.

Yao was duly accepted into Qingji's entourage and pledged his allegiance to the Prince. For a while nobody suspected anything.

Then, while the group was crossing the Yangtze River, the assassin made sure he was standing directly behind Qingji. The weather was bad and the ship began rocking in what had become a fierce gale. Qingji, his eyes closed against the wind and rain, did not see Yao Li raise his spear. One handed, the assassin plunged his weapon into the Prince's back.

Qingji managed to pull out the spear and, knowing that he was dying, congratulated Yao on his courage and skill. He ordered his guards not to kill the assassin and slid slowly to the deck. Then, without another word, he died.

Seeing the bravery of Prince Qingji, Yao Li was overcome with remorse. He knew that he had committed a number of unforgivable offences. Firstly, he had killed his closest family, secondly he had assassinated Qingji, a man he had sworn to serve, and thirdly by mutilating himself he had insulted the honour of his parents.

Knowing he was damned, Yao Li walked calmly to the ship's rail and threw himself into the raging waters of the river. He was quickly swept out of view and never heard of again.

The Sacred Ridge Massacre

We are used to hearing about massacres of Native American People, usually at the hands of the US Cavalry. But recent research on Sacred Ridge outside Durango, Colorado, offers something of a variation on the old story.

Archaeological exploration, carried out in 2010, has uncovered a massacre of the Anasazi Puebloan people dating to circa 800 BCE, long before the cavalry appeared on the scene.

Skeleton remains, along with a number of two-headed axes spotted with the remnants of blood, showed that the massacre was a planned event, something that was carried out over two or three days. In other words it was a mass assassination, one that despatched over 3000 people.

Examination of the remains showed that there was evidence of torture before death and mutilation of the corpses afterwards. Arms and legs of the victims were cut off and presumably taken away as trophies. Killing pits had been dug ready for the assassination of men, women and children and the entire village, containing some twenty structures, was burned in the wake of the massacre.

Reasons for the mass assassinations have not yet been discovered, although several suggestions have been laid out. Teeth and other parts of the skeletal remains have shown that the victims were all of a different ethnicity from the assassins – that is certainly one possible cause.[2]

Then, inter-tribal tensions might have played a part. Weather conditions, notably a long-running drought, might also have been a contributing factor. It is hard to know but perhaps at some stage in the future something more will be learned.

Death in the Warring States Period

The Warring States Period was a long stretch of time in China's history ranging from approximately 475 until 221 BCE, nearly 300 years. It followed the Spring and Autumn Period in Chinese history, a time which was certainly not the peaceful and harmonious time the name suggests.

The Spring and Autumn Period, named after a chronicle of the State of Lu, may have been shorter than the Warring States Period but it was almost as violent and bloody.

In the Warring States Period, seven different states or regional clans competed for control. Some, like the Han, were quite small and relatively weak, others – notably the Qin - were far more powerful and better equipped to fight a civil war.

Several major battles were fought during the Warring States Period resulting in thousands upon thousands of deaths and injuries. Finally, the time of war was brought to an end when the victorious Qin State unified China. It was the conclusion of an era although for men and women whose whole life had been spent in violence and killing it was hard to put weapons of war aside.

Jing Ke and the Great Failure

Even the best sometimes get it wrong! As a final example of assassination in far distant places, a failed assassination attempt during China's Warring States Period must be mentioned.

By the third century BCE the Chinese state of Qin was so supreme that Crown Prince Dan of the rival north eastern State of Yan, decided that drastic measures were called for.

Perhaps remembering Sun Tzu and *The Art of War*, he came to the conclusion that King Zheng, the Qin ruler, needed to be removed from his seat of power. Consequently, in 227 BCE the renowned assassin Jing Ke was chosen to carry out the deed.

The resulting plan was two-fold. If possible Jing was to kidnap King Zheng, bring him back to Dan and force him to release many of the territories recently conquered and now controlled by the Qin clan. If that was not possible then, and only then, was Jing to kill his victim.

A complex cover story was invented to help Jing achieve success. He was to pretend to be a nobleman, someone exiled by the Yan State, begging for mercy and help. In order to ensure acceptance he would present two gifts. The first of these was a valuable map of Dukeng. The second gift was, to put it mildly, bizarre.

General Huan Li, a notable figure in the Warring States Period, had fallen out of favour with the Qin dynasty following a defeat in battle. Now, furious at the way he had been treated and desperate for revenge, Huan Li offered to commit suicide so that his severed head could be carried to the Qin palace and presented to King Zheng.

Jing was also given an assistant, a young man called Qin Wuyang. He had already committed a murder, some time before when he was just thirteen years old, but when compared to Jing he was inexperienced, maybe even something of a liability.

Meanwhile, the Crown Prince had laid his hands on the sharpest dagger he could find. Having had it coated with poison, he presented it to Jing Ke. Everything was now ready.

Jing Ke and Qin Wuyang were seen off by Prince Dan and his courtiers, all of them wearing white clothing to mark the occasion.

The poisoned dagger was hidden inside the rolled up map and the bloodied head of Huan Li was carried by Jing. It was a triumphal departure but it was grossly premature as things soon began to go wrong.

When the two assassins were presented to King Zheng, the young Qin Wuyang was clearly nervous. He was shaking and sweating, constantly glancing over his shoulder, so nervous in fact that officials were immediately wary and he was forbidden to approach the King.

Jing stepped forward, offering the head and the map. As Zheng reached out to take them, Jing pulled out the dagger. He grabbed at Zheng, taking hold of his sleeve but the King pulled away and Jing's blow missed the mark. Jing was left holding the torn sleeve as Zheng tried desperately to draw his sword which had slid around his waist and was now at his back.

The guards were outside the room, furiously trying to batter their way inside, as Zheng took refuge behind a pillar. He finally managed to get his sword out of its sheath and moved towards the assassin. Jing, realising things were going badly wrong, hurled the poisoned dagger at Zheng but it failed to hit the mark and clattered off a pillar to the floor.

By this stage, the only other person in the room was the royal physician. In desperation he threw his medicine bag at Jing, distracting his attention and allowing Zheng to get in a blow that struck the assassin in the thigh.

Jing staggered back, trying to staunch the flow of blood from his leg, and Zheng struck him again and again. In all, eight blows landed on his body. The weakened assassin slid to the floor, his back against a pillar and with his legs, wide open, stretched out in front of him. It was a deliberate dying pose, apparently regarded as an insulting position at the time.[3]

As the guards finally managed to batter their way through the doors and pour like advancing ranks of legionaries into the room, Jing spent his last moments hurling abuse and insults at the Qin King. The guards finished him off and then turned their attention to the terrified Qin Wuyang who had taken no part in the attempted assassination.

Qin Wuyang had, however, been in the wrong place at the wrong time. He may have murdered in his youth but this was different, this was cold blooded assassination and he had neither the heart nor the stomach for the affair. He, too, was quickly despatched by the guards.

The attempted assassination had been an unmitigated failure. King Zheng was shocked at how close he had been to death and went into a comatose state for a short while. He soon recovered, thanking the physician for having had a hand in saving his life. There was little else that could be done.

After the failed assassination attempt Zheng simply got on with his principal mission in life, uniting the various provinces of China into one major force. He put the attack down to occupational hazard. As the first emperor of the Qin Dynasty he reigned until 210 BCE.

Chapter Five

In the Shadow of Alexander the Great

Alexander the Great, the renowned and much revered King of the Greek state of Macedon, was arguably the greatest soldier of the ancient world. He succeeded his father, Philip of Macedon, in 336 BCE when he was just 20 years old but already his bearing and performance on the battlefield, as a commander in his father's army, had marked him down as the coming power in Macedonia and the Middle East.

Over the ten years following his accession to the throne, Alexander carved out one of the largest empires ever seen in the ancient world. It stretched for thousands of miles, from the deserts of Egypt to the River Indus and the northern borders of India.

Alexander was undefeated in battle, despite often fighting against vastly superior numbers. Arguably, his reign and his activities between becoming King of Macedonia and dying aged just 32, twelve years later, changed the course of history. As one writer has said:

> 'If Alexander had died at the age of twenty-two, instead of ten years later, after having conquered the Persian Empire, human history would have been very different indeed..'[1]

It's a fair point but at the end of the day the idea of Alexander dying even younger than the thirty-two years he achieved remains one of those imponderables that haunt history and make it so fascinating. He did die young but not before he had made a significant mark on the world.

So successful was Alexander that his very existence and reputation created huge problems, both for his successors and, strange as it might seem, for his immediate predecessor. They were all more or less chased by Alexander's shadow, even by those who had not had the time to see that shadow grow. The problems began with Alexander's father, Philip.

Philip II, King of Macedon

Coming to the throne in 359 BCE, Philip of Macedon had already lived a life of danger and adventure. He had fought in many battles and as a Macedonian prince he was the ideal political prisoner for powerful states and cities like Illyria and Thebes, both of which had recently defeated Macedon in war. They required a hostage to ensure the continuation of peace and Philip was just the man to fill the 'hostage role.'

During his period as a hostage Philip studied diplomacy and military tactics with some of the greatest teachers in the ancient world before being returned to Macedon in 364 BCE. During his time in 'captivity' Philip's brother had died in battle and, first as Regent for his nephew, then in his own right, Philip finally took the throne in his own name.

Over the next twenty or so years Philip II used diplomacy and military skill to take Macedon to the pinnacle of power in ancient Greece. He reformed the Macedonian army, doubling it in size, developing the cavalry and, in particular, revolutionising the infantry through the invention of the Macedonian Phalanx.

This amazing manoeuvre comprised a phalanx of twenty-one foot long spears wielded by sixty-four infantrymen, front, sides and rear, combined into a protective square. They advanced a wall of interlocking shields that acted both as a defensive manoeuvre and as an offensive tactic, literally battering the opposition out of the way – those who had survived the spears. It was a revolutionary tactic that shocked the world and brought Philip victory after victory in conflicts like the Peloponnesian War of 431-404 and Third Sacred War (346-356 BCE).[2]

Philip's premier achievement, however, was the creation of the League of Corinth, effectively uniting the Greek city states in a pact of peace. It secured the Macedonian underbelly and allowed Philip and then his son Alexander the Great to roam far and wide in what became nothing less than a bid to conquer the known world.

Philip was assassinated on 31 October 336 BCE, in the town theatre of Algae. He had gone there to celebrate the wedding of his daughter, unprotected by his usual squad of soldiers so as to be approachable by dignitaries and officials who were gathered in the theatre to welcome him. He was also, as it turned out, totally vulnerable.

When Philip paused to talk to someone in the crowd, Pausanias of Orestis, one of the seven bodyguards who had come with him as his only protection, reached over and stabbed him in the ribs. Philip died instantly.

In the chaos and surprise following the assassination Pausanias made a run for it, getting as far as his hidden and tethered horse. His intention was to get clear of the city and meet up with fellow conspirators waiting outside the city limits. They would then return and make a bid for power.

Unfortunately for him, Pausanias's horse tripped on a vine. He was thrown from the saddle and immediately pounced on by three of Philip's bodyguards. He was stabbed repeatedly and died where the guards had caught him. The motive behind the assassination of Philip remains unclear but Pausanias had apparently become a bodyguard with the express intention of assassinating the unsuspecting King.

A variety of reasons for the assassination have been suggested. One of the most feasible is that Philip's uncle Attalus had once got Pausanias drunk and then raped him. Pausanias could not get at Attalus who was away campaigning on behalf of his nephew so he looked for the next easy target for his revenge, Philip of Macedon. Another possibility is that Pausanias was the rejected homosexual lover of Philip but there is even less evidence for this than there is for the first option.

At the time of his death Philip was already becoming conscious of the skill and courage of his son. Their relationship was far from good, Philip growing more and more jealous of his son's abilities and Alexander lamenting that if his father did not stop conquering other lands it would leave him with nothing to do when he became king.

Father and son fell to quarrelling, events culminating in Alexander poking fun at Philip during a wedding banquet. Weapons were drawn but with Philip already drunk the argument came to nothing. As a result of the spat Alexander took his mother Olympias back to her home in Epirus while he endured self-imposed exile until Philip eventually relented and asked him to return.

Alexander and his mother Olympias were ambitious and, quite possibly, may have been aware that Pausanias was planning to kill the king. It has been suggested that they were actually the instigators of the plot, providing horses and weapons for Pausanias and his friends. It has never been proven, just as Philip's growing fear of his son also remains a matter of conjecture.

What is clear is the simple fact that Philip was growing older and more and more settled in his lifestyle. If he had remained alive he would have been far more circumspect in his attack on Persia and the other countries that Alexander went on to invade.

Philip would probably have been happy with a victory or two before making the offer of an enforced treaty – which may or may not have been broken at some stage in the future. He had not lost heart exactly but his desire for battle and conquest had diminished with age.

On the other hand, Alexander, young and eager for glory, wanted nothing less than complete victory, regardless of who the enemy actually was. He could see that his father was slowing down, just as Philip realised Alexander's ambition would bring death and submission to thousands. He was right in that. Estimates vary on the number of men killed during Alexander's wars of conquest, ranging between 300,000 and 400,000. Philip could not have suspected such casualty figures but already he was beginning to walk in Alexander's shadow.

Assassination, Multiple Examples

Alexander's first act on coming to the throne in 336 BCE was to eliminate anyone he considered a potential threat to him. This involved him in a number of assassinations, including that of his cousin Amyntas and two Macedonian princes from the region of Lyncestis who were rumoured to have taken part in the conspiracy to assassinate his father, Philip.

Perhaps the most significant opponent assassinated at this time was Attalus, the commander of the advance guard of the army then campaigning in Asia Minor. He was uncle of the King and the brother of Cleopatra Eurydice who happened to be married to Philip. At the wedding Attalus gave a public prayer hoping that Cleopatra would give birth to a legitimate heir. It was a clear insult to Alexander – and Alexander the Great never forgave an insult.

As well as having insulted the new King, Attalus was apparently in communication with Demosthenes of Athens regarding the possibility of defecting to the Greek city state. And then, of course, there was the oft-repeated rumour that he had raped Pausanias, the assassin of Philip. In Alexander's eyes, he was clearly too dangerous to live.

Philotas, commander of the elite Companion Cavalry, was another early victim to Alexander's paranoia. At the King/Emperor's behest, Philotas was condemned by the army which was quickly informed they would also have to kill him. Philotas' second in command was charged to carry out the act. Assassination or execution, it hardly mattered.

Alexander had always loved to exhibit his skill and courage. Making a statement that others would see and appreciate was high on his agenda. That was the reason behind his taming of the wild horse Bucephalus and the cutting of the Gordian Knot. People might forget many of his battles, they would never forget those two relatively minor events.

The Destruction of Thebes

Alexander the Great was not just a great soldier, he was also completely ruthless. His destruction of Thebes was a classic case of his brutality, the assassination of an entire city – purely for show.

In 335 BCE, after being placed at the head of the League of Corinth in place of his father, Alexander found himself pulled in several different directions as rebellions against Macedonian rule erupted in many of the Greek states.

He was north of Thebes with his army when he was given the news that Thebes, one of the most important city states in the country of Greece, had risen in revolt. Alexander immediately marched south, covering 300 miles in just two weeks and astounding the inhabitants of Thebes when he suddenly appeared outside their walls. They could hardly believe their eyes. Apart from anything else, Demosthenes of Athens had told them that Alexander was dead.

He was far from dead. From the beginning Alexander had known that he needed to make an example of Thebes. But to begin with he tried diplomacy. Prompted by Demosthenes, who had also provided Athenian weapons and material support, all of his advances and offers were rejected. It would have to be military action.

The Theban army marched out to face Alexander. They were reinforced by hundreds of slaves who had no choice in the matter, they were forced to fight. The only problem came when many of those slaves promptly decamped and joined Alexander's army. Even so, the Theban soldiers were still no match for the Macedonian Phalanx, and were quickly destroyed. Alexander then turned his attention on the city itself. Normally city bases like Thebes were left intact after a victory. Not this time.

The inhabitants were butchered and the city destroyed by fire. In all nearly 6000 soldiers and civilians were killed and 30,000 sold into slavery. Assassination is not too strong a word. Alexander knew exactly what he was doing, knew the purpose of his actions. It was ruthless butchery on a grand scale. And it worked.

Learning about the fate of Thebes, the other Greek city states quickly capitulated, leaving Alexander free to pursue his aims elsewhere. Only Athens resisted and with them Alexander was able to use his diplomatic skills to bring about their subjugation.

War and Death

Once he had removed the potential threats to his throne Alexander the Great was happy to begin the series of wars that kept him busy for the rest of his life.

After ensuring the safety and reliability of his Greek city states, Alexander invaded Persia. His army at this time consisted of 30,000 infantry and just 5,000 cavalry. It was the hordes of scientists, philosophers, engineers, historians and architects who accompanied his troops that gave away Alexander's true intentions. Victory in battle would be followed by subjugation and admission to the Macedonian Empire.

India was never far from Alexander's mind. In all honesty, he did not know a great deal about the country, protected as it was by the Himalayas, when he crossed the Indus in 327 BCE. It just happened to be next on the list after Egypt and the areas around the Mediterranean.

In battle Alexander had always led from the front. Given the furore and chaos involved in battles and skirmishes at that time, leading the charge inevitably put him at great personal risk. He was nearly killed on several occasions, often wounded and during the Indian campaign his lung was pierced by an arrow. Small wonder that his life was short.

Rumours that Alexander was assassinated have always abounded. His death in Babylon at the early age of thirty-two, still young and seemingly fit, was unexpected and shocked everyone. The actual drop into death from active military leader to comatose and helpless patient was a relatively lengthy one, eleven or fourteen days depending on whichever storyline you choose to believe.

The fourteen day version has Alexander sliding gradually into fever which worsened so that in the end he could barely speak. The eleven day version sees Alexander drinking a large bowl of unmixed wine, then being suddenly seized by a sharp stomach pain. It grew worse and worse, Alexander getting weaker by the hour. There was no fever but he died in agony.

Amazingly, Alexander's body which was left lying in state for six days while funeral arrangements were being made, did not decompose in any way.

The weather was hot and humid so that some sort of wasting of his flesh was to have been expected. When that did not happen, Alexander's soldiers immediately fell back on the old belief, one that Alexander himself partially accepted – he was not a human at all, he was nothing less than a god.

The immediate reaction by everyone, his comrades, his family, the politicians and diplomats, was that Alexander had been poisoned. That was eventually dismissed as the poisons then in use would have acted far quicker than the eleven or fourteen days of decline that Alexander reportedly endured. There were no chemical poisons in existence at that time and all of the 114 different poisonous materials available to assassins would have brought about death in a day or so.

While the actual cause of death remains unknown, it was probably not assassination. Malaria or typhoid, possibly even meningitis, aided by exhaustion after ten years of almost constant campaigning along with several serious wounds, would seem to be the logical cause. Alcoholism, leprosy and syphilis have also been suggested. Grief over the death of his friend and homosexual lover Hephaestion along with a dose of West Nile Virus, not identified until the twentieth century, have also been suggested.

The list of possible causes goes on and on. One thing, however, is clear. If Alexander the Great was assassinated then it was a sure case of self-assassination.

His relentless drive for action, the damage to his body in battle, the even more deadly abuse he courted and endured from copious amounts of alcohol and food, the signs are all there. They simply have not yet been proved to be the cause of Alexander's death.

Nevertheless, there are still many historians who claim that Alexander met his end at the hands of an assassin. One of the most persistent rumours or beliefs is that the philosopher Aristotle, in an act of revenge for the killing of his disciple Kallisthnes, sent the poison that was eventually used to assassinate Alexander. Antipater, who received the poison, supposedly administered it via a bowl of wine. The story is unlikely to be true but there are still people who believe it implicitly.

Roxane, Alexander's wife, has recently been 'put in the frame' for the assassination of her husband. He had taken another wife, cause enough for a jealous woman like Roxane. Then, she was bitterly hurt by his public display of sorrow and desperation at the death of Hephaestion. Alexander reportedly lay on his body for several days, not alongside it but actually on top of Hephaestion before he would allow his friend and partner to be buried. It would have been enough to push Roxane over the edge but, yet again, there is no proof.

One recent suggestion is that Alexander died from Guillain-Barre Syndrome, an auto-immune disorder where the immune system attacks healthy cells and often results in paralysis.

That has been offered as the reason for Alexander's six days of 'lying in state.' Put simply, he was not yet dead. He was certainly sick, incurably so, and could not move a muscle but was still able to hear and understand everything that was going on around him.³ The anger and fear that such a condition would have caused Alexander can only be imagined. How to tell everyone that he was still alive must have been a greater concern than conquering India or Persia.

Alexander died before the birth of his only child so that the succession was always going to be a problem. As he lay dying he was asked 'Who succeeds you?' His answer sparked off fifty years of almost incessant warfare between his generals. In what were his final words he managed to gasp out 'The strongest one.' He may have had someone in mind but died before he could name him.

Philip II of Macedon had brought the Greek states into one empire, Alexander took that Empire to totally new levels. The Hellenism developed and displayed during his reign was, arguably, his greatest achievement of all.

Greek culture was spread across the whole of the known world, men like Aristotle and Socrates spearheading the advance. Drama, poetry, the love of the human body, displayed through things like the Olympic Games, were revolutionary concepts that changed the world and greatly aided the growth of civilisation.

Regardless of that, it remained a brutal and dangerous time to be alive. Even erudite and thinking people like Aristotle held views that many of us would despise. They were not uncommon in the final years of the ancient world:

> 'There must be a law that no imperfect or maimed child should be brought up. And to avoid an excess in population, some children must be exposed. For a limit must be fixed for the population of the state.'⁴

Foe 'exposed' read 'left outside to die.' Shades of Hitler's Third Reich seem to surface very easily once you read those words.

The Wars of the Diadochi

On the death of their all-powerful leader, the Diadochi, the successors as they have become known, began the unofficial but ruthless business of dividing up Alexander's Macedonian Empire between them. The matter of the succession was sorted out first. This, it was decided, would fall on Alexander's unborn son. After birth and until he reached an age where he could rule, a Regent would be appointed.

Obeying Alexander's last 'instruction' the immediate matter of control within the Empire came down to who was the fittest, the strongest and most capable. Almost as a side-issue, the wars that took place over the next fifty years marked the end of the Alexandrine Age which Alexander had created and saw the beginning of the Hellenistic Period.

Four men – Ptolemy, Antigonus, Cassander and Seleucus – had been gifted territories by Alexander in the years before he died, four territories that they would rule as Satraps or Governors in his name. These territories were, respectively, the old empires of Egypt, Asia Minor, Macedonia and Persia.

To use Alexander's definition, the appointment of the four Satraps effectively meant that they were, initially at least, the leaders of the Empire, the strongest generals and administrators. Seleucus was excluded from the four, a position he would soon change. There were other men, ambitious and cunning, biting at the heels of the four. Seleucus was just one of them.

A number of separate wars took place during this period, one general attacking another and achieving temporary leadership and overall control. A pattern was soon established. War would erupt, then it would end and, after a period of uneasy peace, conflict would begin again.

A number of the generals and war leaders died in these battles. These included figures like Perdiccas, the Regent for Alexander's son Philip who, it soon became obvious, was intellectually disabled. Successful at first, Perdiccas soon found himself wrong footed many times. His army was dissatisfied with the results of his campaigns leading to a situation that Seleucus, serving Perdiccas as one of his strongest officers, headed up an assassination plot. Perdiccas was duly stabbed to death.

As Seleucus I Nicator, the 'new man on the block' went on to greater things, hauling himself up from the position of secondary player to lord and master of Asia Minor, Syria and Mesopotamia. In the process he carved out an empire for himself, one that grew to virtually replicate that of Alexander.

It was never made official but as his conquests continued it was clear that he was attempting to revive Alexander's Empire. Only Egypt, where Ptolemy remained strong, managed to avoid his grasp.

Seleucus was renowned as being the founder of several new cities. These included Antioch, which replaced Babylon as the centre of the empire, Edessa and Seleucia on the River Tiber. By the winter of 282 BCE his Empire stretched from Asia Minor to the northern extremities of India.

In India, which he invaded in 306, Seleucus found himself at war with Chandragupta Mauga, founder of the Indian Mauga Dynasty. The war ended in something of a stalemate and with a treaty that saw Chandragupta marrying the daughter of Seleucus. It also saw Seleucus presented with 500 war elephants, complete with mahouts. Seleucus would use them in the battles to come.

When, in the last year of his reign, Seleucus marched into Thrace he did not realise it would be his final campaign. He was assassinated by Ptolemy Ceraunus, a man he had befriended and just admitted to his inner circle.. Ptolemy slid a knife into his back as Seleucus was sacrificing to the gods.

For some time Antipater, the Satrap of Greece, had also been one of the most significant figures in the post-Alexander world and in 320 BCE he was elected Regent of all Alexander's Empire.

The promotion of Antipater should have brought peace and harmony but just one year later, in 319 BCE, Antipater died suddenly. The one man with enough prestige and ability to hold the Empire together had gone.

From that point on it was a downhill trajectory all the way for the great Macedonian Empire. Unfortunately, it just so happened that the Macedonian decline coincided with the rise of the Roman Empire. And that was a force that none of the Middle Eastern Dynasties could hinder or defeat. It was, barring the odd hitch or two, all one-way traffic.

The Antigonid Kingdom, established by Antigonus soon after Alexander died, quickly fell to Rome. So too did the kingdoms of Seleucus (the Seleucids) and of Ptolemy of Egypt (the Ptolemites). Unable to halt the break up of his Empire, Alexander the Great was probably turning in his grave.

Seleucus' creation of a new Alexandrian Empire was a reasonable enough achievement. He did, at least, establish and, for a while, retain his Empire – retain being the appropriate word. When compared with the great empires of the ancient world – Rome, Egypt, China - it was retention for just a small window of time.

The only one who manged anything like the achievements of his mentor was Cassander who founded the Antipatrid Dynasty. He managed to survive by a process of clever diplomacy and assassination or murder, notably of Alexander's infant, disabled son. He was succeeded by Philip IV.

The Dynasty did not last long once Philip died, the Antipatrid Dynasty growing weaker by the year and eventually falling back on their native Macedon. The kingdom was eventually conquered by the Romans in 168 BCE.

Chapter Six

Brutality in All Things

All assassinations are brutal. That is unavoidable in a process which involves the unexpected taking of a life, cutting short another person's time on the planet without permission, acting outside the law, perhaps even going against public opinion. Having said that, it seems an obvious statement but some assassinations were more brutal than others.

Over time, justification for assassination developed into a necessary evil, not just for the assassins but also for those who paid for and perhaps planned the whole event:

> 'Sometimes the murder is conceived – by others as well as the murderer – as a duty, and is justified by ideological arguments. The victim is a tyrant or a usurper; to kill him is a virtue, not a crime. Such ideological justification may be expressed in political or religious terms.'[1]

The logical extension to such a rationale is that, in the minds and eyes of the assassins or the planners, the greater the crime the more deserving is the victim of a vicious and brutal slaying. The killing or assassination is no longer a means to an end. It is a statement.

In the ancient world most assassinations were over quickly; a knife in the ribs, a swift dose of poison, a club or hammer over the back of the skull. Occasionally, however, the brutality of the murder – shown by its violence, by the length of time it took to complete the actual deed, by the clearly perverted enjoyment the assassination gave to the perpetrators - still retains the power to shock.

Phalaris and his use of the Brazen Bull is a classic example of 'assassin shock.' Painful, prolonged, noisy and available for public entertainment, it was brutality of the finest order. Its use did not always constitute an assassination although the Bull's final appearance and use certainly was.

Planned, thought through, the final use of the Bull was executed by the rebels who overthrew Phalaris to end the tyrant's life. They did it to perfection. Hardly surprising when the apparatus, in the shape of the Brazen

Bull itself, was already there to hand. There were many other examples, some well-known, some obscure.

The Ottoman Fratricide

Technically outside the remit of this book, the Ottomans came to power in Turkey towards the end of the twelfth century. They were, however, descended from the Turkic people, a race with origins that can be traced back to the first century CE.

Both Pomponius Mela and Pliny the Elder refer to the Turkic tribes in their writings, so perhaps there is good reason to mention them here. As predecessors to or forerunners of the Ottoman's they might have practiced, perhaps irregularly, perhaps more commonly, some of the tropes that later became a significant part of the Ottoman Empire.

What makes the Ottomans special, and possibly the Turkic people too, is that the leaders and sovereigns of their Empire practiced a form of safety netting that others in the ancient world would have done well to adopt. It was fratricide on a grand scale, aimed at supporting a policy of one-man sovereignty:

> 'The political and historical pressures forced the Sultans to destroy and kill their rivals. This sad compulsion meant that, either willingly or unwillingly, they murdered even their own brothers … The process of brother-killing actually became legal, with a law stating it was right and proper for the administration of the Empire.'[2]

As it lies outside the span of this book, it is probably wrong to delay too long over the Ottoman policy of brother-killing. Suffice to say that no matter what were initially 'good' intentions, brother-killing was something which quickly escalated to whole-family assassinations. It does, however, beg the question – should, could and would the rulers of the ancient world have gone down the same path?

Brute Force and Ignorance

And yet, despite the theory that brutal behaviour demands a brutal response, many of the more vicious assassinations took place because the perpetrator, and sometimes even the victim as well, simply did not know any better.

The ancient world was a small world, perhaps not in terms of the territory it covered, but certainly in the depth of understanding displayed by any one particular culture to the detriment of others. Nine times out of ten understanding began and finished in the home environment, in other words the country from where the individual came. It was better, it was more useful and it was certainly more accessible. Conquests might have brought the occasional new set of values or behaviours but mostly it involved simply the imposition of home values upon a beaten foe.

Warriors and politicians might have known about the expected response of brutality breeding brutality - an eye for an eye, as the Bible declared. To continue the metaphor, they would have been singularly one-eyed if they had not. But the customs and traditions of other nations were largely an unknown world.

If you looked for it, the message was there. You accidentally insult the traditions or the ruler of a kingdom and you are courting danger. Deliberately insult those traditions and you had better have a good escape plan ready to go into operation.

Very rarely did one nation invade another because it had better facilities for things like education or health care, better standards of living, better infrastructure and so on. War and invasion had more basic roots than that. Land grabs, bullion theft, a desire to hit the enemy before he hits you, those were the basic tenets of ancient warfare.

A Bodily Function

The Greek historian Herodotus, writing in 569 BCE, declared that a single bodily action once caused a revolt against King Apries of Egypt and, ultimately, brought about his downfall. It was a simple enough story, but one that quickly became admired and loved by the storytellers of the age.

King Apries sent his general Amasis to quash a rebellion in the ranks of his troops. The rebels quickly decided that they preferred Amasis to Apries and, almost before anyone knew what was happening, crowned him King.

Apries next despatched his advisor Patorbemis to try to talk some sense into Amasis. But the new King was enjoying his position. He raised one cheek of his backside from the couch, broke wind and declared 'Take that back to Apries.'

It is not known if Patorbemis demonstrated the answer from Amasis but when he passed on the comment Apries lost all sense of reason. He had the messenger arrested, bound and then brought before him. Without further argument or debate, Apries then ordered his nose and ears to be cut off as punishment for bearing such unwelcome news.

News of the brutal treatment towards a man who was simply doing his job quickly spread and Apries was faced by open rebellion. He was literally torn apart by a furious crowd. Brutality clearly breeds brutality.

Mithridates and The Boat

The death of a soldier called Mithridates (not to be confused with the Persian Emperor of the same name) is one of the most brutal of all recorded assassinations. His fate is worth noting. To begin with, what was the reason for the assassination?

There are two parts to the answer. First, Mithridates had accidently killed Cyrus, brother of King Artaxerxes II. The King agreed to forget the matter as long as everyone assumed it was him who had fired the fatal arrow.

That was fine until, second part of the answer, Mithridates got very drunk at a royal banquet and betrayed the confidence of King Artaxerxes II. Furious that everyone now knew of the deception, Artaxerxes decided that the young soldier needed to die. The method of assassination was known as Scaphism or, in translation, The Boat.

Mithridates was laid in a small boat, half full of water. Another identical boat was upturned and nailed on top of the first one, creating something resembling a shell. Mithridates' arms, legs and head were left sticking out.

Once both parts of the boat were in place Mithridates was force-fed several cannisters of honey and milk, a mixture of which was also rubbed into his limbs and cheeks. This sickening process was repeated every day the victim survived.

With his face turned towards the blistering sun, flies, wasps and other insects immediately settled on Mithridates' head and limbs and it was not long before he began to suffer from diarrhoea. Worms and rats could be relied on to add their involvement to the pain of Mithridates.

Within a few hours dozens of different vermin, worms and sea-snakes in particular, began to appear, feeding on the excrement now lying in the boat and then beginning to gnaw at the victim's vulnerable body. Amazingly Mithridates survived for seventeen long days before, mercifully, dying.

The Humiliation of Valerian

Emperor Valerian, full name Publius Licinius Valerianis, was the first Roman Emperor to be captured alive by the enemy. Most beaten or defeated Roman leaders would kill themselves rather than be captured. Not Valerian, however. Emperor between 253 and 260 CE, Valerian was campaigning against the Persians when he was defeated at the Battle of Edessa.

Desperate for freedom, Valerian tried many ways to escape. It was all in vain, he spent the rest of his life in captivity. During his imprisonment Valerian suffered horrendous humiliations such as being used as a footstool by the Persian King Shapur. He was also used as a mounting block whenever Shapur wanted to mount his horse.

Finally, after several years as a prisoner, in 260 CE Valerian offered Shapur a huge sum of money if he would only set him free.

The Persian King was disgusted by what he saw as the Roman Emperor's lack of courage and honour and immediately had Valerius killed. Molten gold was poured down his throat, his skin was flayed from his bones and then stuffed with straw. The grisly trophy remained on show in the Persian palace.

The Prophet Muhammad

The prophet Muhammad was a man of many parts. Holy man, religious, spiritual and secular leader to his people, founder of the Islamic religion and, when necessary, organiser of assassinations, he never claimed to be either divine or immortal, only a messenger from God.

Born in Mecca in 570 CE he lived in a brutal age, and was himself brutal when the occasion demanded it. However you regard him, by the time Muhammad died on 6 June 632 he had laid the foundations of the Islamic faith and most of the Arabian Peninsula had already converted to Islam.

The stories about Muhammad and his activities are legendary. On one occasion he was entertaining a group of eight men from the Banu Urayman tribe. They complained about the heat and, as a balm to soothe burned and blistered skin, not as a drink, Muhammad offered them a mixture of camel urine and milk. It was an offer made for the comfort of the visitors.

Those visitors, metaphorically at least, threw Muhammad's offering back into his face. Later that night, they left their tent and stole eight of his camels, killing the animals' attendants in the process. Muhammad tracked them down and had their eyes gouged out, their limbs hacked off. They were then thrown out into the desert to die. It was a brutal process but Muhammad was avenging an insult as well as the murder of his staff members.

Shortly before his death in 632 CE Muhammad ordered the assassination of Asma bint Marwan and the Jewish writer Abu Afak. They were both poets whose recent verses had offended Muhammad. Another poet who suffered the same fate was Abu Rafi ibn Abi Al-Huqaiq after he had mocked the Prophet in one of his verses.

A Warlike Foursome

Whether or not you regard the Biblical stories, particularly those from the Old Testament - more of this later – as an extended parable or as a piece of historical fiction, the tales are certainly riveting pieces of literature. Many of them have a brutality that is frightening. Nowhere is that more clearly seen than in the story of Jael, Deborah, Barak and Sisera.

Sisera was the commander of the Canaanite army of King Jabin. The Canaanites invaded Israelite territory and fought them for nearly twenty years. The Israelites fought furiously but were constantly on the back foot against superior numbers and better tactics.

The real strength of Sisera's Canaanite army lay in his 900 iron chariots, against which the Israelites had no real answer. On the open desert plains the chariots cut a swathe in any defensive formation they encountered.

Eventually the prophetess Deborah managed to persuade the reluctant Israelite General Barak to face Sisera once more, this time at the head of an army made up largely from the tribes of Zebulun and Naphtali. Deborah was the only one whose voice and opinions could stand up to Sisera and after much debate Barak began to listen to her.

Barak needed some convincing but eventually he took to the field, with 10,000 warriors. He managed to defeat Sisera in the Battle of Mount Tabor on the plains of Esdraelon, just as Deborah had predicted. He was greatly assisted by a cloudburst and overflowing water from Wadi Kishan which made the iron chariots of the Canaanites ineffective. The Biblical comment on the victory was simple - 'The stars in their courses fought against Sisera.'[3]

Sisera fled the scene of his defeat on foot, his chariot having been bogged down in the mud and water of the battlefield. He sought refuge in the campsite of Heber the Kenite, being welcomed by Heber's wife Jael. Heber and his people were technically non-belligerents which meant that Sisera felt safe in their company. He should have known better. Jael, in particular, had seen the depredations of the Canaanites and secretly supported the Israelites in their efforts.

Sitting in her tent, Jael plied Sisera with warm milk and, according to some sources, had sex with him on at least seven occasions. If she was hoping to tire him out, Jael was successful. With a promise that she would keep him hidden, she then covered Sisera with a rug and watched, satisfied, as he fell into a deep sleep.

Then Jael took a tent peg and hammered it into Sisera's temple. The peg went clean through his head and pinned Sisera to the ground. As Jael's actions, both in sexually abusing Sisera and in killing him in such a brutal fashion, were regarded as being done for the sake of Heaven, she was forgiven, her actions classed as praiseworthy.

Barak, on the other hand, was punished for his reticence and lack of intent. As he was still so reluctant to come face to face with the Canaanites, Deborah went with him in the chase after Sisera was beaten. She was there when Jael emerged from her tent saying 'The man you want is here.'

Deborah had already prophesised that Sisera would fall at the hands of a woman; Barak because of his reluctance to fight would receive none of the glory. And so it was.

On the day of his death, once Sisera's corpse was discovered in Jael's tent, Barak and Deborah did sing a song commemorating the defeat and death of the Canaanite general. That, however, was the end of Barak's fame:

> 'Through the window peered Sisera's mother.
> Behind the lattice she cried out
> Why is his chariot so long in coming?
> Why is the clatter of his chariots delayed?[4]

As Deborah had predicted, Jael's name went down in history. Poor Barak, not frightened but clearly cautious after so many defeats, was forgotten.

Jael's actions found their way into paintings by people like Tissot and into fiction written by, amongst others, Geoffrey Chaucer, Anthony Trollope, Agatha Christie and PG Wodehouse.

Li Si's Brutal Death

In ancient China punishments for serious crimes like treachery and betrayal were brutal in the extreme. Death by processes like The Five Punishments (see below) were renowned across the country and were nothing short of horrific. The specific punishments varied over time but invariably included amputation of one or both feet, cutting off the criminal's nose, castration and constant whipping with bamboo sticks.

Li Si was a philosopher and politician who became Chancellor or Prime Minister to Emperor Quin Shi Huang in 246 BCE. After enjoying several years when he was clearly in control of government-led political enterprises, Li Si began to fear that he had had it too good for too long. Fuelled by court gossip, he was worried that he might lose his position. It was a clear case of chicanery, whispered words of caution and 'dirty dealing,' all common enough in the Imperial Court at that time.

After the death of Emperor Qin Shi Huang in 208 BCE Li Si became tied up in a series of connected plots involving fake news, induced suicides and the deposing of the true successor. He was eventually betrayed by his accomplice the eunuch Zhao Gao and sentenced to death. Not any normal hanging or beheading, this was to be death by The Five Punishments.

In the public market place, as the spectators roared and urged on the executioners, the Five Punishments were inflicted. Li Si was first tattooed across his face, then had his nose cut off. This was followed by the amputation of his feet and castration.

The final stage of The Five Punishments saw him cut in half by sharp saw, the process being known as the waist chop. He was probably beyond caring and thought little about it but Li Si's own death was followed by the execution of his family to the third degree.

The Wicked Empress

Empress Lu Zhi supposedly held all of the evil traits required to become China's un-official 'wicked queen,' a role well worthy of any of Walt

Disney's carton creations. Commonly known as Empress Lu, she was the consort of Gaozu, the first Emperor of the Han Dynasty, and when he died in 195 BCE she took on the role of Empress Dowager. It gave her all the power she had ever wanted.

First on the agenda was revenge. Empress Lu hated with a vengeance any of her dead husband's other consorts, particularly his favourite Lady Qi. It was, she felt, time to act.

Without any semblance of a trial, Lady Qi was literally dismembered at Lu's prompting. Her hands and feet were cut off, her eyes gouged out and her ears were burned off. Poison or acid was poured down her throat, not enough to kill her but enough to destroy her vocal cords and make her dumb.

Already half dead, Lady Qi was then flung into a pig sty so that the people could see what the Empress Lu referred to as 'the human swine' or 'the human pig.' When Lu's son, the Emperor Hui, saw what his mother had done he was driven into deep depression, into what might now be referred as a blast of mental breakdown, and withdrew from public service. It merely gave the Empress Lu more power and control.

The Empress continued on her wicked way. She controlled everything during the reign of her son Hui and during the infancies of two very young Emperors who succeeded him on the throne. Finally, she died in 180 BCE when she was sixty-one years old.

A Consort War?

In the middle years of the seventh century CE, the consorts of Emperor Gaozu were a powerful group of ambitious and deadly women.

Consorts like Xiao, Wang and Wu – none of their other names being known - not only held great power, they also knew how to use it. Emperor Gaozu was invariably entranced by one consort after the other, something which was quite acceptable to any of the new arrivals, not so welcomed by those who felt they had been left behind.

Consort Wu was introduced into the Chinese harem of the royal dynasty and Gaozu was, naturally enough, soon besotted. The Chinese harem was a very different beast from the Sultanate devices of Egypt and, later, of the Ottoman Emperors.

Unlike the harems of Egypt and Turkey, the system for the Chinese was not related to the forbidden quarters of the women. Those were known simply as the back or rear palace.

The term harem related to a hierarchical organisation of the women in the inner court and palace life. It was a closed, specifically tight world that saw men ranked in order of succession to the throne by, amongst other things, the prominence of their mothers.

Chief amongst the women was the empress, followed by the consorts, of which there were usually many, and, finally, by a whole raft of concubines.

When Consort Wu suddenly appeared on the scene it meant that the other ladies of the harem were gravely put out. Xiao and Wang immediately tried to rid the court of this new threat but Wu was far too clever. Before they knew what was happening, the two women were arrested, charged with witchcraft and set up for execution, all on the orders of Consort Wu.

Wu was created Empress in 655, the same year as Xiao and Wang were imprisoned. It was a combination of her influence on Gaozu and, perhaps, as a reward for ridding the court of two concubines who might just prove to be difficult in the years ahead.

As Empress, Wu's anger and bitterness knew no bounds. She soon realised that her position was still tenuous and that she had better take steps to ensure her safety.

The obvious threat to Wu came from the previous favourites, Xiao and Wang. Consequently, Wu sent soldiers to cane the two consorts, 100 strokes each, and then, while they were still in agony, had their hands and feet cut off.

As if that was not enough, the mutilated women were then thrown into two large wine jars where they were supposed to drown. That did not happen, the women survived the ordeal and showed no sign of dying.

Empress Wu commented simply 'Let the two witches be drunk to their bones.' After a few days Xaio and Wang were still alive, even if just barely. They were then taken out of their wine jars and beheaded.

The Empress Wu went on to enjoy a career of glittering success. When she was finally able to look back and assess what she had achieved it was clearly a violent but phenomenal progress from concubine to Empress, success based on ruthlessness, brutality and intelligent manoeuvring.

Wu was the undoubted power behind the throne of Gaozu and of his two successors before, in 690 CE, finally being gifted the throne in her own right.

She had begun her 'royal' life as a concubine, little more than a professional lover for the Emperor, and climbed carefully up the social ladder, reaching the pinnacle as China's first and only female emperor.

She ruled from 690 until being deposed by a palace coup in December 705. By then she was happy to go and died peacefully a few months later.

Over the years, from her early days as a concubine and consort, Wu had developed a network of spies, based in the royal court and throughout the empire. They were highly efficient and kept her informed on the state of her domain, one of the reasons she remained in power for so long.

Wu totally revised the hierarchical system of government promotion in China, appointing officials and officers on their ability rather than their family position and background, a change that helped propel China to a position as one of the great powers in the world. That was her greatest achievement.

Tiger Women

The achievements of Empress Wu, brutal and unforgiving as they were, need to be considered alongside the Confucian Tradition, as detailed in *The Book of Rites*.

This tome declared that women in Chinese society should be gentle and obedient. Unmarried women should obey their fathers while married women became subservient to their husbands. If the husband was dead, then authority passed to the sons.

It was a sexist society where any woman who failed to adhere to these rules was regarded as a 'Tiger Woman,' someone who was tough, dynamic and, above all, unreasonable when people, men in particular, attempted to be logical and understanding.

Tiger Women were elegant, knew what they wanted out of life, and were totally fearless, even if a little impulsive. As far as the average Tiger Woman was concerned men were of secondary importance and she was certainly not going to adhere to the rules of Confucius. Whatever else she might have been – and the list for that one is both long and varied - Empress Wu was certainly a Tiger Woman.

Chapter Seven

A Biblical Interlude

The Old Testament stories, particularly those which are based on historical fact rather than on myth or legend and an unapologetic desire to teach and indoctrinate, provide a treasure trove of fascinating information. The Deuteronic Books as the 'historical' sections or chapters are called are invariably well written, holding the reader's attention to the end.

Above all, however, the Deuteronic books are tales which put meat on the bones of long-gone lives and events. They highlight motives and intentions which most of us first heard about in our childhood and which still resonate with us today. They catch the mood of the time, presenting facts and allowing readers to make whatever judgements are required.

Historically based, the stories are still clearly linked to the teachings of the church. As such the deuterocanonical tales of the Bible, along with various small passages from other works, are books which were considered to be canonical or fitting the standard of accepted ecclesiastical law. Even in these books there are occasions when history takes a back seat.

The accepting or approving agencies were the highly influential Catholic Church, the Eastern Orthodox Church, the Oriental Orthodox Churches and the Asyrian Churches of the East. The deuterocanonical stories do not feature as separate entities in the Hebrew Bible.

Depending on which source you take for your base line, out of the 39 books that feature in the Hebrew Bible either twelve or seventeen are volumes that we would class as historical or Deuteronomic documents. The actual *Book of Deuteronomy,* the third book in the Bible, may have been begun by Moses, possibly being finished by Joshua.

The discrepancy regarding the number of Deuteronomic books is due, in the main, to certain of them having multiple purposes and subjects. Any account of the work of a prophet, for example, is bound to include various aspects of history. So where is it recorded, which category does it reflect? It comes back again to the business of listing and logging

Taking twelve as the exact and most accurate number of historical tales, that leaves five that are concerned with Jewish Laws, five which concentrate on poetry, five on the major prophets and twelve on minor prophets - total 39! The Catholic Old Testament later added four more, including the otherwise often ignored Book of Judith.

Written, or at least made public, between the appearance of the Old and the New Testaments, the stories depend on hindsight and research for their accuracy. When first made public, they were accepted by the Pharisees who regarded them as historical records but not necessarily as divinely inspired messages.

Whatever your specific beliefs and opinions regarding religion, the Old Testament's Deuteronomic tales certainly read like works of historical fact. Bearing in mind the old truism that history belongs to the victor, like many early works of history they might not all be one hundred percent accurate but there is enough there to establish a core of belief.

However you look at the stories, it is impossible to escape or avoid the fact that they were written in the period of time we term as the ancient world. Truth or fiction, they influenced thought and belief. They were real to the people of the ancient world, as real as the times in which they lived, and were viewed as examples of good and bad behaviour. As such, the tales of the Old Testament, the Hebrew Bible and other sacred tomes can only be viewed as genuine articles.

And that brings us back to the issue of assassination. The area of the Middle East which we now know as Palestine was originally a united kingdom. However, for many years after approximately 900 BCE it was split into two, Judah in the north and Israel in the south.

Judah existed as an entity for 362 years, Israel for 204, before they were re-united under, firstly, King Saul and then his successor David as the combined kingdom of Israel. The veracity of both Saul's and David's rise and successive reigns have been questioned as whatever primary facts and information that we possess come solely from the Hebrew Bible. Regardless of this, it remains a passionate and fascinating period and there seems to be no reason why the events as we know them should not be believed or accepted. They are not to be put up like skittle pins simply for the sake of being knocked down.

The years of separation were difficult and dangerous. During that time, in Israel alone, no fewer than eight out of the nineteen kings who ruled were assassinated, each one being murdered by his successor. Judah was not far behind, five of the twenty rulers of the kingdom being removed from the throne in the same manner.[1]

The secession of Judah from the original combined kingdoms had taken place in the time of King Jeroboam of Judah and King Rehoboam of Israel. The stoning to death of Adoram, chief officer and the man in charge of forced labour for King Rehoboam, was a crucial moment. He had been sent into Judah to restore order after rioting and to enforce the heavy tributes Rehoboam confidently expected from the people of the north.

The death of Adoram, his name sometimes spelled Adoniram, was a political killing or assassination, although it was unlikely to have been planned and thought through like so many of the other assassinations in the ancient world. A chance presented itself to the furious crowd and while they had always hoped for such an opportunity they were probably as surprised as Adoram when that opportunity presented itself.

The anger and hatred of the crowd towards Rehoboam and his officials was real enough but the actual killing was more of an upsurge of emotion than cold blooded murder. However you define it, Adoram's murder was the final straw in an increasingly fraught relationship between the two kings and resulted in Rehoboam fleeing for his life and taking refuge in Jerusalem. The age of the separate kingdoms had arrived.[2]

When you consider that some of the kings who ruled in Judah and Israel reigned for only very short periods of time, the violent death of one monarch after another was hardly a surprise in a region that saw violence, warfare and assassination as an occupational hazard of rule:

> 'Persons living 50 or 60 years in either kingdom during their parallel existence would, on average, have experienced no less than three royal assassinations in their lifetime.'[3]

It was hardly a situation designed and implemented for stability and security, either for the population of the two states or for the monarchs who ruled them.

Acknowledging that there are errors in the Old Testament tales, some accidental, others deliberate falsifications, it remains with the writer and historian – ultimately, of course, with the reader – to decide where they put their metaphorical crosses.

Cain and Abel

In a Biblical epistle like *The Book of Genesis*, which is claimed by some historians to be an historical account but which contains many fables and ancient legends, there are a large number of stories that are clearly works of fiction. The depiction of the creation of the world, the appearance of Adam and Eve, the intervention of Satan and the serpent, are all obviously inventions, put in to entertain, illuminate and terrify early believers. In effect, they are metaphors linking humankind to the work of God and Satan. So, too, is the legend of Cain and Abel.

According to *Genesis*, Cain and Abel were the eldest sons of Adam and Eve. Supposedly the first man and woman on the planet, Adam and Eve had a little known third son, Seth. He does not feature in the story.

The legend as we know it declares that the two brothers made a sacrifice to God, a sacrifice that saw preferment going to Abel's offering. A jealous and bitter Cain lured his brother out to the fields that he farmed and where the Devil had first told him to smash in Abel's head with a stone. With Abel suspecting nothing, the assassination was soon performed.

When the body was hidden, Cain returned home. The question of Abel's whereabouts brought about one of the best known of all Biblical quotations when Cain, asked about the location of his missing sibling, replied 'I do not know. Am I my brother's keeper?'

Once the assassination was uncovered, it led to Cain being marked by God, exiled from his natural family and left to live a life of wandering the world without a clear home base. He supposedly died in the great flood that drowned everyone apart from Noah's chosen few.

The story is exactly what it claims to be - a story. It appears in the Quran but does not feature largely in the rest of the Hebrew Bible. It is symbolic rather than real but there are elements of what could be actual motives behind what was designed to be the archetypical example of fratricide.

According to some non-Biblical sources, Cain was besotted with Aclima, a beautiful woman betrothed to his brother. The only way that the emotionally disturbed Cain could see of claiming her was by ridding the world of Abel.

While there is little doubt about the two brothers being fictional characters, the twin motives, religious and secular, were to surface many times in the lives of men and women. And the writer or writers of *Genesis* were very well aware of the problem. This early morality tale was a warning for people to control their basic instincts.

Ehud and the Death of Eglon

Eglon was the head of a military confederacy consisting of soldiers from Moab, Ammon and Amalek. He and his powerful army invaded Israel and ruled ruthlessly over the country for eighteen years, although the exact dates remain unclear. Indeed, the lack of specific dates is one of the reasons that many Biblical scholars doubt the accuracy of the story. It is, they claim, a colourful legend written and presented to entertain rather than inform.

For the moment, however, we will take it as a factual account of one of the more gruesome Biblical assassinations. Ehud ben-Gera was a Judge sent by God to free the Israelites from Moabite oppression. In other words he had been chosen to assassinate the Moabite king.

Ehud had one distinct advantage over most assassins. He was left handed. He prepared himself by fashioning a two edged dagger, ideal for stabbing, which he then hid by strapping it to his right thigh. Most men were right handed, carrying their weapons on their left leg. Consequently, the guards failed to find any hidden weapon when they came to search the assassin.[4]

Ehud arrived at Eglon's palace on the pretext of paying the annual tribute to the Moabites. Ushered into the presence of Eglon he declared that, as well as the tribute, he had a message for the King from God. Eglon stood up – no easy task for a man like him, grotesquely overweight – and told his servants and guards to leave the room.

Strangely, the interview between the two men is said to have taken place in Eglon's bathroom. Certainly the reaction of the servants would seem to indicate that this was indeed the case. Wherever it occurred, as soon as the two men came close, Ehud drew his dagger and stabbed Eglon in the abdomen. The knife went straight in, probably piercing the King's bowel, allowing *Judges, Chapter Three*, to claim that 'then the dirt came out.' For 'dirt' read faeces.

Try as he might, Ehud could not free his dagger, the blade of which had entered Eglon's body, along with a large part of the handle. In the end, he left it enveloped in the King's flesh. Twisting and turning of the weapon to get it out of Eglon's fat belly would only have hastened the man's death.

The assassination over, Ehud locked the door and left. The guards and servants did not enter Eglon's private apartments for some time, believing their monarch was relieving himself. The smell exuding from the bathroom confirmed this belief. Eventually, when Eglon did not emerge, they broke down the door and found the King dead on the floor.

Ehud made haste to quit the region while he still had the chance. He went to Seraiah where he rallied the Israelite forces. His army invaded Moab, blockading the fords on the River Jordan and totally defeating the now-leaderless Moabite forces. Peace apparently descended on the country for over eighty years.

Saved but Not Saved

Jehoida was High Priest of Judah during the three consecutive reigns of King Ahaziah, Queen Athalia and King Joash, a period of nearly fifty years lasting from 842 to 796 BCE. Married to Jehosheba, sister to King Ahaziah, Jehoida watched as his mother-in-law Athalia usurped the throne, killed her son Ahaziah and, in 841 BCE, proclaimed herself Queen Athalia.

In order to secure her position on the throne Athalia promptly had all of the royal family – or, at least, those she could get her hands on – put to the sword. Jehoida, however, managed to save and protect his wife along with Joash, the six year old son of Ahaziah and grandson of Athalia.

He hid Joash in the Chamber of the Jewish Temple, the innermost and most sacred of all Jewish holy places but hardly a comfortable sanctuary. While he was in hiding, Joash's grandmother Athaliah decided on spiritual as well as secular reform and went about strengthening the position of Baal as the supreme religion in Judah. It could not last.

Jehoida and Jehosheba organised a coup d'état, a plot that took Athaliah totally by surprise. She was hunted down by soldiers armed with shields and spears. The soldiers gathered in a ring around Joash, protecting him with their shield wall but allowing him to see what was going on.

All Athaliah could do was to cry out 'Treason' before she was pulled outside the palace and stabbed to death. Joash, the son of the assassinated Ahaziah, was then proclaimed King of Judah.

To begin with Joash, aided and advised by Jehoiada, seemed to be doing well. He outlawed worship of Baal, executed Mattan, the High Priest of the sect, destroyed the Baal temple and brought back worship of Yahweh, declaring that the people of Judah should be 'The Lord's People.'[5]

Soon, however, his natural ego and belief in his invincibility took over. He began to believe that he was a god. It was a belief that was strengthened by the princes of the region, men who had more inclination to worship Baal than Yahweh. 'You have to be a god, they told him, or else you would not have come out alive from the Holy of Holies.'[6]

The longer he reigned, the more dictatorial Joash became, his behaviour eventually verging on the bizarre. Assassination seemed to be the logical way forward. It was the easiest and quickest way to despatch unwanted monarchs, in this case a man who had forgotten or chosen to ignore the basic rules when assuming the role of tyrant and absolute ruler:

> 'Whatever latitude an absolute monarch may assume in his own conduct, whatever indulgence he may claim for his own passions, it is undoubtedly in his interests that all his subjects should respect the natural and civil obligations of society.'[7]

Consequently, in 796 BCE yet another way forward was mapped out. It was a simple enough idea, taking the standard route of killing through the auspices of those closest to the victim. Joash was duly assassinated by two of his servants, one the son of an Ammonite, the other an unknown man from Moab.

The tragedy of Joash and his decline into a self-interested and deluded belief in his invincibility remains one of the least known of all Biblical tales – which may or may not have been appropriate given his belief in his own divinity.

The reign of Joash lasted for nearly forty years and was a reign that could and should have given so much more to the people of Judah. As it turned out Joash and his time in power ended in bloodshed and death.

The House of David

The great heroic figure, both in the Hebrew Bible and in the Christian Old Testament, has to be David, the shepherd boy who slew Goliath and rose to be king of a unified state of Israel. Most of what we know about his life and times comes from Biblical sources which proclaim him to be, mainly, a selfless leader, a great soldier and a man of compassion and understanding.

David's reign and his life, however, were certainly not peaceful interludes. The son of Jesse the Bethlehemite, his family was not poor but neither were they wallowing in riches. Similarly, his character was far from the perfect example of God-fearing innocence that many people still hold close to their hearts and believe implicitly.

Courageous, gifted and intelligent, David was a man of intense passions, emotions that drove him and often put him 'outside the pale' within his own time frame and culture. It was a personality flaw that was to prove fatal for many of his subjects and for members of his own family.

The story of how David rose to prominence is well known. In many respects, the young shepherd boy and harpist who became, firstly, armour bearer to the king, then champion of his people by defeating the Philistine Goliath in single combat is a classic rags to riches tale.

In approximately 1065 BCE the Philistine army invaded Judah. Goliath, ten feet tall and champion of the invading Philistines, challenged any of Saul's soldiers to a one-to-one confrontation in the valley separating the two armies. Nobody took up the challenge, at least not until David appeared on the scene and offered himself. He refused Saul's offer of body armour and 'took out' the Philistine champion with his sling shot.

Following his victory, David's reputation escalated rapidly. He was acclaimed and feted wherever he went, rising in importance to such an extent that he was allowed to sit at the side of King Saul and his son Jonathan, with whom he had developed an intense friendship.

Inevitably, perhaps, Saul grew jealous of the young man who, against the odds, had defeated an unbeatable giant of a man and quickly assumed a position of honour and popularity amongst the soldiers of his kingdom. He was, Saul thought, laying the foundations of an attempt to snatch away his crown. Why else would he court such popularity and fame?

Antagonism led to anger and David, warned by his friend Jonathan, was forced to flee from the increasingly paranoid king. Jonathan knew of his father's weaknesses but did not have the strength of personality to do something about them. That could be left to his friend David who now took refuge in the hills.

For some time David was a hunted man. He had several opportunities to kill Saul, notably one occasion where they both found themselves taking refuge in the same cave. David recognised the King but an exhausted Saul was unaware of his rival's presence. David cut off a portion of Saul's cloak while he was sleeping and later showed it to the King as proof that he could have killed him during the night but had chosen not to do so.

David's refusal to commit murder eventually led to a reunion of Saul and the man he still considered his potential nemesis. A little reluctantly,

David was recognised by Saul as the future king of Judah, successor to his throne. It was an uneasy alliance, neither man totally accepting the truce and each treading more than carefully in the other's presence.

When Saul and Jonathan were killed at the Battle of Gilboa, part of the seemingly endless war against the aggressive Philistine forces, it was the end of a united Israel. For a few years the kingdom was divided into Israel in the north, Judah in the south.

As Saul had decreed, following the death of Jonathan and himself, David was proclaimed King of Judah. It effectively marked the beginning of the royal House of David.

The Assassination of Ish-Bosheth

On the death of his father, Saul's surviving son Ish-Bosheth, then forty years old, was anointed as King of Israel. After his father, he was the second man to hold the position, ruling for just two years before being assassinated by Rechab and Baanah, two of his own officers.

Ish-Bosheth's brief reign had been marked and marred by constant conflict with David and the kingdom of Judah. The incessant warfare was draining on both states, on Israel in particular, and dissatisfaction with the King and his obvious hatred of David grew steadily amongst the populace.

Rechab and Baanah were serving officers in Ish-Bosheth's army but they were driven by greed as much as by political and military necessity. They would kill their King but they expected to be well rewarded by David.

Knowing that the King took a rest each noon, when the heat of the day was at its most intense, the two assassins waited until Ish-Bosheth was lying, comatose, on his bed and then they struck. The first blow caught the King in his groin, mortally wounding him. They then cut off his head and took it south to Hebron where they proudly presented it to David.

The Judaean king had not wanted or asked for the death of Ish-Bosheth and refused to reward Rechab and Baanah for their treachery. He had them both executed, after having had their hands cut off, a punishment that was almost a traditional method of torture and punishment.

Despite David's anger and rejection at the sight of Ish-Bosheth's severed head, the assassination was a significant event in the history of Israel. It ended the dynasty or House of Saul and paved the way for David to become king of both Judah and Israel.

The unification of the two countries was not long delayed after the death of Ish-Bosheth. Within a few weeks the crown of Israel was offered by the Israeli elders, religious leaders and officials to King David of Judah, the one man who, everyone hoped, would bring peace to the region.[8]

David and Bethsheba

David was a man of passion, particularly where women were concerned. He had numerous wives and concubines, as was acceptable, even expected, for reigning monarchs at that time. His sexual promiscuity produced many children, at least sixteen boys and one girl.

Walking on the roof of his property in Hebron, one morning David saw Bathsheba, the wife of Uriah the Hittite, bathing in an adjacent house. Captivated by her beauty, the lustful David vowed that he would claim Bathsheba for his own.

With Uriah away fighting for his country, David soon found the opportunity to consort with the new woman in his life. For a while he was perfectly happy but then Bathsheba announced that she was pregnant. David was in a dilemma. Once people began to notice her swollen belly, they would also begin to talk. That was not good for the King's reputation or his adherence to the laws of the land. There was also a very real danger that he could even be accused of rape.

And so David summoned Uriah back from the front lines of war. His scheme was that after months of absence Uriah and Bathsheba would fall into each other's arms and make love. Bathsheba could then claim that the coming child was a result of coupling with her husband.

Uriah refused to leave his post at the front, however. Repeated requests were ignored, Uriah firmly believing that duty came before pleasure. Finally, in desperation, David wrote a letter to his general Joab who was about to commence the siege of Rabbah:

> 'And he wrote in the letter, saying "Set ye Uriah in the forefront of the hottest battle and retire ye from him, that he may be smitten and die." And it came to pass, when Joab observed the city, that he assigned Uriah unto a place where he knew the valiant men were. And the men of the city went out and fought with Joab and there fell some of the people of the servants of David, and Uriah the Hittite died also.'[9]

Bathsheba mourned her dead husband but David, still smitten, brought her into his house. He married her, keeping her secluded until she had given birth.

According to the Bible, the prophet Nathan promised punishment for David. Someone close to him, Nathan declared, would seize all his wives and concubines and rape them in public so that everyone could see and appreciate the enormity of what David had done. As further punishment Bathsheba's son fell ill and, despite pleading and prayers from both David and Bathsheba, soon died.

David accepted his punishment. He had no option and became a somewhat more honest and respected monarch. His lust and his dreams of glory remained, however, and soon the promised punishment started to become reality. David and Bathsheba had other children, notably Solomon who became King of Israel after his father. Others, like Absalom and Amnon, were destined for other fates.

Amnon and the Rape of Tamar

The eldest son of David by his second wife Ahinoam, Amnon was born in Hebron and was heir apparent to the throne of Israel. A glorious future beckoned but it was not to be.

Amnon enjoyed the life of a prince of the realm, wallowing in the privileges and the power he was given. Whatever else David might have been he was a loving father. Nothing was too good for Amnon and his brothers.

Amnon had inherited David's lustful character and soon, more than anything, he began to lust after his half-sister Tamar. The daughter of David and Maachan, Tamar was a beautiful but naïve young girl who accepted Amnon's jocular but suggestive comments, his physical contact and lustful glances as nothing more than acts of friendship.

Amnon's desire grew to an overwhelming level and finally, almost distraught, he sought advice from his cousin Jonadab. The advice he received was simple - lure Tamar into your quarters by pretending to be ill. She, Jonadab said, would be happy to cook a special meal for you.

Amnon did as Jonadab suggested. Once Tamar was in his power, Amnon raped her and then expelled her from his house. Having had his way with her, love quickly turned to dislike, even hatred, thus suggesting that Amnon's initial desire was one of lust, not love.

When he heard the news King David was furious but could not bring himself to punish his eldest son. It was a weakness that he would come to regret. Absalom, Tamar's full brother and the most significant of David's other sons, was appalled by what Amnon had done. He harboured his desire for revenge, however, allowing it to fester and grow. For two years he did nothing but wait and plan.

Two years after the rape of Tamar the vengeful Absalom was ready. He invited all of his brothers and half-brothers to a feast.

It was sheep shearing time, an occasion for celebration and fun. Amnon suspected nothing. Absalom plied him with glass after glass of wine, watching as the alcohol began to take effect. When he finally collapsed on the floor Absalom's servants leapt on the prostate body of Amnon and killed him.

Realising that David would be enraged at the assassination of Amnon, Absalom immediately fled to Geshur where he put himself under the patronage of King Tamal and where his father could not touch him. And there, once more, Absalom waited. In time, David came to terms with the death of Amnon and invited Absalom to return to Jerusalem.

Absalom, Death and Glory

Third son of David, Absalom was widely regarded as the most handsome man in the kingdom. He was a favourite of the people, much as David had been in his youth.

Whenever he was out on his chariot he had fifty men to run before him, clearing his path and announcing his coming. Spectators, which was what the people on the streets quickly became, would stand at the roadside, cheering as Absalom drove past, graciously acknowledging the cheers of the crowd.

Like his father and siblings, Absalom loved the finest things in life. In particular he had a fondness for beautiful women. Not for him the monogamy of one-on-one relationships:

> 'In pious times, ere priestcraft did begin,
> Before polygamy was made a sin,
> When man on many multiplied his kind,
> Ere one to one was cursedly confined.' [10]

With Amnon dead, Absalom quickly assumed his position as David's favourite son. His charming manners and love of pomp and glory made him a perfect companion for a king who had set himself the same standards. Absalom, however, had ambitions that lay way beyond friendship with his father.

Four years after his return from Geshur, Absalom struck. He declared himself King of Israel and raised an army in the southern town of Hebron.

On the advice of the royal advisor Achitophel, he deliberately engaged in sexual acts with his father's concubines, apparently having sex with ten of them in public, thus making sure that his people knew what he had done. Not only did this public display show his contempt for David and all of his family, it also fulfilled the prophesy made by Nathan many years before. Having done all he could to shame his family, Absalom then marched on Jerusalem.

On the march northwards Absalom was joined by thousands of citizens and David, seeing that the situation was hopeless, fled the country. The Priests Zadok and Ablathar remained in Jerusalem where they and their sons doubled as highly effective agents and spies for David.

Absalom was also joined on his march by Achitophel. He had been, for some years, one of David's most trusted and intelligent advisors. The Bible (*2 Samuel, 16:20*) declares that Achitophel might have been exceptionally intelligent and quick witted but he had no piety. And that soon became his downfall.

Achitophel had switched his allegiance to Absalom, a betrayal that David knew he had to destroy – and take Absalom with it. David sent Hushai, another trusted lieutenant, to Absalom's camp where he was to pretend loyalty to the young would-be king. He was to offer advice that was deliberately contrary to Achitophel's. It worked perfectly.

Achitophel's advice to Absalom was that he should attack David now, while he was still retreating in disorder and confusion. That was logical, the sensible thing to do. Hushai, however, deliberately took the opposite view, advocating a policy of waiting and building the strength of the rebel army. Absalom, perhaps reluctant to see his father destroyed by an unsuspecting attack, chose to accept the advice of Hushai.

Seeing that he had over-reached himself, Achitophel flounced away and fled to his hometown of Giloh. There, after consideration, he realised that he had backed himself into a corner and that there was no way out. Sooner or later King David would come for him. He took a rope and hanged himself, one of the earliest recorded suicides.

Right: Pharaoh Teti, victim of the first recorded assassination

Below: The tomb of Ramesses

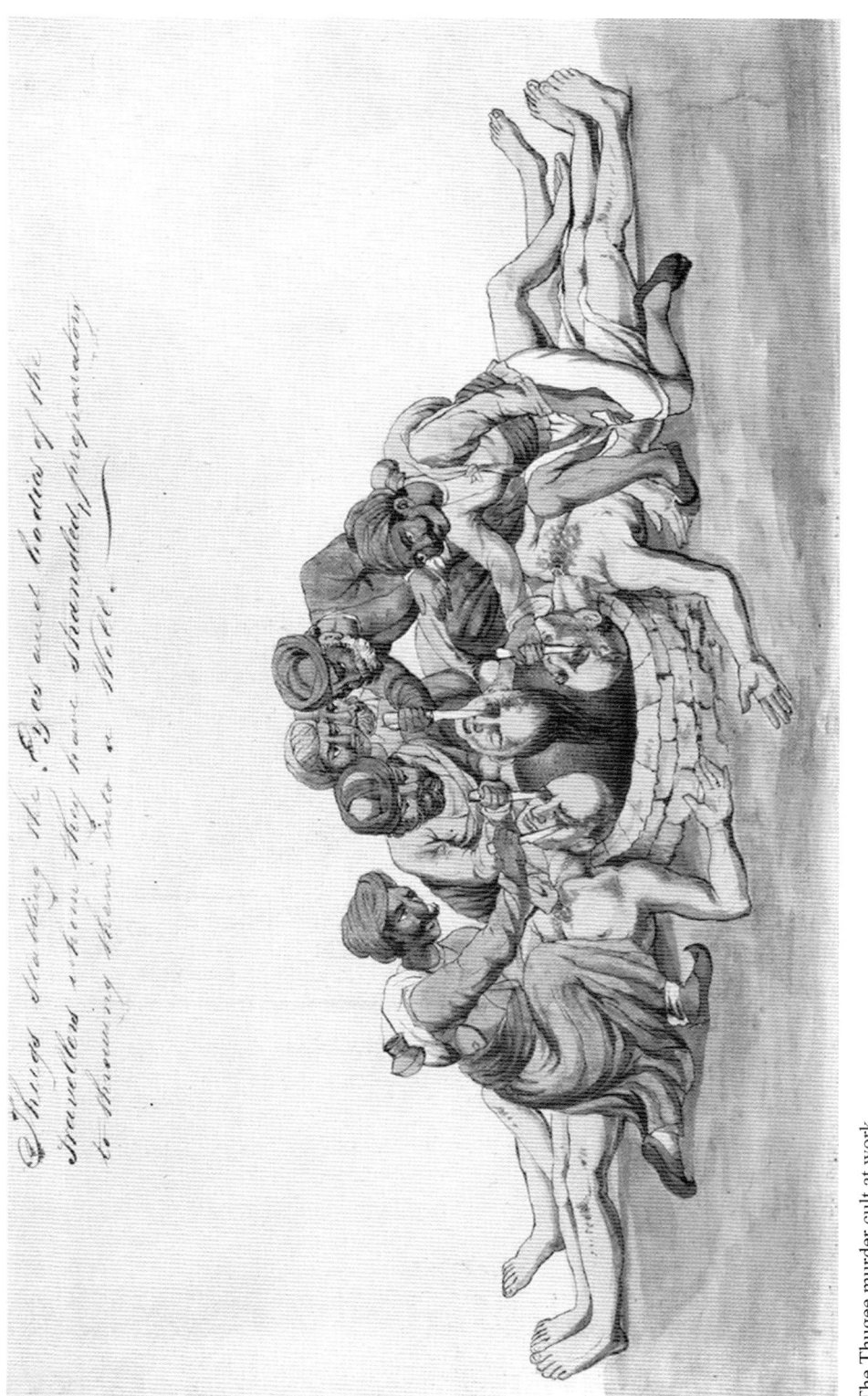

The Thugee murder cult at work

The assassination of Philip of Macedon

Alexander the Great

The Battle of the Delta

Left: Commodious, the Gladiator Emperor, dressed as Hercules

Below: The Cadaver Synod

Above left: Emperor Caligula, the most vicious of all Roman rulers

Above right: Emperor Nero

The Death of Julius Caesar

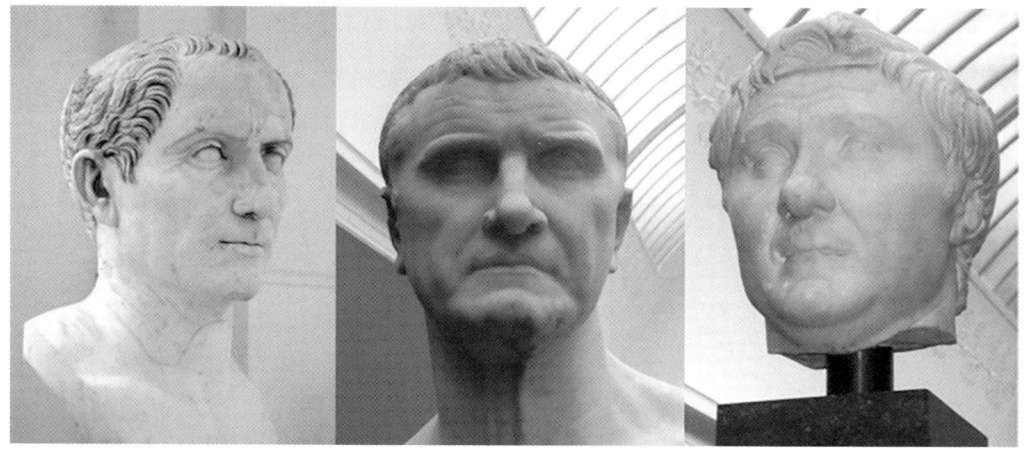

The First triumvirate - Julius Caesar, Crassus and Pompey the Great

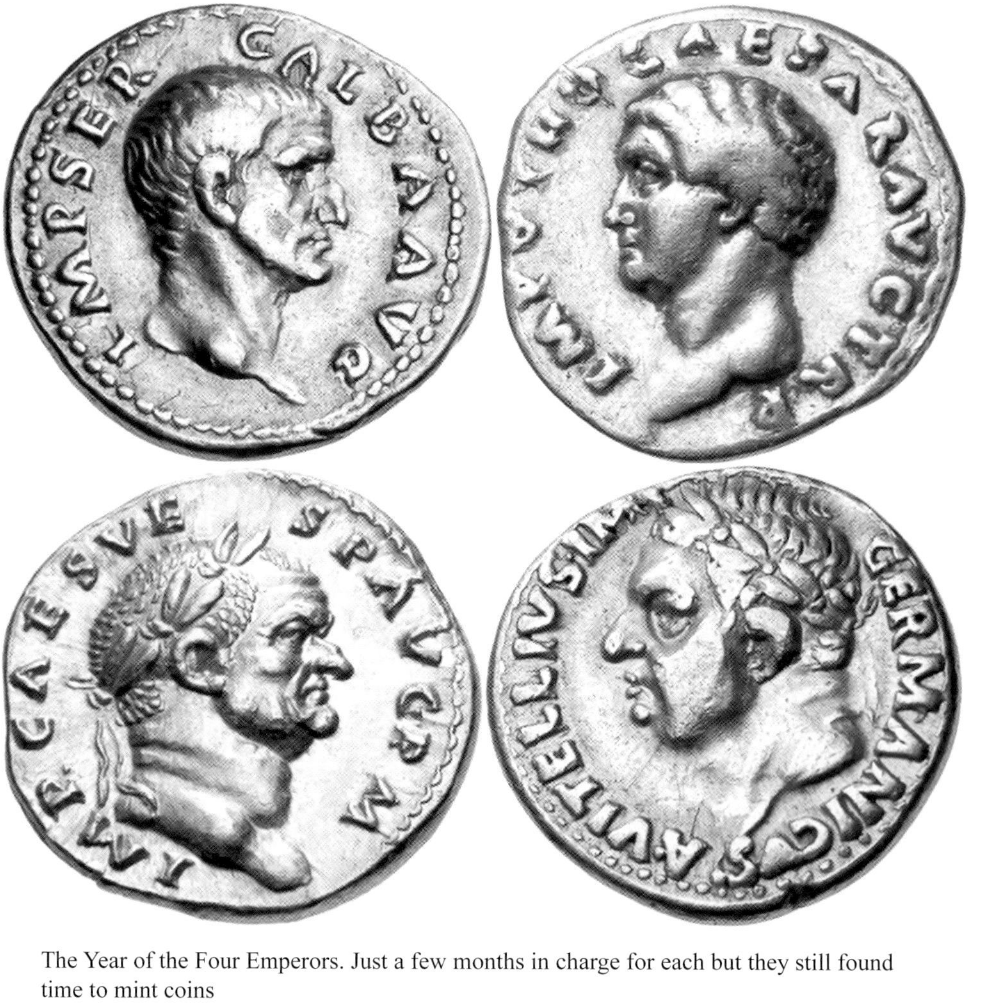

The Year of the Four Emperors. Just a few months in charge for each but they still found time to mint coins

Artists impression of the assassination of Caesar

The death of Pompey

The Macedonian Phalanx, a revolutionary tactic

The Emperor Tiberius on Capri

Left: The writer and historian Tacitus

Below: An artists impression of the massacre of Thessalonica

The assassination of the Druids on Anglesey

Memorial to Pompey

Witchcraft, strong throughout the Dark Ages

The death and martyrdom of St Boniface

The Coliseum in Rome

Meanwhile, David had reformed and regrouped. He swung back into Israel, arrived at the Jordan and met Absalom's forces west of the river. The battle in the wood of Ephraim was bloody and brutal and, after several hours, Absalom's troops were defeated.

Absalom fled but on his way out of the wood his long hair caught in the branches of an oak tree. He was pulled off his horse and left hanging, totally vulnerable, in the air. For what seemed like hours he hung there, pinioned by the luxurious mass of hair that had always been his pride and joy. Nobody came to help and the pain must have been unbearable. Finally, he came to the reluctant conclusion that he would have to cut himself free.

He was about to cut off the long strands of hair, enabling him to drop to the ground, when he was discovered by the soldiers of Joab, King David's chief commander. To Joab seeing Absalom hanging helplessly in front of him would have been like taking hold of the Ark of the Covenant.

The killing of Absalom had been expressly forbidden by David. Defeat him in battle by all means but ensure that he came safely out of the conflict. David had already lost several sons, notably Amnon, and did not want to go through the agony of such grief yet again.

However, Joab saw a chance for revenge. Absalom had once set fire to a field of barley owned by Joab and his family. It was a joke, an off-hand piece of fun or a mindless prank as far as the pampered and thoughtless prince was concerned but the total decimation of a crop that was worth a fortune to Joab's family was nothing less than destruction of a way of life.

Orders from the King were one thing but the chance to pay back the spoiled and treacherous Prince Absalom was more than Joab could bear. He would explain it later but for now the sight of a hanging and struggling Absalom was like target practice to the general..

Three darts into Absalom's body were enough to cripple him. He was finished off by Joab's armour bearers. David was beside himself with grief:

> 'And the King was much moved and went up to the chamber over the gate and wept. And as he wept, this he said "O my son Absalom, my son, my son Absalom. Would God I had died for thee, O Absalom, my son, my son.' [11]

The story of Absalom is one of selfishness, greed and total lack of thought by parties on both sides of the political divide. David's reluctance to make hard decisions, even though they were clearly called for, and the people's acceptance of Absalom's good looks and charm in the place of integrity brought about disaster for all concerned.

The story has been commemorated by many artists and writers. Paintings by people like Tissot and Giaquinto are complemented by plays from Peter Shaffer, songs and music from singers such as Leonard Cohen and numerous novels and poems.

The most notable of these written works are the novel *Absalom, Absalom* by William Faulkner and John Dryden's seventeenth century satirical poem – claimed by many to be the finest long satirical or ironic poem ever written - *Absalom and Achitophel*. It remains an allegory, written in early Jacobite times but still has the power to stand alone.

Chapter Eight

Women, More Deadly Than the Male?

Women, more deadly than the male – is that a cliché or a truism? The answer is probably a bit of both. The Japanese certainly thought so, going so far as to create an all-female assassination corps which worked alongside their squads of male Ninjas. They were the infamous Kunoichi, who operated for many years under the mistaken belief that women were less noticeable than men and consequently less harmful than their male counterparts. Until, that is, they revealed themselves as some of the deadliest assassins of the ancient world.

Several of Egypt's assassinated pharaoh's were victims of plots laid, or at least contributed to, by their wives. Notably amongst these were Teti and Ramesses III, both victims of assassination plots fashioned and put into practice by their wives, women they had imagined to be supportive, loyal, caring and, of course, submissive.

There are many more examples, women taking the main role in plots to rid the various kingdoms of their rulers. The Hebrew Bible and the Old Testament are full of such stories. One of these tales is about the now infamous Queen Jezebel.

Jezebel, If Ever a Devil was Born

Daughter of Ithobaal of Tyre, wife of King Ahab of Samaria, the most northerly kingdom within Israel, Jezabel remains one of the most renowned and influential female characters from the past – influential, that is, in a decidedly unpleasant way! She was a Phoenician by birth, exceptionally beautiful and totally ruthless.

Along with her husband Ahab, Jezebel instituted the worship of Baal and Asherah throughout Samaria, purging the region of its prophets and the many temples of Yahweh. Jezebel, as the High Priestess of Asherah, was intimately involved in the suppression of Yahweh and his Christian followers.

When the prophet Elijah invited Jezabel's priests and prophets to take part in a challenge or contest between themselves and the believers in Yahweh she immediately agreed. It was the ideal opportunity to firmly establish belief in Baal and to rid Samaria of early Christianity for ever.

The challenge was simple. It was to take place on Mount Carmel and was to decide which of the two branches of prophesy could summon Yahweh or Baal to appear before them. Despite cries, curses and self-mutilation Jezabel's prophets failed dismally, Baal did not appear. Elijah, however, succeeded in summoning Yahweh and, immediately, the supporters of Baal were slain. Furious, Jezabel ordered the killing of Elijah but he escaped and fled into the desert.

The greed of Jezabel and Ahab was soon revealed when they attempted to acquire the vineyards of one of their citizens, a man by the name of Naboth. Threats, bribery, even the offer of good money could not persuade Naboth to part with his beloved land. It was, he declared, ancestral property and he would not part with any of it.

Jezabel's next move was to have Naboth arrested on false charges of blasphemy. It was a carefully planned assassination which eventually saw Naboth convicted, taken outside the city and executed. Dogs apparently licked and chewed bits of his corpse. Shades, perhaps, of what was soon to come! Meanwhile, Ahab happily seized the vineyards and added them to his already bulging portfolio.

Three years later, in approximately 848 BCE, Ahab was killed in battle. His first successor, his eldest son Ahaziah, also soon died, leaving Joram, another son, to take the throne. The prophet Elisha, successor to Elijah, persuaded Jehu, commander of the Samarian army, to rebel against Joram in an act of divine judgement on the family of Ahab.

Joram was defeated and assassinated by Jehu who fired an arrow into his back, killing him instantly. Having disposed of the King, Jehu turned his attention to Jezabel, now widely acknowledged as Queen Mother. Being informed of her son's defeat, she dressed in her finery, put on a wig and makeup and then taunted Jehu from her window. She guessed what was going to happen to her and she was determined to go out of life as a Queen.

Jehu entered the palace, ate and drank in style and considered his options. Then, having made up his mind that Jezabel must die, he ordered the palace servants to throw her out of the window, the same window from which she had taunted and teased him earlier in the day.

It was the first recorded de-fenestration in history. The Czech people later made it something of a speciality, several *De-fenestrations of Prague* taking place when the people became dissatisfied with their rulers. Jezebel's assassination was the first but right to the moment of her death she did not know that she was about to become the first of many.

Jezebel's blood was splattered on the palace walls and courtyard. Jehu's horse deliberately trampled on her body. Then Jehu went back inside to finish his meal.

When he came out a few hours later, supposedly to remove Jezebel's body for burial, all that could be found of her were her skull, the palms of her hands and her feet. Scavenging wild dogs had finished what Jehu had begun. Some years before her death, the prophet Elijah had prophesised just such an ending for Jezebel.

Mistress Marica

Marica Aurelia Ceionia Demetrias was the chief concubine of Emperor Commodus who ruled Rome in the late second century CE. He succeeded to the position as joint Emperor, along with his father and was initially quite popular. However, when his father died things began to change. Commodus was a difficult and strange man who was at his happiest when competing in the gladiatorial arena where, because of his status, he knew that no-one would hurt him.

Outside the arena, Commodus ruled tyrannically. In CE 192 he even tried to rename Rome by giving it the title of Colonia Commodiana. Inevitably, the people of Rome turned against him. Marica attempted to persuade him to stop competing in the arena, knowing that sooner or later somebody would seize the chance to kill him. It simply made Commodus angry and he put Mistress Marica's name on the list of those to be executed the following day.

Marica found the list and, in conjunction with several others, laid plans to assassinate the Emperor. That night, after his hot bath, she gave him poisoned wine. It simply made Commodus sick and he promptly threw up the poison. Having made her move, Mistress Marica felt she had no option but to turn to her fellow conspirators and Commodus was actually strangled by his wrestling partner. Without the input of Marica, however, it is doubtful that the assassination would ever have taken place.

Bring Me the Head of Holofernes

The story of Judith and the death of Holofernes divides opinion. Is it a work of actual history or is it a piece of fiction? It could be either; it certainly captures the spirit of bravery and the willingness of the main character to put herself in danger, even to sacrifice herself should the need occur.

There are no firm dates attached to the story, although some sources have suggested that the death of Holofernes occurred in 650 BCE. Several writers have claimed that Holofernes was actually a general by the name of Nicanor. If that were so it would put the events in the second century BCE, sometime during the revolt of Judas Maccabeus, probably circa 150 BCE.

The story and the book were excluded from the Hebrew canon but included in the Eastern Orthodox Old Testament. The story does not feature in any of the Dead Sea Scrolls but the *Book of Judith* was accepted by the Council of Rome in 382 CE and again at Florence in 1442.

So, the story has led a chequered life but, when looked at closely, it tells a tale as powerful and potent as the killing of Sisera by Jael.

Judith, a God fearing and beautiful widow is disgusted at the lack of spirit and fight amongst the people of Israel when the Assyrians invade their land. Led by Holofernes, the Assyrian army pauses outside Judith's town of Bethulia, high in the mountains on the road to Jerusalem.

The people of Bethulia, led by the town Governor Uzziah, want to surrender, an action that Judith adamantly rejects. She demands opposing the Assyrians, something that is reluctantly done. The town gates are shut and the siege of Bethulia begins.

The siege is in its thirty-fourth day when Judith and her maid, never named or identified, slip out through the locked gates and make their way to the camp of General Holofernes. Promising to guide the Assyrians through the wilderness to Jerusalem, Judith spends three days in the enemy camp. Holofernes, the man who has burned and mutilated his way into Israel, is captivated by her beauty and entertains her lavishly each night.

On the final night, full of drink, lust and passion Holofernes passes out and Judith strikes. Using the Assyrian's own sword, she cuts off the head of Holofernes. It takes two blows with the sword and the comatose general does not realise what is happening until it is far too late.

The severed head is then covered with a jewelled canopy, placed inside a food-sack and carried back to Bethulia by the unnamed maid. Judith had been given permission to leave the Assyrian camp at night, supposedly to bathe, an excuse that she now uses to make her way back home.

Judith is received by a rapturous crowd, her promiscuous behaviour excused as it was done with the Lord's blessing. The now leaderless Assyrians are defeated in battle, the siege is raised and the invaders flee out of Israel. The power of an intrepid, not to say dangerous, woman is clear for all to see and, for the men and women of the Ancient world, to read about.

Women With No Names

Nameless female assassins were not exactly commonplace but there were many instances of their work in the ancient world. Arguably, the lack of a specific identity summed up the place and position of women in many of the societies of the time where beauty, a la Judith and Jael, seemed to be more significant than courage!

The story of what the *Book of Judges* calls the Unnamed Woman of Thebez remains a classic example. It is exactly what the title of the story suggests.

The tyrant Abimelech murdered his brothers and set himself up as king, causing the town of Thebez to protest and offer resistance. Abimelech immediately marched on Thebez where a large section of the population, realising they had pushed Abimelech too far, took refuge in a tall tower on the outskirts of the town.

Rather than begin the long, drawn out process of setting up a siege of the tower, Abimelech decided to burn it down. He did not want mistakes, he would start the fire himself. Huddled close up to the tower wall, where arrows and spears could not touch him, he thought himself safe and did not bother putting on his armour:

> 'But one woman threw a millstone on Abimelech's head and crushed his skull. He called hurriedly to the young man who carried his armour – Draw your sword and kill me, lest they say of me "a woman killed him".'[1]

The sword thrust finished him off but Abimelech's dread of being known as the victim of a woman ensured him a place in history. Hardly surprising, a heavy millstone thrown from the top of the tower, a height of fifty or sixty feet, was guaranteed to cause serious damage to the human body. The identity of the woman who threw the stone has never been revealed.

Another unnamed assassin is the killer of Pyrrhus, the man credited with causing the accidental but lasting invention of the phrase 'pyrrhic victory.' According to the writer Plutarch, at the close of an urban battle in the town of Argos, Pyrrhus was riding blithely through the streets when an old, and unnamed, woman hurled a roof tile at him.

The tile struck Pyrrhus on the head. Stunned, he fell from his horse and lay bleeding to death on the ground. Enemy soldiers found him and finished him off. Nobody ever asked for the name of the old woman – a truly pyrrhic victory for her.

The Carthaginian general Hannibal is famous for his victories over the Romans and for crossing the Alps with his elephants. A little-told tale about him concerns a group of unknown, unnamed women from the town of Sarmatia.

In 220 BCE Hanibal was besieging Sarmatia, something that could only end with the town's capture and a huge loss of life. Requests for the town to surrender were, initially at least, of a negative sort. Hannibal prepared to storm the city.

Then, however, a group of women pretended to surrender and left the town with weapons concealed inside their clothing. Outside the town walls, they rounded on their captors and took them totally by surprise. One of the victims was the Carthaginian interpreter Banno who was stabbed and, finally, attacked with his own spear.

The victorious Sarmatian women took to their heels, heading for the mountains. From there they began negotiations with Hannibal. The Carthaginian general was so impressed by their courage and cunning that he gave them back their city. He did not, however, record their names.

The all-female poison groups, particularly the aptly named Poison Damsels who were used extensively in ancient India, did not expect recognition. Indeed, publicity of this sort was the last thing they needed in a world that believed their body fluids were poisonous to other human beings. It was a strange world.

Greek Mythology

Greek mythology is full of stories about women who killed. They killed for love, they killed out of hatred, and they killed for revenge. The general thrust of almost all of the tales, however, is one of treachery and betrayal, again showing men's over-riding negative view of women in the ancient world.

Clytemnestra, the wife of Greek king and war chief Agamemnon, exacted a painful revenge on her husband. Before going off to fight in the Trojan War, Agamemnon apparently sacrificed his and his wife's daughter in order to appease the goddess Artemis for the accidental killing of one of her stags. While Agamemnon was away at the siege of Troy, Clytemnestra and her lover Aegisthus plotted and planned their revenge.

On Agamemnon's return, he was welcomed back into his palace by a seemingly loving wife. Lulled into a drowsy state with wine, as Aegisthus held his arms, Clytemnestra suddenly leapt on Agamemnon and slit his throat. Like many of the Greek heroes of the ten year long Trojan War, Agamemnon was clearly not destined for a happy return home.

Circe, in Greek mythology, was a sorceress who lived and ruled on an island some way off the mainland shore. She hated men and lured them into her home where she gave them food and drink and then used magic to turn them into hogs. Only Odysseus, forewarned about the danger, was able to avoid the fate of so many others.

Medea was another vengeful Greek wife and mother. Sometimes referred to as a witch, more commonly as a sorceress, Medea helps Jason in his search for the Golden Fleece.

On his return from a successful expedition, Jason and Medea marry and live together in Corinth for ten years. Then Jason's roving eye leads him to another woman. Medea poisons her rival, flees to Athens and there, seemingly happy, marries the King.

Samson and Delilah

No account of the power and strength of women would be complete without some reference to Delilah and her emasculation of the Israelite hero Samson.

The last of the Israeli Judges or leaders, before kings took over ruling the country, Samson was a man of immense strength. The Philistines feared him, much as the Israelites were later to fear Goliath. They bribed Delilah with 1000 silver coins to find out the cause of his great strength.

A street woman, a high class prostitute, a courtesan, we know little about Delilah's background. What we do know is that Samson was soon totally smitten by her beauty and by her charms. His duties and his position as an Israelite leader were forgotten. All that mattered was Delilah and the pleasures she could bring to the bedroom.

Delilah made three attempts to uncover his secret but Samson, despite his fascination with the woman of his dreams, was wary of her. He was even a little distrustful, and offered up only false information. That was no more than what was expected of him by his country and his binding religious beliefs.

At last, after a passionate hour or two in bed together, he told her that the secret lay in his long, uncut hair. When an exhausted and blissfully happy Samson fell asleep Delilah cut his hair and gave it to the Philistines. He awoke, supposedly as weak as a baby kitten and fell without protest into the hands of the Philistine soldiers. A lifetime of captivity awaited him.

The moral of the story lies not in the cause of Samson's great strength being revealed but in his inability to remain pure. He has lost his state of spiritual grace, the cutting of the hair being merely symbolic.

By passing on a so-called 'secret' Samson had let down himself and his people. He clearly loved Delilah but it is highly unlikely that she reciprocated the emotion. He was, effectively, a victim of assassination without death. He had been emasculated by a wicked and treacherous woman.

Although Delilah's motives were clearly evil, standing as the emotional opposite of Jael and Judith, she used sex and her personality to defeat a strong and powerful male opponent. In that at least she was just like the two pro-Israelite women.

Her story showed assassination without death. However, the postscript offers a full-on bloody ending for many of the participants.

Chained, his eyes gouged out, a blind Samson is forced to spend his days turning a millstone in the Philistine capital. As his hair grows once more he is moved to the Temple of Dagon where, resting against one of the pillars that hold up the temple roof, he prays to God. His strength returns and, next morning, he pulls down the column.

The temple roof collapses, killing everyone who is underneath it, Samson included. Assassination in numbers! Whether or not Delilah was in the temple at the time and therefore became one of the victims remains unclear.[2]

Chapter Nine

The Death of Julius Caesar

The Roman Empire brought peace and prosperity – a taste of them at least – to the people of the ancient world. However you look at it, Pax Romana was a huge step forward in the development of human civilisation, bringing unheard of benefits to those fortunate enough to reside within the confines of Rome and what was, from the beginning, the city's expanding empire.

In particular it brought physical and emotional safety, along with improved education, for those who wanted it. There were advances in culture, in cuisine and in higher standards of living. Rich markets and protected sea lanes enabled extensive trade to and from the Italian mainland, making the people of Rome one of the most privileged nations in the world.

It was, to a large extent, privilege for the chosen few. Privileges were there, ready and waiting but only if you wanted them. For many of the Empire's lower classes, the men and women who made up the much-feared Roman mobs, there was little direction towards a better way of life.

The availability of simple things like untainted water and luxuries such as improved sanitation and comfortable clothing, might have been taken for granted by the citizens but they were hard-won benefits. However, like freedom of expression and citizens' rights, Pax Romana was not a divine gift from the gods. It came at a price. In this case the price was weighted on the point of a sword, a Roman sword. That was perfectly fine if you were a Roman citizen, not so positive or productive if you lived outside the rule of Roman law:

> 'The legions, whose responsibility it was to keep the dominion
> won by the Roman people secure against the savages who lurked
> in barbarous darkness, were patently fulfilling their duty.'[1]

Apart from the barbarians of northern Europe, the tribesmen of northern Africa and Arabs of the Middle East, there were also violent forces of discord much closer to home. Within the confines of Rome's streets, mobs and gangs of angry citizens, mostly disorganised but always eager to display their power, were a constant threat.

The plebs – common or ordinary citizens with little official position or rights – were a useful tool for ambitious politicians and statesmen. It was simply a case of knowing how, why and when they were best controlled and used.

The early history of Rome remains shrouded in legend and myth. The story of Romulus and Remus, the twin boys who were abandoned and left outdoors to die, was a perfect fairy tale. The boys were found and brought up by wolves and then moved on to found the city of Rome. The legend became standard fare for all Romans of whatever station in life.

Assassination arrived early in Rome, even in the fictional version, as the twins, debating the founding of their own city, fell out regarding its location. Debate dissolved into crime with the result that Romulus killed Remus, the first assassination in Roman history, and went on to create his city on the Palatine Hill. The similarity to the tale of Cain and Abel cannot be avoided.

In reality, Rome was founded as a city state on the banks of the Tiber in approximately 753 BCE. The Republic of Rome was first ruled by a series of kings, a Senate or advisory body of magistrates being created early in the city's history. Magistrates were elected annually. However, Rome and its provinces were, from the beginning, under the mantra of military commanders, tribunes as they became known, establishing and then maintaining a long tradition of strong links between the governing regime and the army.

The first king of Rome was Romulus, not the fictionalised wolf-boy but a powerful politician who ruled for over thirty years. He was followed by six other monarchs, most of whom also ruled for considerable periods. The last leader of the Republic was Lucius Tarquinius Superbus, a tyrannical overlord who was deposed in 509 BCE.

Following the removal of Lucius, the Roman Republic was created, the title of king being retained for the leading Priest in the city - title, yes; power, no. The Republic was what has become known as a represented democracy, overseen by three important elements. These were a system of magistrates, a senate comprising patrician (upper class) representatives and several lower assemblies. Two elected consuls held the highest positions.

The Roman Empire developed slowly, city leaders making sure its grasping fingers were, until the middle years of the third century BCE, retained and restrained within the Italian Peninsula. After that, an increasingly acquisitive and warlike Republic began to flex its muscles and expand out across and around the Mediterranean.

Edward Gibbon in his monumental *Decline and Fall of the Roman Empire* was clear that everything and anything was available for the people of Rome, as long as it was useful for the continuation of the Empire. And that included produce and culture from the countries and territories annexed while the Republic still existed:

> 'The safety and honour of the empire was principally entrusted to the legions, but the policy of Rome condescended to adopt every useful instrument of war.'[2]

It was a dramatic and yet disciplined environment. Many, if not most, of the Roman dignitaries had been soldiers at some stage in their careers. The routines and ambitions they would have encountered in the army were ideal training for men who were both expected and expecting to take the reins of control in the Republic.

Julius Caesar, Background Story

When discussing assassinations, Julius Caesar is the one name everyone remembers. Assassinated by a group of his friends and colleagues on 15 March 44 BCE, just a few months after he had been appointed Dictator for life, the dire warning of 'Beware the Ides of March' has remained in popular usage ever since.

Gaius Julius Caesar was born in 100 BCE, coming from Patrician parents who claimed to be descended from the goddess Venus. It was a claim that was willingly accepted by the Roman people. Another claim, that he was delivered by Caesarean section, was believed at the time but has since been disproved, just like his fictional descent from Venus.

Not a great deal was expected of the young Julius Caesar. He was proclaimed priest of Jupiter while still very young, the priesthood being one of the higher non-political honours in Rome. At that time it was clear he was going nowhere.

The final decades of the Roman Republic were turbulent, a civil war won in 82 BCE by the dictator Sulla, calling the whole concept of elected rulers into serious question. Caesar had opposed Sulla who was strongly in favour of despotic, one person rule. And in the wake of the civil war he found himself in a precarious position.

Within weeks of Sulla's victory, Caesar was immediately presented with an ultimatum. It was simple enough. If he wanted to remain in Rome he must resign his position as a priest and divorce his wife Cornelia, the daughter of Cinna, long-time enemy of Sulla.

Caesar refused both options and was forced to go into hiding. Only when influential relatives intervened on his behalf was he able to return to Rome where he and Sulla agreed that he would abdicate from the priesthood but stay married to Cornelia. He remained married to her until her death in 69 BCE when he re-married, this time in a purely political move, to the daughter of Pompey

Caesar went on to serve in Bithynia, winning the Civic Cross for bravery during the siege of Mytilene. The award whetted his appetite for further honours and when Sulla died in 78 BCE he returned to Rome to begin his slow but steady climb up the political ladder.

Caesar was both ambitious and opinionated. When sailing to Rhodes in 76 BCE his ship was attacked and captured by pirates. Told he would be ransomed for just 10 talents, he took umbrage and demanded that they ask for more. It was a classic 'Don't you know who I am?' moment. In the end a figure of 50 talents was agreed.

Despite apparently getting on well with the pirates, Caesar was not one to ignore an insult or an affront. After being set free, he promptly returned to the pirate stronghold, this time with a fleet of warships, and utterly destroyed the pirate force.

Caesar was elected one of Rome's military tribunes in 71 BCE but took no part in the war against the rebellious slaves of the gladiator Spartacus. At this stage in his career Caesar was a confirmed supporter of Pompey the Great but made sure that his political profile was as well-known as Pompey's in Rome. He did this by staging a series of lavish games and by reinstating many of the past trophies that had been taken down by Sulla.

The appointment of Caesar to the post of Pontifex Maximus, followed by a posting as governor of Hispania Ulterior, added to Caesar's glory. Finally the grant of a consulship saw Caesar move from temporary to permanent strength. Winning the consulship put him firmly at the top of the political tree and in 59 BCE, along with Pompey and Crassus, the latter being the general who had defeated Spartacus, he became part of the all-powerful First Triumvirate.

Caesar still found time to write. His ten-volume series of commentaries on the Gallic Wars are still considered to be Latin literary masterpieces, even though their accuracy is sometimes questionable. Roman victories are acclaimed in the books and defeats ignored or treated with minimal attention. Hardly surprising when the central figure in the histories is Caesar himself.

Julius Caesar had already managed campaigns in Gaul, fighting mainly against the Belgae. He returned to his task and by the time he had finished nearly all of Gaul was under Roman control. An expedition to Britain, 'the Land of Mystery,' in 54 BCE was abandoned because of uprisings in Gaul but, even so, Julius Caesar had shown Rome the way across the Channel.

While Caesar was fighting and defeating Germanic and Gaulish war leaders like Vercingetorix, there was chaos on the streets of Rome. It was largely at the instigation of Clodius, a popular plebian tribune who was opposed to Caesar's expressed wish for a second consulship.

Clodius also made use of the defeat and destruction of five cohorts of a Roman Legion in Germany. Given credibility by Clodius and his rantings, doubts were beginning to be expressed about Caesar's ability as a commander. Caesar, of course, ignored them.

It was a time of in-fighting and failed partnerships. Notably, this was seen in the arguments and lack of co-operation amongst the members of the First Triumvirate. Each of them was too self-centred and ambitious to give in to the demands of the others. It began to splinter when Crassus was killed in battle against the Parthians. They, apparently, poured molten gold down his throat, a symbolic gesture reflecting his greed.

Between 52 and 49 BCE, as the relationship between Caesar and Pompey deteriorated, there was real concern that the Republic might slide once more into civil war. The remains of the Triumvirate finally disintegrated when Pompey was instructed to defend Rome from Caesar who was believed to be marching on the capital.

Pompey had little inclination to fight Caesar but reluctantly accepted the task. He drew up his forces outside Rome and waited for his former comrade to arrive. In January 49 BCE Caesar crossed the Rubicon, the northernmost border of Roman territory, and headed south. It was a symbolic and a practical action.

Despite commanding only one legion, the Legio XIII Germana, the defenders of Rome quailed before Caesar's advance. They fled the city, most senators 'heading for the hills,' Pompey taking refuge in Greece. Caesar spent two weeks in Rome, attempting unsuccessfully to open peace negotiations, before leaving Italy in charge of his colleague Lepidus and heading for Pompey's holdings in Spain. These were quickly captured and, in 48 BCE, he turned his attention to Greece.

Caesar defeated Pompey at the Battle of Pharsalus and saw his great rival now head for Egypt. Pompey's world seemed to have fallen apart, supporters like Cato, Cicero and Marcus Junius Brutus begging for pardon from Caesar. Provided they asked for such an amnesty, Caesar was happy to grant it. Brutus, in particular, became a friend and colleague.

Pompey the Great was assassinated as he came ashore in Egypt, Caesar arriving just three days later. He would probably have spared Pompey but he never had the chance.

Assassination

In Egypt, Caesar began an affair with Cleopatra, Queen of Egypt, who ruled alongside her brother Ptolemy. Caesar helped her to victory over Ptolemy, a victory which left her as the sole sovereign. He then moved on to achieve a series of victories over King Pharnaces who was attempting to reclaim lands lost by his father. It was a minor campaign but one which led to Caesar's famous quote 'I came, I saw, I conquered.'

More significantly, however, in 48 BCE he was appointed Dictator of Rome. Such a position was normally just a year-long honour but in this case it was a position that was granted for ten years. It was given in Caesar's absence but the award was welcomed by his soldiers and by his supporters back in Rome.

Caesar's friend and comrade Mark Antony took over management of Italy while Republican elements under Cato and Scipio were brought to battle and defeated in Africa. Caesar had formed an alliance with Gaius Octavian, his grand-nephew who he now named as his principal heir and, together, they mapped out their plans for the future. They were three-fold.

Firstly their aim was to supress armed resistance in the provinces. This would help in the success of their second aim, to knit the provinces together and bring order to the Republic.

Finally came the need to create a strong central government in Rome. In order to achieve these aims the final one was crucial. Caesar, the prime mover in this decision, needed to ensure that his control over Rome was undisputed. In other words, even at this early stage in his political career, he intended to create a permanent, long term dictatorship.

The Death of Julius Caesar

This dictatorship for life was a position to which Caesar was elected in 44 BCE. From his golden chair in the senate he immediately began a series of reforms.

The reforms started with the appointment of new senators, men who he and Octavian felt they could trust, and quickly moved on to things like a reformation of government. Caesar even reorganised the Roman calendar. Yet all was not as comfortable as it seemed.

On 15 March 44 BCE, the Ides of March as the day was known, Caesar was due to appear before a session of the senate. He went, suspecting possible danger but not knowing that a conspiracy involving some 60 of the senators had been hatched against him. If he was scared he certainly did not show it, as the later Roman historian and writer Plutarch was to claim:

> 'A soothsayer had warned Caesar to beware the Ides of March, a traditional deadline for settling debts in ancient Rome ... On the way to the senate, they passed the soothsayer. Plutarch says Caesar greeted him with a jest and remarked "Well, the Ides of March are come." Softly the seer replied "Aye, they are come but they are not gone."'[3]

Mark Antony had also heard of the conspiracy, this time from Casca, one of the assassins, and attempted to head off the doomed man. He was intercepted as he approached the portico of the Theatre of Pompey where the meeting was to take place and kept talking until a loud commotion was heard from inside the building. Guessing what had happened, Mark Antony promptly fled.

As soon as he arrived Caesar was presented with a petition from one Tillius Cimber, begging to recall his exiled brother. The plotters gathered around the pair as Cimber caught Caesar by the shoulders and spun him around. In doing so he pulled down part of Caesar's toga. It was the signal the other assassins had been waiting for but in the noise and chaos few saw Cimber's actions.

Casca was one who did and he struck the first blow, a glancing swipe with his dagger across Caesar's neck. 'Casca, you villain,' Caesar shouted, 'what are you doing?' It was a sign for the other plotters to attack and within moments blow after blow was being aimed at the dictator.

In all, 23 wounds were inflicted although only one blow – the second one as it happened - was in any way fatal. Caesar fell to the floor, blinded by his own blood. Shakespeare's line of 'Et tu Brute,' aimed at Marcus Junius

Brutus, the man he had pardoned not long before, is a dramatic piece of theatre but is unlikely to be true.

Most of the senators and the plotters fled the scene. Not all of them, however. Brutus and Cassius, the latter being the other main conspirator, went to the Capitol building where Brutus declared 'People of Rome, we are again free.' He was greeted by silence. And then the people of Rome fled to their houses, locking themselves in for safety.

Caesar's battered and blood splattered body lay on the steps of the portico at the theatre for several hours before officials finally summoned up enough courage to remove it. Several of the conspirators had wanted to throw the body into the Tiber, a traditional way of dealing with dead enemies. Mark Antony, however, had Caesar's corpse preserved for a public burial and funeral ceremony.

The Aftermath

Even to begin with the conspirators were received coldly by the people of Rome. Fickle and changeable as they were, the citizens had thought the advent of Julius Caesar meant a degree of stability for the city. It was, they hoped, going to be a clear case of 'benevolent dictatorship.'

Rome had undergone more than enough chaos over the past few years and now, with the assassination of the one man who promised a degree of stability, it all seemed to be kicking off again. They were right to react coldly. Fourteen years of yet another civil war lay ahead.

It may have begun with something of a cold shoulder to the plotters but public opinion soon turned violently and totally against them, particularly once the terms of Caesar's Will were made public and Mark Antony's passionate speech at the funeral had inflamed the plebs. Caesar had left three pieces of gold to every citizen, more than enough to buy the support of the Roman mob. Public unrest began to spread throughout Rome.

Houses were burned, shops looted and those conspirators still in the city were hunted by large, baying mobs. Mark Antony and Octavian Caesar sat back contentedly, knowing their time would come but, for the moment, happy to leave destruction in the hands of the mob.

The motives of the plotters were varying and this quickly became apparent to everyone. Brutus, a man of standing and importance in Rome, was the main conspirator. He was, as Shakespeare had Mark Antony declare 'an honourable man' but in the wake of the assassination that mattered for very little.

Despite his friendship with Caesar, Brutus was clear in his own mind that the dictator had designs on kingship, something that ran in totally the opposite direction to his own plans for Rome. He was a republican through and through and believed that once Caesar was dead and out of the way, the Roman Republic would resurface.

Mark Antony had offered Caesar the crown on three separate occasions, an offer that was refused every time. Yet the dictator was increasingly adopting regal postures, even his statues around Rome being adorned with crowns, laurel leaves and other marks of kingship.

It was, Brutus knew, only a matter of time before Caesar would be offered the crown once more. And this time it might just prove to be once too often. Brutus and his partners had already taken one chance, now it was time to act again.

So much for Brutus, who does seem to be a man of honour. Cassius, on the other hand, was no republican. He was motivated by personal greed and by a desire for revenge - a payback for real or imagined slights – for wrongs done to him and to his family.

Above all, he held Caesar in contempt, considering him a coward. 'How he did shake; tis true, this god did shake' he declared when describing Caesar in a fit of despair and worry when they were campaigning in Spain. He went on to compare him to a sick girl:

'Ye gods, it doth amaze me
A man of such a feeble temper should
So get the start of the majestic world
And bear the palm alone.'[4]

The jealousy and anger Cassius displays in the above speech might simply be a dramatic invention of William Shakespeare but from the accounts made by Plutarch and others it does seem to be an accurate judgement.

Caesar noticed it, of course, Shakespeare giving him one of the most potent lines in his play about the assassination:

'Let me have men about me that are fat;
Sleek headed men and such as sleep o' nights.
Yon Cassius has a lean and hungry look;
He thinks too much: such men are dangerous.'[5]

The other plotters fall somewhere between the attitudes and desires of Brutus and Cassius in their aims and intentions. They are pliable individuals, men who are too easily swayed by the oratory of the main conspirators.

The assassination of Julius Caesar sparked what might be termed a surge of 'assassination fever' in Roman history. Political killing had been widely used in the ancient world but never in such force and fury as in the Roman Empire.

Of the coming half dozen emperors, at least five were illegally executed or assassinated. Tiberius, Caligula, Claudius and Nero all fell to the assassins blades, metaphorical or literal. They were not alone, dying with many other significant Roman characters whose potential rise to power was cut short.

Assassination remained common for the rest of the Empire with future emperors like Galba, Titus and Vitellus all being assassinated by poison, knife or spear. In all, out of 82 Roman Emperors over 30 of them met their death via assassination. That was an amazing figure of approximately 20% and it all began with Julius Caesar.

There is even a school of thought declaring that Augustus, the founder of the whole concept of Roman emperors and single person dictatorship without the inconvenience of elections, was killed by his wife Livia.

She smeared poison, many believe, on the figs growing on trees in the Emperor's garden. Augustus, who had grown fat and gluttonous in his old age, could not help himself and kept picking at the ripe fruits that he loved so much. A clear case of job done.

Robert Graves certainly thought the rumour to be true, using it as part of the plot for his revolutionary historical novel *I, Claudius*. Livia, as Graves describes her, was certainly capable of such activity but it has never been confirmed.

The Roman historian Tacitus was non-committal about the death of Augustus but was clear about other Livia-led assassinations. In particular, he believed that Gaius and Lucius, stepsons of Livia and her first husband Agrippa but adopted by Augustus and therefore in line for the succession, had been murdered by their step mother.

True or not, the assassinations of other emperors are well recorded. The assassination of Julius Caesar was a landmark moment in ancient history. It took fourteen years to work itself out, fourteen years of warfare, murder and mayhem, but the killing marked the end of democracy in Rome. Brutus and Cassius, along with every other conspirator, did not live to see it.

The two main conspirators fled Rome once they realised that public opinion had turned against them. Despite an amnesty arranged by Caesar's adopted son Octavian, more of a gesture than reality, they were hunted down and brought to battle.

After being defeated twice in battles at Philippi, in October 42 BCE both Brutus and Cassius chose to kill themselves. It was already being considered the 'noble' way to die.

One by one the other conspirators either preceded or followed them. The republican cause died with them.

By the end of 43 BCE Mark Antony and Octavian, along with the consul Marcus Aemilius Lepidus, had clearly become the strongest, most powerful of all Roman officials. There was little affection or respect between them, however, and in an attempt to stay on friendly terms Antony married Octavia, sister of the nineteen year old adopted son of Caesar.

It was an uneasy peace, one that was bound to fester and die at some stage. Despite whatever public announcements they made, none of the three men had any real affection for each other or for the Republic which they were now bound to protect. Octavian, in particular, had very different plans. Sharing power had never been his intention.

Chapter Ten

Early Assassinations In and Around Rome

With Brutus, Cassius and the other conspirators lying dead, Rome promptly descended once more into a pit of open conflict and dynastic ambition. In 43 BCE, in an effort to put a halt to the violence that was still haunting the streets of Rome, the three main players - Mark Antony, Lepidus and Octavian - formed themselves into what is now known as the Second Triumvirate.

The name was not actively employed until the seventeenth century but viewed now, in hindsight, it nails home the strength and power of the three-man junta that assumed power and came to rule in Rome. Members of the Triumvirate were the holders of ultimate Roman power, granted on a five year tenure. Within that space of time, the three men were given consular power and the right to make decisions without even consulting the senate.

Their first act was to prescribe and execute 200 men who, it was felt, had contributed to the chaos. Amongst the victims was the writer Cicero. He had only recently delivered the Philippic Orations, criticising Mark Antony and calling him a threat to law and order in Rome. This was Antony's opportunity for revenge.

The members of the Triumvirate next divided up the Empire between themselves, Mark Antony taking the eastern section, Octavian the west and Lepidus being sidelined in Africa. For a while it appeared to be a sensible solution – until raw ambition began to burn away any cords that still bound the Triumvirate members together.

With Mark Antony making snide comments about Octavian and Octavian replying in kind, it was a time of dramatic tension in Rome. Lepidus, never really part of the group, was exiled. Clearly the situation could not last much longer. At that point, enter Queen Cleopatra.

Antony and Cleopatra

Mark Antony had led a somewhat dissipated youth and adolescence but pulled himself together in order to become a cavalry leader of note during various campaigns in Judea and Egypt. He went on to serve with Julius Caesar during the Civil War of 49 BCE.

Despite the formation of the Second Triumvirate, open conflict between Antony and Octavian seemed sure to break out. Antony retired to Egypt where, always open to the advances and attention of beautiful women, he made the acquaintance of Cleopatra. He spent the winter and spring of 41-40 BCE in Alexandria as her lover and gave her the first of two children.

In 35 BCE Octavia, Antony's wife, journeyed to Egypt, resulting in Antony and Cleopatra abandoning their affair for the length of her stay. Two years after her arrival Mark Antony felt he had endured enough and sent Octavia back to Rome. It was a decision made mainly because her brother had not fulfilled his obligations in sending troops to help Mark Antony in his campaigns. It was, however, a foolish, ultimately a humiliating, move on Antony's part, particularly as with Octavia now absent, he turned again to Cleopatra for comfort, solace and sex.

She and Mark Antony had not seen each other for nearly three years but their affection for each other remained very real. He declared that Cleopatra was all a man could want, she was the new Aphrodite, the Roman goddess of love. They also had need of each other politically. Antony needed Egypt as a source of supplies for a proposed assault on Parthia while Cleopatra needed him to support her in her efforts to revive the boundaries of the old Ptolemaic kingdom.

A furious Octavian consoled his sister and declared that Mark Antony had no right to civilised western women. He had chosen an oriental paramour. Using his influence, Octavian persuaded the senate to take action. In 32 BCE Antony's powers as a member of the Triumvirate were revoked and Rome declared war on Egypt. Meanwhile Antony carried blithely on, barely recognising Roman power and control.

He made Alexandria his base and in 34 BCE mounted a successful expedition into Armenia. He celebrated with a Triumph through the city and by pronouncing Cleopatra Queen of Kings. Her son Ptolemy was announced King of Kings at the same time. Not surprisingly, Octavian saw it all as an attempt by Mark Antony to move the Roman power base to the east.

The Triumvirate formally ended its days in late 32 BCE. Importantly, Octavian had huge support in the senate, Antony almost none. He and Cleopatra were, increasingly, putting themselves out on a limb, a situation made even worse when Antony divorced Octavia and married Cleopatra, even though the marriage was not recognised under Roman law.

Further incensed at what he regarded as an unforgivable insult, Octavian and his chief lieutenant Agrippa crossed the Ionian Sea with a large body of legionaries, their forces landing, unopposed, in Greece and Macedonia. Octavius clearly had ideas about single-person control although the term 'emperor' had not yet appeared in his vocabulary. For the moment, with Lepidus exiled and out of the game only Mark Antony stood in his way.

Cleopatra insisted on being at Antony's battle headquarters. It was a mistake. Her haughty attitude antagonised and alienated many of the Romans under Antony's command, large numbers of them switching sides to join Octavian and Agrippa. Antony was a capable commander but not so efficient and as ruthless as Octavian or as experienced and wily as Agrippa. As the numbers of his men switching sides grew, the more discontent developed in the ranks and the more morale declined.

Cleopatra had been born in approximately 70 BCE. She came to the throne after the death of her father in 51 BCE and ruled Egypt with her brothers Ptolemy XIII and IV. Her son Ptolemy Caesar later joined the list of Ptolemy monarchs. An autocratic ruler, she had little care or concern about her appeal to the Legionaries. She had been in Rome when Julius Caesar was assassinated and regarded the Romans with contempt.[1]

Now, when Antony was ready to face Agrippa at sea, Cleopatra insisted she should be there alongside him. The Battle of Actium was fought on 2 September 31 BCE. Agrippa's ships were smaller than Antony's and greatly outnumbered. However, they were far more manoeuvrable and when Cleopatra, sensing that defeat was close at hand, slipped away with 60 of her vessels, it was the end of the encounter.

In the wake of Cleopatra's desertion, Mark Antony was also soon in flight. A further victory for Octavian and Agrippa, on land at Alexandria, made the end result inevitable.

Cleopatra killed herself by clasping a venomous snake to her chest, Antony taking the more usual and traditional Roman way of ending everything by stabbing himself in the belly. The poignancy of the situation allowed Shakespeare to produce perhaps the most powerful ending to any of his historical or classical plays:

> 'Unarm Eros; the long days task is done
> And we must sleep ... Off, pluck off;
> The seven-fold shield of Ajax cannot keep
> The battery from my heart.'[2]

Following the death of Antony and Cleopatra, Octavian's forces spread out across Egypt. There was little or no opposition to what was now a relatively painless invasion.

Neither the death of Antony, nor that of Cleopatra, both deaths occurring in the end as independent from each other, was an assassination in the traditional sense of the word. And yet it is impossible not to categorise their deaths as assassinations of a sort.

The two deaths were certainly the result of a conspiracy which led to the removal of two dynamic and influential bodies, people who would have definitely challenged Octavian over what came next. They killed themselves before Octavian could do it for them - self-assassination if ever it was.

With Cleopatra and Antony out of the way, Octavian's route to ultimate power was simple. Returning to Rome in 27 BCE he was proclaimed First Citizen, tribune, censor and commander-in-chief. Outwardly, it was the creation of a free republic with power still vested in the senate. But it was little more than a façade, Octavian being granted his titles and positions for life.

His titles were soon subsumed into that of Emperor, Octavian taking the regal name of Augustus (meaning the venerated). It was the first time an emperor had ruled in Rome and the Julio-Claudian Dynasty he created was to last for 200 years.

Philosophy, Ambition and Hemlock

Assassination in and around early Rome, in its dominions and its satellite states, was not reserved solely for emperors and would-be monarchs. Even the philosophers and the great writers of the ancient world were potential targets for the assassins. That did not diminish the significance of the crime:

> 'Assassination is an act of war and must be acknowledged as such ... (it) is a fantastically leveraged act, a David and Goliath contest where cunning and surprise overcome brute force.'[3]

Socrates

Born and brought up in Athens, the philosopher and scholar Socrates is credited with being the founder of Western Philosophy. He became a victim of judicial assassination in 399 BCE.

An enigmatic figure, Socrates left no books, no writings or texts, his work being known to posterity through the posthumous accounts of other writers and scholars. Acerbic, unwilling to accept fools gladly, he tended to polarise people's opinions and that, inevitably, led to the creation of loyal friends on the one hand, and bitter enemies on the other.

Socrates fell foul of the Thirty Tyrants, a pro-Spartan oligarchy installed by warlike Sparta in 404 BCE after Athens had been defeated in the Peloponnesian War. Even though they ruled for just under a year, the Thirty Tyrants managed to kill off 1500 Athenian citizens, some 5% of the population, without fair trial. Many Athenian citizens fled the city but Socrates chose to remain in Athens where his former pupil Critias was now one of the leaders of the Thirty.

Socrates was a man of principles. He was once, along with four other notable citizens, ordered to bring Leon of Salamis before the Thirty. It was an example of how a man, guilty of only helping and advising others, might be treated in a dictatorship. He would be examined, Critias and the Thirty deemed, and then executed. Socrates refused to participate in any way, an action that caused him to be 'marked down' for future attention. In 339 BCE he was duly arrested and condemned to death for 'corruption of the young and neglect of the gods.'[4]

Socrates spent a month in prison, waiting for 'the sacred ship' to return from Delos. No execution could take place while this venerated vessel was absent and Socrates and his friends took the opportunity of meeting every day for discussion and companionship. Several times someone suggested he should take advantage of the delay and seize the chance of escaping. He refused every time. The law, he felt, had to run its course.

Finally, they heard that the ship had returned and Socrates prepared himself for execution. The chosen method was poisoning and one of the prison guards instructed him in what he was supposed to do:

> 'Drink the poison and walk about till your legs feel heavy; then lie down and the poison will take effect of itself.' He walked about and when his legs were heavy, lay down on his back ...

The man who had administered the poison laid hands on him and after a while examined his feet and legs, then pinched his foot hard and asked if he felt it. He said "No."[5]

After a while the chill reached his heart and Socrates died. It was a peaceful death for Socrates but those friends who were in the prison with him were moved to tears.

Archimedes

If Socrates was the victim of judicial assassination, then the mathematician, scientist and writer Archimedes met his untimely death at the hands of unthinking and unseeing Roman soldiers.

Famous for his invention of the Archimedes Screw and the principle that a body immersed in water displaces weight equal to the amount of fluid it displaces, he is best remembered for what is probably a piece of fiction. Most people recall the story of the excited mathematician, his theory having taken shape, leaping from his bath, running naked through the city shouting 'Eureka!'

There are two recorded versions of his death but it remains clear that he died in 212 BCE at the end of the Roman siege of Syracuse during the Second Punic War.

Version one has Archimedes being accosted by a soldier shortly after the city fell. Marcus Claudius Marcellus, commander of the victorious Roman army, wanted to meet him, the soldier declared. Archimedes refused, he was too busy. Despite Marcellus' orders that Archimedes was not to be hurt, the soldier drew his sword and promptly killed him.

Version two records an abstracted Archimedes deep in mathematical study and contemplation when the summons came. The soldier carrying the message assumed that Archimedes' mathematical diagrams and models were valuable and killed him in order to gain possession. This version of his death records the mathematicians' last words as 'Do not disturb my circles.' It is entirely possible.

Archimedes had greatly assisted in the defence of his city, inventing stone throwing machines that caused heavy casualties amongst the Romans. He modified the giant defensive catapults, again causing many casualties. It is, therefore, entirely possible that his death was something of a revenge issue. The jury remains out.

Marcus Tullius Cicero

The death of writer and politician Cicero took place in December 43 BCE. He had been educated in Greece and in Rome and served, briefly, as a soldier before changing tack and becoming a lawyer. Married to a wealthy woman, money was no real object but in relatively quick succession he was elected quaestor in 75 BCE, praetor in 66 and consul in 63, one of the youngest men ever to reach that rank.

Cicero argued and fell out with Julius Caesar in 63 BCE and when the First Triumvirate was formed he felt he had no option but to flee from Rome. He attempted to persuade Pompey to break with Caesar but to no effect and, reluctantly, he was forced to give the Triumvirate his grudging approval. He was, at heart, a republican but was virtually alone in his belief. He left politics in disgust and for a number of years concentrated on his writing.

After a brief period as governor of Cilicia, by the time of the death of Crassus in 53 BCE and the subsequent war between Caesar and Pompey, Cicero was back in Rome. Both men asked Cicero for support, something that the already biased writer gave to Pompey. The five year long civil war was eventually won by Caesar but despite being pardoned by the dictator, not long after Caesar's death Cicero was once again venting his wrath:

> 'Our tyrant deserved his death for having made an exception of the one thing that was the blackest crime of all ... Here you have a man who was ambitious to be king of the Roman people and master of the whole world. All honest men killed Caesar, some lacked design, some courage, some opportunity: none lacked the will.'[6]

Following Caesar's spectacular funeral and Mark Antony's wooing of the crowd, Cicero like Brutus and Cassius, fled Rome. For a while he believed he had found an ally and patron in the young Octavian and yet again returned to Rome, this time to make fourteen scathing denunciations of Antony, the Philippics as they were known.

The war between Antony and Octavian saw much glory bestowed upon the younger man with Cicero hailed as the hero of the hour. He was borne aloft from his house to the Forum. However, in the furious in-fighting which followed, it became obvious that Octavian was not the man Cicero had thought: - 'The boy (Octavian) must be praised, honoured – and removed.'[7]

When the Second Triumvirate issued its list of proscribed citizens, people who were marked down for future assassination, Mark Antony made sure that Cicero's name was included. The end for Cicero came quickly.

Cicero and his brother were at their villa in Tusculum, intending to take a ship to Macedonia where they would link up with Brutus. When Quintus went back to the villa to pick up extra supplies he was assassinated by the house servants.

Cicero, plagued by indecision, left by ship, then returned, having changed his mind about his destination. Hearing that Mark Antony's soldiers were close at hand, he decided to take the road through the forest to the port of Gaeta.

Having been shown the way by a slave, soldiers led by Popilius, a centurion who had once been defended in court by Cicero, and by the senator Herennius, caught up with Cicero's carriage. He was pulled out and killed. The historian Appian later wrote the following account of the assassination:

> 'As he leaned out of his litter and offered his neck, his head was cut off. Nor did this satisfy the senseless cruelty of the soldiers. They cut off his hands, also, for the offence of having written something against Antony.'[8]

Appian's account does not say if Cicero put out his head voluntarily and allocates no blame on Mark Antony.

Other versions of the assassination state that Antony ordered Cicero's head and right hand should be cut off and displayed on the rostrum in the Forum, the same platform from which Cicero had spoken so brilliantly, so often, in the past.

Pompey the Great

Born on 29 September 106 BCE and arguably the greatest soldier Rome ever produced, Gnaeus Pompeius Magnus came from a background of senatorial nobility. That background gave him confidence and pride in his own ability.

He began his military career when still very young, serving the dictator Sulla in the Civil War of 83-82 BCE. He also became a consul while still young, without following the three steps – the cursus honorum as they were known – normally required to advance a political career.

Elected consul three times, Pompey served in various campaigns and earned himself three separate Triumphs. His success garnered him the name of Magnus (the Great), chosen in honour of Pompey's boyhood hero Alexander the Great. His enemies were not so charitable. They called him 'adulescentulus carnifex' (teenage butcher) because of his youth and utter ruthlessness in time of war or civil disturbance.

In 60 BCE Pompey joined Crassus and Julius Caesar in an informal alliance, the First Triumvirate, marrying Caesar's daughter Julia to cement the arrangement. Julia died in 54 BCE, Crassus was killed fighting the Parthians a year later and the Triumvirate fell apart. Pompey then joined the political faction known as the Optimates, the conservative side of the senate. It brought Caesar and Pompey into direct conflict with each other.

Pompey was a genius on the battlefield but so too was Caesar and on 9th August 48 BCE the two generals came face to face at the Battle of Pharsalus. Caesar emerged as the victor and Pompey fled. He was looking for refuge in Ptolemaic Egypt, a country where he had served before. This time, however, it was different. King Ptolemy, 14 years old and engaged in a bitter war with his sister Cleopatra, was afraid of offending Caesar.

As Pompey came ashore at Pelusium on 28th September 48 BCE, arguably to pay respects to Egyptian officials, he was struck down by Lucius Sextus, a Roman officer serving in the Egyptian army. It had been an adventurous life, Pompey having cleared the Mediterranean of pirates, added many territories to the Roman Empire and fought in countries like Egypt, Africa, Armenia and Palestine.

Pompey's death was witnessed by his son Sextus who remained appalled by what happened after the death. The great general's head was cut off to prove that he was actually dead and sent back to his wife. As the writer Cicero declared 'His life outlasted his power.'

Mithridates VII of Pontus

Mithridates was the ruler of Pontus in northern Anatolia from 120 until 63 BCE. Also known as Mithridates Eupator and Mithridates the Great, he was a ruthless warrior, highly skilled in the arts of war.

He was a formidable opponent for Rome and while his efforts to break Roman dominance of Asia Minor were ultimately unsuccessful, there were many moments when it seemed as if the fate of the Hellenistic world rested solely in his hands.

Knowing the propensity for assassination in the ancient world, Mithridates cultivated an immunity to poison by regularly ingesting small doses of otherwise fatal poisons over extended periods. The practice was later termed mithridatism in honour of its 'inventor.'

Born in what is now modern-day Turkey, Mithridates was present at the large and elaborate banquet where his father, Mithridates V, was assassinated by the use of poison. The perpetrators of the poisoning remained unknown but Mithridates had seen how effective a killing machine it was.

Succession to the throne went to the younger brother of Mithridates. Not surprisingly Mithridates was overlooked. Laodicea, his mother had always had a preference for her youngest child and now she ruled as Regent until he came of age in 116 BCE. Fearing for his life, Mithridates had already left Pontus and gone into hiding.

He returned to his homeland somewhere around the time of his brother's formal succession. By now Mithridates was blessed with great strength and a talent for political manoeuvring.

Before Laodicea and her favoured son could oppose him, Mithridates had them both imprisoned. Both later died in captivity, the brother possibly being assassinated, Laodicea from what appeared to be natural causes.

Mithridates promptly married his younger sister, the sixteen year old Laodice, taking her as his 'first' wife. It was common practice at the time, the idea being to preserve the purity of the blood line. Having secured that, Mithridates went to war.

He began by organising a genocide of Roman and Italian settlers in his country, possibly as many as 80,000 of them, in what became known as the Asiatic Vespers. His activities were supported by Athens and other Greek city states but, eventually, after three wars against Rome, Mithridates was defeated and exiled.

He returned to Pontus in 67 BCE while the Romans were involved in other matters and defeated them at the Battle of Zeba when 7000 legionaries were allegedly killed.

The victory brought him up against Pompey the Great and inevitably, given the quality of Pompey's troops, Mithridates' forces were routed at the Battle of Lycus.

Mithridates then fled to Crimea, an area north of the Black Sea where he began plotting yet another return to Anatolia. His plan this time was to gather his armies, invade Italy through the Danube region and force the Roman Legions out of Asia Minor.

He had just completed the basic organisation when one of his sons, aided by local warlords, suddenly rebelled. Mithridates was devastated and withdrew to the citadel of Panticapaeum.

There, in despair, he decided he had suffered enough. He would kill himself. He tried poison but, of course, he was immune. Desperate, now, he asked Bituitus, an old soldier companion and bodyguard to take his sword and kill him.

The poet AE Houseman, albeit with limited knowledge of Mithridates and his period in power, was moved to write about his death and, in a somewhat hidden or subliminal manner, his scheme for immunity:

> 'They put arsenic in his meat
> And stared aghast to watch him eat;
> They poured strychnine in his cup
> And shook to see him drink it up;
> They shook, they stared as white's their shirt;
> Them it was their poison hurt.
> I tell the tale that I heard told
> Mithridates, he died old.'[9]

The key line is the second one. He had indeed sampled all of the 'killing store.' Preparation and awareness, after all, were not always the key elements, it seemed!

In the technical sense of the word, Mithridates was not assassinated, he was a victim of what might be called applied suicide. But he gave his sword to Bituitus, knowing that the old man would obey his instructions. That, really, was assassination, albeit self-inflicted or self-ordained, thus putting Mithridates in the long list of rulers who lost their lives to killers, willing or otherwise.

Before he was killed by his own sword, Mithridates' two daughters had asked to test the poison. They both took it and both died.

Mithridates, despite walking around and around, supposedly to speed up the effect of the poison, had survived the fatal dose. Ultimately, he took the only way out and effectively requested his own assassination.

Chapter Eleven

Assassinations in the Empire of Rome

Roman society was brutal, an understandable view or attitude when considered in the context of the time. Physical retribution for perceived acts of rebellion, public execution for many seemingly innocuous crimes and a strict observance of state policies were common practices. Anything less was invariably considered to be a show of weakness and that was something no emperor or army commander would tolerate.

Nowhere is that better seen than in the seemingly endless series and lists of assassination victims in the last days of the Republic and in the early period of the Roman Empire.

From emperors and politicians to writers and philosophers, nobody was above the assassins blades, nobody was immune, and everyone was a potential victim. It was a convenient and relatively blameless way of rendering justice.

The first emperor, Octavian or Augustus as he became known, brought a degree of stability to the city and its possessions or territories. It slowed the series of assassinations, did not halt them, but, overall, his reign was a welcomed and much needed period of peace after years of civil war and incessant power struggles. His popularity and a fondness for an easy and mutually beneficial dictatorship were the hallmark of Augustus's long period in control.

The basic premise was simple – keep your nose clean and you'll do alright; offend the system and there will be trouble. In the long term it could not hope to last for ever, as events were to prove, but for nearly 200 years under Augustus and his immediate successors the Roman Empire grew and prospered.

Citizens of Rome revelled in what became known as the Pax Romana. The empire's greatest territorial expanse – culminating in a final total of 1.7 million square miles - occurred under the Emperor Trajan between 98 and 117 CE. It was a far cry from the early days of Romulus and Remus.

During the Pax Romana culture, the arts, literature and architecture all flourished. Rebellions did occur, usually out in the provinces but they were dealt with swiftly, efficiently and ruthlessly. Glory days, indeed.

End of the Old Guard

Tiberius Gracchus was a Roman politician and statesman, born in 163 BCE, one of the last defenders of the old Republic. He was renowned for his interest in agrarian reforms and for championing the process of transferring land from the grip of the wealthy and the state into the ownership of poorer citizens of Rome. It was a campaign that, ultimately, he was to pay for with his life, his death marking the beginning of the Republic's rather rapid decline.

He began a military career in 147 BCE, serving as legate/military tribune to his brother-in-law Scipio Aemilianus. He fought in the Third Punic War, where he was part of the force that spent several years attempting to take Carthage, and in the Numantine War in Spain. The campaigns were not always successful. At the end of the Numantine War, he was forced to negotiate a humiliating treaty with the Numantines, on behalf of the Empire, surrendering the entire Roman force.

Returning to Rome he became conscious of the decline in the Roman population and in the quality of those workmen he encountered. Tiberius Gracchus put it all down to the land-grabbing rich. Now a senator, in 133 BCE he campaigned hard for a reform of the land laws which permitted such unjust persecution of the agrarian poor. Opposition in the senate was furious, arguments and threats becoming the standard order of the day.

Soon the atmosphere in the city of Rome began to mirror events in the senate. Riots broke out as the mobs roared through the streets, destroying property in a seemingly mindless orgy of destruction. As ever, the mob violence was fuelled by the rich and powerful, in this case the rich and powerful enemies of Gracchus.

It was election time in Rome. Tiberius Gracchus had come to the end of his term of office but he now tried to get himself re-elected to the senate. He and his entourage took control of the Capitoline Hill where the voting was taking place but they were immediately challenged by his cousin Publius Cornelius Scipio.

Screaming for anyone who wanted to keep the community secure to join him – a traditional tactic from the time - Publius charged the Capitoline Hill with his toga pulled over his head. He fooled no-one, least of all his cousin.

Tiberius Gracchus and his supporters were stoned and beaten to death with clubs, refusing to fight back against fellow Romans. Their bodies were dumped unceremoniously into the River Tiber. The tactics employed by

Tiberius and the reformers showed that the Republic, in its final days, was not geared for the types of economic reforms required and demanded by Tiberius Gracchus. For that to happen citizens would have to wait for the coming of the Empire.

The assassination of Tiberius Gracchus was a carefully organised affair, senatorial opponents using the Roman mob to carry out the execution. It was the beginning of a long series of assassinations and riots in Rome where political disputes were increasingly settled by violence. Tyrannicide, it seemed, was a justifiable process.[1]

The Death of Germanicus One and Germanicus Two

A popular and highly successful soldier who was renowned for his campaigns in the northern parts of the Empire, Germanicus – full name *Claudius Nero Drusus Germanicus* – was the younger brother of Tiberius, soon to be the second Emperor of Rome.

Both brothers came from an influential and prosperous Roman family. Their father was the politician Tiberius Claudius Nero, first husband of the infamous Livia Drusilla. Emperor Augustus fell in love with Livia. It was love at first sight, apparently and he proceeded to force a divorce on the couple. Both parties accepted the situation with no ill will or rancour.

With her first husband shuffled to one side, Livia then married Augustus and Nero even gave her away at the ceremony. In 4 CE Livia's son Claudius Nero became the legal stepson of the Emperor. In 12 CE he was elected consul and a year later proconsul of Germania Superior and all of Gaul. This gave him command of a large and vitally important part of the Roman army.

He was awarded and accepted the agnomen Germanicus in 9 BCE. He had performed many notable feats in Germany and Gaul and award of the name was regarded as recognition for his campaigns against the northern barbarians.

Most notable amongst his many achievements was launching the first Roman incursion across the Rhine. But as well as defeating many of the Germanic tribes, Germanicus was also the man behind the digging of a canal from the River Rhine to the North Sea. It was an incredible feat of engineering for the time but Germanicus did not live long enough to enjoy his fame or the economic value of his creation.

In the summer of 9 BCE Germanicus was thrown from his horse and received serious injuries. In what was to become a recurring nightmare for the nobles and governors of the Empire, Germanicus looked to be recovering but then took a downward spiral that resulted in his death thirty days later. Even the Empress Livia's own doctor, who was hurried to the spot, could not save him. The accident was genuine enough but the presence of Livia's Doctor and the sudden reversal of recovery do make you wonder if the death of Germanicus was entirely accidental.

Germanicus Julius Caesar accepted the name Germanicus on the death of his father and was soon proving equally as adept in war as the original holder of the name. His father might have led the first Roman incursion north of the Rhine but the young Germanicus soon avenged the Roman defeat at Tannenberg and went on to reclaim two of the infamous lost eagles of the Legions. He returned to Rome in 17 CE, receiving a full Triumph for his efforts.

His stay in Rome was short lived however. Within a few months Germanicus, on the orders of his uncle, the new Emperor Tiberius, was heading east to reorganise the provinces of Asia Minor which were in a more than unhelpful degree of confusion.

He immediately clashed with Gnaeus Calpurnius Piso, the governor of Syria and within a few weeks a full-scale feud had developed.

The arguments became increasingly bitter and, eventually, Piso left Syria to return to Rome. His departure was more to do with respite than with any complaints he might make. Germanicus remained at Antioch.

Shortly after Piso left Germanicus sickened and died, despite the efforts of Livia's own physician who, once again, hurried to the sick bed. It was 18 CE and Germanicus was only thirty-three years old, still a fit young man. Poison was immediately suspected, Piso's wife Plancina being the chief suspect.

Back in Rome, Piso was hauled before the senate to deny or substantiate the charges but committed suicide before any decision could be made. The matter of Germanicus, Plancina and poison were never investigated further.

Rumour, however, continued unabated. Tongue wagging in the forum, in the wine and oyster shops, in the Legionary Barracks and in almost every house in Rome became almost a leisure pastime. Plancina might have delivered the poison but she was hardly the instigator of the plot. Who was behind it? Everyone had their opinion but nobody had the answer.

The Emperor Tiberius, who had always played second fiddle to his brother Germanicus and now, it seemed, to his nephew was known to be jealous of them both – suspect number one. Livia had always preferred Tiberius to Germanicus and had long held visions of her favoured son succeeding to the Imperial throne. This he had done but Germanicus was still a potential threat – suspect number two.

Then there were Piso and Plancina, annoyed at having their world disrupted by the boy hero from Rome – joint suspects number three. Germanicus and his wife had a number of children, amongst them the disturbed but highly ambitious Caligula – suspect number four.

Even Augustus, always pliable and open to suggestion from his wife Livia was a possibility – suspect number five, even though he had been dead for a number of years. That did not stop the gossip mongers and superstitious Roman citizens from suggesting that he was striking from the grave.

And so it went on. Nothing was ever proved and the assassin, whoever he or she might be, remained at large. It was one of the few ancient world assassinations that were never attributed to anyone, even though the options and the choices were many and varied.

The Death of the Successors

The assassin or assassins of Germanicus might never have been identified but there is also some doubt or confusion surrounding the death of the two grandsons of Emperor Augustus. Those grandsons, Gaius and Lucius Caesar, were the nominated joint successors to his throne. Much loved by Augustus, the two boys were raised, educated and housed in the Imperial quarters with Augustus, Livia and the rest of their family.

They were the sons of Augustus' friend and colleague, the renowned general Agrippa, and of Julia, daughter of Augustus. With Julia being in direct bloodline from the Emperor, the nomination of his two grandsons was logical and expected once he had adopted the title of Emperor for himself.

However, things did not work out quite as plainly or as simply as might have been expected. Both Gaius and Lucius died in what could be termed unusual circumstances.

Gaius was betrayed and wounded while leading a campaign in Anatolia in the year 4 CE. Summoned to a meeting with the leader of his opponents, supposedly to discuss their surrender, he was totally unprepared when the enemy chieftain suddenly rounded on him. Knives flashed and Gaius fell.

His lieutenants dragged the bleeding Gaius away to safety and then began a siege of the enemy fortress, an action which eventually proved successful. Gaius was not there to see it.

His wound, at first, appeared to be healing but it soon took a turn for the worse. Doctors could do nothing, his physical and mental health, never strong in the first place, deteriorated and he died in February 4 CE. His brother had preceded him.

In the first century CE Lucius was finishing his military training in Spain when he was struck down by a mysterious illness. Just like his brother, his condition seemed to be improving but then worsened. Doctors seemed powerless and Lucius died on 2nd August 1 CE.

Both Tacitus and Cassius Dio, Roman historians, claimed that the two boys, young men as they had become, were the victims of foul play. More than that, they both hinted at the fact that Livia, wife of Emperor Augustus, was responsible. The sudden swing from full recovery to decline and death is certainly a familiar story.

There was then and is now no proof of Livia's involvement in any of what we might now call her assassinations. However, given an increasingly significant desire for personal power, perhaps in her own right, perhaps through the succession of her only remaining son, it is indeed possible that Livia did have some direct involvement in the deaths.

She was well-versed in the use of poisons and doctors acting on her behalf were present at the death beds of several possible victims. It is, however, mere speculation, the meat and drink of fiction writers like Robert Graves who, of course, made the Empress Livia the evil presence at the centre of the plot in his novel *I, Claudius*.

Fact, fiction, or somewhere in between, the activities of Livia remain a fascinating prospect, particularly when you add to the two deaths of the successors other mysterious deaths like those of her son Germanicus and Germanicus, her nephew – an unlucky name if ever there was one.

The Emperor Tiberius

Following the death of Gaius and Lucius, the two designated heirs to Augustus, his adopted stepson Tiberius was named as Emperor in Waiting. He was now successor to Augustus and thus intended and, as it turned out, destined to become the second Emperor of Rome. In the meantime he and Augustus would rule jointly. Livia was beside herself with joy.

Early in his life Tiberius had been an able administrator and an excellent soldier who, like his brother Germanicus, campaigned successfully in Gaul and Germany. Happily married to Vipsania, daughter of the famous Agrippa, his blissful life ended when Augustus demanded that if he was be his successor then he must divorce Vipsania and marry his own daughter Julia, widow of Agrippa.

Tiberius was not happy at the prospect of a life with Julia and was reluctant to destroy his perfect marriage to Vipsania. However, prodded and pushed by his mother Livia and driven, at that stage in his life, by personal ambition, Tiberius eventually became a submissive party to the arrangement. As might have been expected, this second marriage was a complete disaster.

From the beginning Tiberius knew he had made a terrible mistake. There was no affinity between the two newlyweds and Julia quickly found sexual satisfaction in public exhibitions of promiscuous behaviour. Her hostility towards him had a dramatic effect on the personality of Tiberius. Despising her, he became increasingly morose and introverted. By divorcing Vipsania he had lost the one person who, after his brother, meant most to him in the whole world.

His temperament was not aided by the length of time he had to wait before Augustus died. When that finally happened – with or without the aid of Livia, we will never really know – it was 14 CE, Tiberius was fifty five years old and by that stage was widely regarded as a man with little or no inclination to take on the duties of emperor.

Tiberius had tried for some time to make Augustus and Livia understand his position and his attitude towards the scandalous behaviour of his wife. In the end, Julia was taken to task and actually exiled but there was no respite in the work load imposed upon Tiberius.

In 6 CE, almost in despair, he had given up all his duties as prospective heir and retired to his villa on the Greek island of Rhodes. A furious Augustus attempted several times to cajole him into returning, all to no avail. It was only when he was formally declared joint ruler and eventual successor to Augustus that Tiberius agreed to return to Rome where he began life as a private citizen but soon found himself embroiled once again in the task of helping to govern the Empire.

When Augustus died in 14 CE a bitterly reluctant and unwilling Tiberius finally took up the reins of Empire. Far from content, he was as moody and as unhappy as ever. The writer and historian Pliny the Elder described him as 'The gloomiest man who ever lived.'[2]

The death of his son Drusus in 23 CE was virtually the last straw for Tiberius. Bitterly hurt, he retired from Rome to take up residence on Capri where he quickly degenerated into a sexually perverted old man. While he sat and watched young men and women engaged in sexual activities or delighted in seeing innocent victims hurled from the island's high cliffs, governing Rome lay in the hands of a man by the name of Lucius Aeolia Sejanus. Over the next few years he became virtually a co-ruler with Tiberius. More of him later.

By the year 37 CE Tiberius was clearly fading fast. His bodily strength, once amazing in its power and grace, had left him and he could now do little more than sit staring into space. There was no change in his vicious and damaging personality, however. That remained as sharp and cruel as ever.

Caligula, son of Germanicus, was now the successor to Tiberius and was eager to take hold of power before the Emperor changed his mind. He was living on Capri with his uncle, a virtual prisoner to the whims of the dying man but he, like everyone else, could see that Tiberius was drawing near to the end of his life. It was just a matter of when he would take his dying breath. If he did not go soon, everyone knew that somebody, probably Caligula, would need to help him on his way.

Finally, on 16th March 37 CE, servants entering his sleeping quarters discovered a supposedly dead Tiberius. He was not breathing and a jubilant Caligula set off with a group of companions to let everyone in Capri and the provinces know that he was now Emperor of Rome. According to Tacitus what happened next was a major shock:

> 'Suddenly news came that that Tiberius was recovering his voice and sight, and calling for food to revive him from his faintness. Then ensued a universal panic and while the rest fled hither and thither, everyone feigning grief or ignorance, Caius Caesar (Caligula) in silent stupor passed from the highest hopes to the extremity of apprehension.'[3]

Quick thinking was required and nobody acted faster than Macro, the new replacement for Sejanus as Prefect of the Praetorian Guard. Already a favourite of Caligula, Macro saw that fate had given him the chance to extend his influence:

'Macro, nothing daunted, ordered that the old emperor be smothered under a huge heap of clothes and all to quit the entrance hall.'[4]

The killing was opportunistic but it was also an inevitable assassination, one that had been pending for years. Tiberius died in his seventy-eighth year and Claudius, the new Emperor, seemed to promise a bright start for Rome. He was popular, both with the soldiers of Rome and the citizens. However, in his reaction to the Emperor's unexpected recovery Caligula had shown a distinct lack of courage and fortitude. Rome did not yet know it but the future beckoned bleakly.

The Praetorian Guard

The Praetorian Guard was founded by Augustus, the original intention being that they would operate as the Emperor's personal bodyguard. However, under the command of Lucius Aelius Sejanus, who rose to become Prefect of the Guard in 20 CE, there were immediate reforms and developments in their organisation and role.

Sejanus, a native of Etruria who had served in Armenia with Gaius Caesar, was an eager and ambitious man. Initially joint commander of the Praetorian Guard along with his father Strato, he became sole Prefect when his father was sent to govern Egypt. Now, he saw an opportunity to create an empire within the empire, one with him firmly in control. And the Praetorian Guard was the ideal weapon or tool to wield.

Under Sejanus, the Praetorian Guard became heavily involved with policing Rome, maintaining public security and overseeing civil administration and political intercession. It was a far cry from their original brief which had been simply to protect the Emperor Augustus.

The power and influence of the Praetorian Guard often centred on the process of replacing rather than protecting emperors. It was always a possibility. Granting an excess of power to men with ambition but not necessarily the status to achieve high position needed very careful handling. Few emperors ever really managed it.

Nearly forty Roman emperors are thought to have been assassinated during the life span of the Empire. Of that forty at least twelve perished at the hands of the Praetorian Guard, ranging from early emperors like

Caligula who was eventually assassinated by his bodyguard to those, like Caracalla who came later:

> 'In 217, for example, the Emperor Caracalla, having had his own brother killed as their mother tried desperately to protect him, was stabbed by one of his guards as he urinated by the roadside.'[5]

It was not just the Praetorian Guard that became powerful. Their leader Sejanus also accumulated massive personal power, holding great sway over the Emperor Tiberius and carefully eliminating anyone capable of posing a challenge to his position. That included Drusus, the son of Tiberius.

Drusus was an obvious threat to Sejanus, his privileged position as son of the Emperor giving him immediate access to Tiberius and to the reins of government.

Dislike between the two men soon evolved into hatred and bitter feuding. Sejanus began undermining the position of Drusus in the Roman court, making it public knowledge that he was seducing Drusus's wife. He even attempted to betroth his own daughter Jumilla to Drusus, although she was just four years old.

Eventually, seeing no other way past the problem, in 23 CE Sejanus had Drusus poisoned. Tiberius was distraught at the death but took no action against Sejanus. Indeed, he probably did not know about the part played by the commander of his Guard in the death of his son.

It was not long before statues of Sejanus were appearing all over Rome. Senators and lawyers, public officials, even senior army officials courted him, gave him gifts and were eager to gain his patronage. With Tiberius now happily ensconced in Capri, Sejanus had effectively usurped power in Rome:

> 'He seemed to be the emperor and Tiberius a kind of island potentate, in as much as the latter spent his time on the island of Capri.'[6]

Eventually, however, Tiberius came to his senses. He began to realise that Sejanus had created a power base for himself and was gaining greater control every day. He was a threat and that was something which Tiberius could not allow. In 31 CE the Emperor struck.

Sejanus was arrested under suspicion of conspiracy to rebel. There was no trial, assassinations did not require such legal paraphernalia, but within a few hours Sejanus was strangled and his body, as tradition demanded, thrown down the Gemonian Steps into the River Tiber.

The man chosen to replace Sejanus was Quintus Naevius Cardus Macro. He was originally Prefect of Rome's fire brigade and night watch but was ambitious, anxious to improve his position and status. Being made Prefect of the Praetorian Guard gave him both.

Seeing Caligula as the coming force in Rome, Macro deliberately courted the future emperor. For a while at least, that enabled him to survive the dangerous changeover of regimes from Tiberius to Caligula.

The young Emperor was a dangerous bedfellow, however, and nobody could rest easily, whatever their position or hopes. It was deliberately done on the part of Caligula, even though a growing mania in the young man's personality made his actions almost unchartable.

To begin with all went well for Macro. He now had more power than he had ever thought possible and he was going to use it. After the death of Sejanus, he coldly and succinctly instituted a purge against his predecessors' family, killing all those he could get his hands on.

It was deliberate murder of all those close to the Imperial family, a series of assassinations that included the young Junilla. As Roman law forbade the execution of virgins Macro had her pinioned by a rope around the neck and then raped before she was despatched by a sword thrust.

Senators and friends, anyone who had helped Sejanus in any way, quickly followed his family to the grave. It was brutal and it was horrible to witness but Macro felt that it was inevitable. He certainly did not want vengeful family and friends to come hunting for him.

Most of those not involved in the massacre considered the cull to be nothing more than exactly what Sejanus and his family deserved. As the writer Suetonius declared, the man had been nothing more than 'a rearing vampire for the Roman people.'[7]

Amongst his many other problems, Emperor Caligula was paranoid and the willing Macro was too dangerous an individual to have around for long. Macro thought himself safe, imagined that he was too valuable to Caligula. It was a short sighted view and it was only a matter of time before yet another assassination plot was hatched.

In 38 CE, thinking that he was being sent to Egypt on government business, Macro turned up at the harbour only to be arrested and taken into custody. Before Caligula's assassins could complete their job, he killed himself, denying them the pleasure of the kill but nonetheless achieving the Emperor's wishes.

Chapter Twelve

The Madness That Was Rome

As the Roman Empire developed and established a firm footing for itself during the relatively stable reigns of Augustus and Tiberius, assassination continued to be a well-used tool. Swift, easy to use, always attributable to suicide, assassination was an occupational hazard for those who sought power and a surprisingly effective weapon for those who wanted to take away that control.

However, nothing quite prepared the citizens and administrators of the Empire for what came after the death of Tiberius. With Caligula installed as emperor, the death toll rose significantly, innocent and guilty alike finding that there was nowhere to hide once the new Emperor got a notion or an idea into his head.

Later opinions about Caligula and his behaviour have varied considerably. Many people have claimed that he was suffering from epilepsy, a condition known then as the 'falling sickness' and which had even affected men like Julius Caesar. He certainly talked regularly and openly to the full moon, something that was then associated with epilepsy.

In the opinion of others Caligula was simply certifiably insane. To some he was filled with a craze for power, neatly confirming the adage that all power corrupts, absolute power corrupts absolutely. He was incredibly irritable and often stared at people for long periods of time, not blinking and not speaking. That alone was one of his more unnerving habits.

The condition now known as hyperthyroidism, over production of hormones by the thyroid gland in the neck, has recently been suggested as a possible cause of what was, to those who saw Claudius in action, full-scale madness. At the time, of course, the condition was unknown and not treatable.

Caligula had fallen seriously ill just eight months after his reign began. Even now, nobody knows the nature of the illness but on his recovery the Emperor's behaviour, always cruel and disturbing, had changed drastically. It was now far more extreme, far more deadly.

Caligula's reign as Roman Emperor was mercifully brief, lasting just over four years. But in that short period of time he caused more damage to the citizens of Rome than Atilla the Hun and all his comrades put together.

Little Boot Flexes His Muscles

On the death of his uncle Tiberius, as he expected, the young Gaius Caesar Augustus Germanicus, better known to history as Caligula, became the third Emperor of Rome. He ruled from the year 37 until his own death in 41 CE.

His background was regal in the extreme. His mother, Agrippina the Elder, was the granddaughter of the Emperor Augustus; his father Germanicus was the grandson of the famous Mark Antony and of Octavia, the sister of Augustus. Caligula had spent all of his life being acclaimed and feted, loved by almost everyone he met.

His antecedence combined with this popularity, particularly with the legionaries of Rome's armies, should have ensured a happy and productive reign. Nothing could have been further from the truth. What actually occurred was a slide into insanity, culminating in one of the most brutal and infamous assassinations ever to take place in the ancient world.

When he was just three years old the future emperor accompanied his father on his first campaign in Germany. Others quickly followed. He was presented with a miniature soldier's outfit, complete with boots, which he wore proudly around the various soldiers camps. The outfit earned him the nickname Caligula or 'Little Boot' as it translates. The name was bestowed by the soldiers of his father's Legions who loved and cheered him whenever he appeared in his uniform, screaming out his new name as a symbol of his popularity. The nickname stuck even though Caligula himself eventually grew to hate it.

After the death of his father, Caligula lived with his mother Agrippina. She fell out of favour with Tiberius, however, after he forbade her to re-marry. In 29 CE she and her son Nero, brother of Caligula, were charged with treason and banished to the island of Ponza where Nero later starved to death. That left Caligula relatively homeless until he was sent to live with his grandmother Livia, a poisonous relationship if ever there was one!

After Livia's death he lived with his other grandmother, Antonia Minor, until in 31 CE he was 'remanded' to the care of Tiberius. He spent the next six years on Capri, his considerable acting skills enabling him to hide his fear and dislike of his uncle, the Emperor.

Caligula began his own time as emperor two days after the death of Tiberius, having spent almost a decade observing the increasingly erratic and dangerous behaviour of his uncle. Learning how to be a dictator at first hand, you might say.

He was originally one of two designated heirs, the other being his younger cousin Tiberius Gemellus. However, the Senate nullified the accession of Gemellus, allowing Caligula to rule alone.

Gemellus did not survive for long. In late 37 CE he was, 'set up' by Caligula for an imaginary plot and ordered to take his own life. He did not know how to hold his sword in order to achieve this and so members of Caligula's newly established Germanic Guard, more deadly and more loyal to the Emperor than the Praetorians, showed him the way. It was yet another assassination, possibly the first after Macro's brief reign of terror.

Caligula's first year as emperor saw his popularity increase hugely. It was not without cost, mostly financial. Tiberius had left 500 sesterces to each member of the Praetorian Guard. Caligula doubled it. He then gave 75 sesterces to every Roman citizen and staged a series of lavish games for the enjoyment of the people.

Launching a massive building project along the Palatine Hill, designed to increase the magnificence of the Roman Empire, further decreased the contents of the National Treasury. It was reckless spending of the reserves which Tiberius had carefully built up during his years in power.

Political and public reforms including things like lifting the need for Imperial confirmation of court sentences and increasing the number of jurors at trials, were welcomed but, again, it was a huge expense for the Treasury. It has been suggested that over two billion sesterces were spent on such matters during the first year of Caligula's reign – even half that sum would have been debilitating for the economy.

There was only one way to recoup such expenditure. Taxes were soon being levied across the full range of Roman society. There were taxes on weddings, taxes on lawsuits, even taxes on prostitution. Rather than face death in the Circus Maximus and other venues, defeated gladiators were soon being auctioned off as slaves.

Inevitably, people began to mutter and complain. The good which Caligula had done during the first year of his reign, projects such as improving the harbour at Rhegium and building a series of new aqueducts around Rome, were forgotten. What people remembered was the heavy taxation he had recently imposed and the increasing number of bizarre behaviours he was now displaying.

In 39 CE he ordered the building of a floating bridge, two miles long and stretching from Baiae to the port of Puteoli, using hundreds of boats as pontoons. He then opened the bridge by riding his horse Incitatus across it several times. It was all a deliberate snub, designed to defy a prediction made by the soothsayer of Tiberius some years before. The prediction had declared that Caligula had no more chance of becoming emperor than he did of riding a horse across the Bay of Baiae. Wrong on both counts!

What really began to worry people, however, was the cruelty and unnecessary violence that their Emperor was now displaying. He clearly killed for pleasure and on one occasion had several notable Senators executed. Others were humiliated and ordered to run behind his chariot through the streets of Rome. It was all for no reason other than that he thought them incompetent.

Quite apart from wars against barbarians, foreign potentates were as vulnerable as anyone. King Ptolemy of Egypt, for example, was invited to Rome on what was supposedly a goodwill visit, then assassinated as soon as he arrived.

An abortive attempt to conquer Britannia resulted in total failure and the rare employment of Decimation, an ancient Roman punishment where one in every ten members of an unsuccessful or defeated Legion were executed on the spot. Rather than embark for the invasion, Caligula had his soldiers collect sea shells from the beaches, claiming that he was capturing 'the spoils of the sea.' He hid the reality of an enterprise that had gone nowhere by declaring to the world that he had attacked and defeated Neptune, god of the sea.

He began to appear in public dressed as one of the various Roman gods, even female ones. He referred to himself as Jupiter and made others call him by that name. The many statues to the gods in temples around the city were subjected to the indignity of having their heads removed and replaced by replicas of Caligula. He was, he declared, 'a living god' and should be worshipped as such. Nobody dared to oppose him.[1]

Having the status of a god, Caligula decided, was something that entitled him to do as he pleased. So he slept with the wives of other men, choosing them at random, then boasting about each 'conquest.' He committed incest with his sisters and had affairs with men. If death had not interceded he even planned to make his horse Incitatus a consul. And so the madness went on.

The final straw came when Caligula announced that he was leaving Italy to settle in Egypt, a much more artistic country for a poet, singer and actor like him. Cassius Chaerea, leader of the Praetorian Guard, was a man who had suffered many insults from Caligula who constantly mocked him for his weak voice and called him Venus. The message was simple. Caligula could claim to be a woman but to everyone else femininity was the ultimate insult.

The idea of an emperor leaving Rome for a life in foreign parts was totally unacceptable, particularly for members of the Praetorian Guard whose very existence depended on the presence of the Emperor. Now Cassius Chaerea decided to use the power of his soldiers to remove this blot, this blight as he considered Caligula, from Roman life.

On 24th January 41 CE Caligula was attacked in a tunnel leading to the Imperial Box during a festival of games and dramatics. Cassius stabbed him first, quickly followed by other members of the Guard. In all, Caligula was struck thirty times, his toga smeared and the floor beneath the lifeless body swimming with his blood.

The Emperor's screams for help alerted his newly formed band of Germanic Guards. These elite and well-armed professionals were devoted to Caligula who paid them well and ensured they were treated like kings in every tavern in Rome. Racing into the tunnel, they found themselves in a pitched battle with the Praetorian Guard over and around Caligula's body. Several conspirators and Guards were killed, along with a number of innocent bystanders. It did not end there.

What followed was an orgy of murder that swept out from the stadium across the city. The Praetorian Guard sought out Caligula's family and killed as many of them as they could lay hands on. His wife Caesonia was stabbed to death, his young daughter Julia Drusilla killed by being lifted by the ankles, her head then smashed against a wall.

Cassius Chaerea had intended the assassination of Caligula to put an end to the whole concept of emperors. Unfortunately for him, a band of roving Praetorian Guards found Caligula's uncle Claudius hiding behind a curtain.

Nothing if not conservative, the Guard had always required a leader and now, rather than kill Claudius, they simply picked him up and proclaimed him as their new Emperor. Physically disabled and with the reputation of being a little simple, Claudius was the ideal man for the Praetorians. He would be a leader without much power, leaving them to act and behave exactly as they pleased.

Before Cassius could prevent it, the quivering and terrified old man was being carried around the Forum and the streets of Rome on the shoulders of the Praetorian Guards. People everywhere acclaimed him as Rome's fourth emperor.

Clau – Clau- Claudius

The strangest but possibly the greatest of all Roman Emperors, Tiberius Claudius Caesar Augustus Germanicus ruled from that fatal moment in the bloodletting of 41 until his death in October 54 CE. He was the nephew of Tiberius, the grandson of Livia, and in many respects a perfect successor to Caligula. Then again, in the eyes of many, Claudius was nothing more than a damned fool.

As a child, his appearance – lame, bent double, stuttering speech, deafness – made him an embarrassment to his family. He was therefore left to his studies and to his writing. He survived because of his supposed ineptitude but underneath the outward façade lurked a brain and an intellect as sharp as a knife. He wrote over thirty books on history and culture and was far happier doing that than heading up the greatest empire the world had ever seen.

Many explanations have been proposed for the medical condition of Claudius. For a long while he was thought simply to be suffering from the effects of polio. It remains a possibility but Tourette's Syndrome has now been added to the list of afflictions. Claudius himself admitted that he had deliberately exaggerated his symptoms in order to keep himself safe during the reigns of Tiberius and Caligula. That, too, is possible as his condition did seem to improve once he became emperor.

His reign as emperor saw the annexation of Mauretania and Thrace, the creation of Judaea as a Roman province and the invasion of Britannia. Claudius accompanied his troops across the Channel to Britain and was present at the battles when his Legions crossed the Thames and created the town of Camulodunum (Colchester).

Perhaps his greatest political success was in the creation of client kingdoms in places like Judea, a relatively inexpensive but effective way of protecting new Roman provinces. He also developed the harbour at Ostia, reorganising the supply of grain into Rome.

Claudius was married four times, notably to Valeria Messalina, a woman of dubious virtue by Roman standards. She once competed against a renowned prostitute to see who could enjoy the most men in a single night. Messalina won easily. Eventually, when she conspired against him and took part in a public marriage ceremony to a Senator by the name of Gaius Silius, Claudius was forced to finally do something about his errant wife. Reluctantly, he had her executed.

The last wife of Claudius was his niece Agrippina the Younger who brought with her into the marriage her son Nero, later adopted by the Emperor as his successor. That disadvantaged Britannicus, the actual son of Claudius. Britannicus took his reduction in rank very personally but Claudius had done it in order to keep him safe from his wildly ambitious and cruel step-brother Nero.

In the end it was his wife who killed Claudius, an assassination which he seemed to suspect and even know about in his final hours. From Agrippina's point of view she needed to dispose of Claudius before he granted power and returned Britannicus to favour rather than Nero.

Details of the assassination vary but it seems, now, that Claudius was given poisoned mushrooms prepared for him by Agrippina. His taster – who remained in post to serve Nero – did not identify anything wrong with the food, seeming to indicate that he was also involved in the plot.

However it was done, on 13th October 54 CE, the Emperor Claudius, a man never intended for Imperial rank, died in agony. He was, as Agrippina had always wanted, succeeded by Nero, her sixteen year old son. She had worked hard to get Britannicus dropped from favour and now, on the death of Augustus, called on the Praetorian Guard to proclaim Nero as Emperor. It left the Senate with no option but to agree, the perfect fait accompli.

The Emperor Nero Fiddles

Viewed now, in hindsight, the new Emperor Nero was not really all that different from predecessors such as Tiberius and Caligula. At various times he was self-centred, vicious, paranoid and tyrannical, so that history has marked him down as the typical mad Roman Emperor. To some extent that is an accurate picture but there is rather more to his character than that simple, one dimensional view.

Nero Claudius Caesar Augustus Germanicus ruled for just over fourteen years, the fifth Emperor of Rome and the last of the Julio-Claudian Dynasty. From the beginning of his reign the nobility of Rome hated him, saw him as beneath them in class and breeding.

Almost as soon as he became emperor Nero organised several athletic games for the citizens of Rome at the Circus Maximus along with drama and music performances, taking part himself as an actor, musician or poet. Occasionally he even drove a chariot in the races. It infuriated and scandalised the nobility even more. They viewed his activities as beneath the dignity of the Imperial leader but the plebs and members of the Praetorian Guard loved him for it all.

Being a young and inexperienced adolescent when he came to power, Nero was particularly interested in what benefits he could gain from being the head of the Empire. Personal pleasures were his main aim in life. Consequently, he left much of the running of the government to his two advisors, the philosopher Seneca and Afranius Burrus, Prefect of the Praetorian Guard.

In his early days as Emperor, perhaps due more to the efforts of Burrus and Seneca than Nero himself, there were major improvements in Roman life. Capital punishment was banned or at least its instances greatly reduced. The Senate was given more independence and the process of holding secret trials, brought in during the last days of Claudius, was outlawed. Even death and bloodshed in the Circus were banned. The patrician members of the Senate viewed the behaviour of their leader as scandalous and undignified.

Rumours now begin to spread about the nocturnal habits of the Emperor. It is hard not to see the hand of the Senate in what was clearly a campaign of hate but, it was claimed, Nero would spend hours prowling the streets of the city, consorting with women of the night and drinking huge quantities of wine. The rumours in this matter were undoubtedly true. Nero, it seemed, would just not help himself.

Nero has always been regarded as the man who started the Great Fire of Rome which destroyed much of the city in the summer of 64 CE. Having begun the blaze, legend declares, he then sat and played his violin as the city was destroyed. It remains a great story but it is just not true. Nero was not even in the city when the fire broke out but was thirty miles away at his villa in Antium.

The fire began on 18th June, in a shop selling inflammable goods on the Aventine overlooking the Circus Maximus. Very quickly the wind fanned the flames and it spread along the full length of the Circus. Counter measures were basic and soon the fire was roaring down the narrow streets and passageways of the city. Shrieking in terror people ran for whatever safety they could find:

> 'When people looked back, menacing flames sprang up before them or outflanked them. When they escaped to a neighbouring quarter, the fire followed ... finally, with no idea where or what to flee, they crowded on to the country roads, or lay in the fields. Some who had lost everything, could have escaped, but preferred to die. So did others who had failed to rescue their loved ones. Nobody dared to fight the flames.'[2]

Quickly summoned back to Rome, Nero did what he could to help the fleeing masses and give them somewhere to find refuge. He threw open The Field of Mars and his own private garden and welcomed in the peoples. He ordered food to be brought from Ostia and the price of corn was cut. Despite these measures the rumour machine quickly got into top gear and wildly inaccurate stories began to spread. While the fire raged, it was said, rather than help his people Nero had stood on his private stage and sung about the destruction of Troy.

The fire blazed for six days until it was finally extinguished at the foot of the Equiline Hill and people breathed a sigh of relief. And then it broke out again. More lives were lost, more buildings were destroyed – and more rumours spread. Nero was intent, the gossip mongers said, on destroying Rome and then founding a new city, named after him.

Blame was eventually fixed on the leaders of the new Christian faith but to begin with causes for the disaster were to be found bobbling uncomfortably before the senate and the Roman populace in general. And they were pointing directly at the Emperor. These ludicrous rumours marked the end of Nero's stance as the popular Emperor.

Nero never noticed and ploughed on with his set way of life. Increasingly attracted to bizarre and novel cults, he also grew more and more interested in displaying his artistic pretensions. He even began giving public concerts as a poet and lyre player. He saw nothing wrong with this but to the nobles and Senators of Rome all of his dignity as the Imperial leader had gone.

His period of real brutality, however, lay in the eighteenth month period between two deaths. The first came in 59 CE when Nero's mother Agrippina the Younger was assassinated. The second was the death of his wife Octavia in June 62 CE.

The Death of Agrippina the Younger

In the early days of his time as emperor, Nero's mother had been a significant presence. She had been instrumental in bringing him to the throne and now thoroughly enjoyed wielding power in Rome. She saw herself – and acted - as unofficial Regent, her behaviour becoming increasingly tyrannical. She even had her image engraved on the obverse side of some Roman coins.

As Nero grew older, however, Agrippina's influence over him was lessened. That decline in her power was probably fuelled by Seneca and Burrus who did not enjoy her interference in their governance of the Empire. Slowly but surely, they began to undermine her position.

Agrippina's life had been adventurous. Daughter of Germanicus, sister of Caligula, she had been exiled in 39 CE for taking part in a conspiracy against her brother. She was allowed to return to Rome in 41 CE and married twice, in all probability poisoning Passienus Crispus, her second husband, in the year 49 CE.

Agrippina then set her sights on her uncle, the Emperor Claudius. Roman law forbade the marriage of uncle and niece and so Claudius had to rewrite that law before they married in 49 CE. Always pliable, Claudius soon fell under the spell of his new wife with, ultimately, drastic consequences.

Now, as her influence over Nero faded, it seemed as if she was altering her allegiance. Agrippina began spending more time with Britannicus, the son of Claudius and the true successor to the Imperial throne. Nero obviously thought this was the case as in 55 CE Britannicus died in mysterious circumstances. In all probability Nero had him poisoned and shortly after the death of Britannicus, Agrippina was removed from court.

She and Nero had fallen out over a romantic affair he was having with Poppaea Sabina, then the wife of Roman Senator Otho. It was the ideal excuse. By exiling Agrippina, Nero had removed her direct presence from court but she remained a threat, publicly criticising her son for the affair with Poppaea. For Nero there was only one way forward.

He had already tried to antagonise her by employing rowdies to stand outside her house and jeer and catcall at her. It had made little effect on Agrippina and so he decided on the final solution. Agrippina must die.

According to the historian Suetonius, he made three attempts to poison her but all failed as she had already taken an antidote. Then he designed a machine that would cause the ceiling tiles of her bedroom to drop and kill her while she slept. Agrippina caught wind of that one and it, too, failed.

The plan he eventually hatched was ingenious and unique. In 59 CE he invited her to join him in Baiae in order to celebrate the Quinquatrian Festival and even sent his fleet commander to fetch her in a brand new yacht. Agrippina was delighted at the prospects of a reunion. What she did not know was that this was a very special type of boat and that reunion was the last thing on Nero's mind.

The account of Tacitus states that the yacht was designed to fall apart and sink when the commander gave the order. Agrippina, sitting in the main cabin, was attended by two servants, Crepereius and Acerronia. All of them were appalled when the ceiling of the cabin suddenly fell:

> 'At a given signal the ceiling of the place, which was loaded with a quantity of lead, fell in and Crepereius was crushed and instantly killed. Agrippina and Acerronia were protected by the sides of the couch which happened to be too strong to yield under the weight.'[3]

The two women were thrown into the water as the yacht rocked and pitched. A strong swimmer, Agrippina was able to make it to shore where crowds of watchers and well-wishers welcomed her magical escape. Her attendant Acerronia Polla was not so fortunate. She was bludgeoned to death by oarsmen from the death ship as she tried to follow her mistress ashore, screaming that she was Agrippina and needed help.

When Nero heard the news he was furious. His ingeniously designed ship had failed him. He decided that enough was enough and immediately sent three assassins to kill his mother. Faced by the killers Agrippina stood upright and allegedly told them to aim at her womb that had produced such an evil killer as Nero. They were happy to oblige.

The End of Nero

Nero did not outlive his mother by too long. From 66 to 68 CE he spent eighteen months in Egypt, enjoying the culture of the country but distancing himself from Rome.

In 67 CE, a series of rebellions, notably one by Gaius Gulius Vindex, supported by Galba, Governor of Hispania Tarraconensis, weakened his position as supreme commander and the Senate declared him a public enemy. The rebellion failed, Vindex was killed and, for the moment, Galba retired to lick his wounds. In absentia, however, the Senate condemned Nero to death. When he returned to his capital he found it in a state of utter confusion.

He promptly fled from Rome, hoping to gather at least some support from his traditional allies, the Praetorian Guard, only to find that they had abandoned him. They were now his most potent adversaries. A plan to go to Ostia and from there take a ship to one of the provinces came to nothing when army officers refused to obey him. 'Is it so dreadful a thing to die?' Nero supposedly exclaimed.

Returning to the Imperial Palace to consider his options, he awoke at midnight to find that his guards and servants had gone, leaving the building eerily empty and echoing. He thought of drowning himself in the Tiber but decided against it. Then he was offered a villa some six or seven miles outside Rome and travelled there with four faithful attendants. His intention now was to kill himself.

In the end, he lacked the courage to end his own life and his secretary Epaphroditus was ordered to do it for him. The blow was fatal but not immediate. Nero lingered long enough to make his famous dying statement – 'What an artist they have lost in me.' Soldiers despatched from the Senate arrived and attempted to stop the bleeding but it was no use. Emperor Nero died on 9th June 68 CE.

Assassination or suicide? With the whole of his world turned upside down and seemingly with everyone against him, it could have been either. The Senate clearly wanted him dead and planned what should and would have been an assassination if they could have got their hands on him. Nero wanted to die, knew it had to happen, but lacked the bravery to end things at his own hands. By ordering Epaphroditus to carry out the deed it became an act of assassination, albeit a willing one.

The Year of the Four Emperors

The death of Nero saw the end of the Julio-Claudian Dynasty and the removal of a deranged despot. It did not bring the peace and calm many had expected but, rather, it ushered in a period of utter chaos, confusion and turmoil when no fewer than four different emperors sat on the throne in just over twelve months.

The first of these was Servius Sulpicius Galba, a man who had already rebelled against Nero. He seized the throne on the death of Nero, reigning from June 68 until 15 January 69 CE. From the beginning of his brief period as emperor his hold on the Imperial throne was tenuous. He had a reputation for cruelty and avarice, a reputation that was both well-earned and feared.

Unpopular with the people, easily swayed and dominated by others, Galba also suffered from gout. He soon lost the support of his Legions and the Praetorians. His unpopularity was not helped by the fact that he seized land from Roman citizens, disbanded the armies in northern Germany and failed to pay members of the Praetorian Guard.

When the Legions of northern and southern Germany refused to swear loyalty to him it was clear that Galba could not hold on much longer. On 15th January 69 CE, acting on the orders of Otho, he was lured to the Forum and assassinated by members of the Praetorian Guard.

As had been planned, Galba was succeeded by Marcus Salvius Otho. He had been a close friend of Nero but following the affair of the Emperor with his wife, Poppaea Sabina, Otho had been 'banished' to the remote province of Lusitania. To begin with he was an ally of Galba, then made his own grab for power.

From the beginning of his three month reign, Otho was challenged by Aulus Vitellius who was the favoured candidate of the Germanic Legions. They finally came to blows at the Battle of Bedriacum when it was rumoured there were 40,000 casualties. Otho lost the battle and committed suicide on 16th April 69.

The reign of Vitellius was another short one, lasting just eight months from 19th April until 20th December 69 CE. To begin with he tried to emulate the tactics and policies of Nero who was still amazingly popular in the provinces. It had little effect on the popularity of Vitellius and it soon became apparent that he would have to fight to retain his position.

It was not long before Vitellius found himself challenged by the power of the Legions from the East. These soldiers favoured their own commander, Titus Flavius Vespasian, who had a proven record as a general and as a leader of men.

Although recognised as Emperor by the Senate, Vitellius was not confident he could retain his throne. He was right. The forces ranged against him were too powerful.

While Vespasian was campaigning in Egypt, Vitellius was defeated by the armies of Vespasian's fellow commander Marcus Antonius Primus at the second Battle of Bedriacum. It was another bloody affair and Vitellius, ever conscious of his position, decided he had no option but to seek peace with Marcus Antonius and abdicate in favour of Vespasian. His supporters, in particular the Praetorian Guard, refused to allow it.

The result of the refusal was yet another bloody battle and another defeat for Vitellius. The soldiers of Antonius entered Rome, sacked much of it and destroyed the Capital. Vitellius was taken prisoner and on 20th December 69, was executed by soldiers and members of the Praetorian Guard.

Vespasian was proclaimed Emperor whilst he was still at Alexandria and before the assassination of Vitellius. He went on to found the Flavian Dynasty which, after the death of Vespasian, existed for nearly thirty years and brought peace and prosperity to Rome.

He also instituted a vast building programme for the city, partly to repair the damage caused by the war of 69 and partly to ensure that the glory of Rome was noticed and acclaimed by everyone who ever saw it.

Vespasian ruled for a relatively short period of time, just 69 to 79 CE but managed to bring stability and structure back to the Empire after the chaos caused by the Year of the Four Emperors.

Commodus, the Gladiator Emperor

Some of the Roman Emperors, men like Claudius, ruled wisely; some like Caligula and Nero governed with all elements of sanity and justice dispelled and forgotten. Some were both bizarre and vicious in their exercising of the role. Commodus is one example of the latter.

In 176 CE Commodus was made co-emperor alongside his father Marcus Aurelius. He was just fifteen years old and he and his father ruled together quite effectively for some years.

A wise and just ruler, Marcus fought border wars and managed Rome through a severe outbreak of plague. Commodus learned precisely nothing from his father's skills, however, and rumours began to circulate stating that he was actually a coward. Even at this early stage he had a tendency to seek out disreputable elements, spending considerable time in the taverns and brothels of Rome.

To some extent Marcus kept Commodus in check but he died, probably from plague, when his son was just nineteen. Then serving on the frontier, Commodus immediately returned to Rome and arrested and executed all those in the senate that he considered his enemies. And so his twelve year reign as dictator and tyrant began.

Almost immediately, Commodus began to display his interest in the gladiatorial games that were held regularly in Rome. He participated regularly, sometimes armed with a wooden sword and facing gladiators who he knew would go easily in the combat against their Emperor.

When he did fight for real it was invariably bloody. He killed wild animals, as gladiators often did in the Circus – but in his case from a distance, firing arrows or throwing javelins into the beasts before they could come near. On several occasions he matched himself against men with deformities and missing legs, opponents he termed as giants. They perished quickly.

Soon Commodus began calling himself the Roman Hercules and strutting around as if he were a god. Sex and violence had become his life. It was rumoured that he had over 600 concubines, boys and girls as well as women. The figure is probably a gross exaggeration but it shows how people felt about his scurrilous behaviour.

The very antithesis of his father, who was respected and loved by the people of Rome, there were several attempts on the life of Commodus. One of these was organised by his sister Lucilla. Commodus showed no mercy and she was executed once the plot was discovered.

By the autumn of 192 CE his chief mistress Marcia was gravely concerned about Commodus. He was, she felt, going mad, something that was certainly not good for the Empire of Rome, let alone her own position. When she discovered her name on a list of potential victims to be executed at the next Games, it was the final straw. And so, she poisoned his food. It had no effect as Commodus simply made himself sick to throw up the poison.

Marcia had shown her hand, however, and further steps now had to be taken. Narcissus, the wrestling partner of Commodus, was brought into the plot. Paid a huge sum of money to finish what Marcia had begun, on New Year's Eve 192 CE Narcissus strangled Commodus while they were practicing wrestling moves. Some accounts say the assassination took place while the Emperor was bathing. Wrestling seems more likely.

The story of Commodus and his gladiatorial skills was captured in the Oscar-winning film *Gladiator* of 2000. He was not the hero of the movie but Commodus would have undoubtedly enjoyed seeing himself on the silver screen.

Chapter Thirteen

Eastward Ho, the Byzantine Empire

The Roman Empire was first divided in 285 CE when the Emperor Diocletian partitioned it's administration into eastern and western sections.

However, it was the Emperor Constantine who in 330 BCE, by transferring the capital from Rome to Byzantium, was the real architect of the Eastern Empire. In many respects it was a logical move with the western holdings of Rome being increasingly open to attack by barbarians from the north.

Unlike the more ramshackle empire in the west, the Eastern or Byzantine Empire as it became known, lasted until the city of Constantinople finally fell to the Ottomans in 1453. The boundaries and borders of the Eastern Empire changed many times, reflecting various defeats, conquests and reconquests but until the end of its days it remained considerably more significant than its dying western neighbour.

Constantinople, as the city of Byzantium was renamed when the Emperor Constantine demolished what was left of the old town and built a new, up-to-date metropolis, was ideally situated on the well-established trade routes between the eastern and western worlds. Sitting on the Bosphorus between Europe and Asia, with easy access to Russia in the north and Africa in the south, the place was a merchant's delight.

Spices, exotic foods, wines and other luxuries flooded into the west through Constantinople, making traders and officials of the city wealthy beyond all expectations. As if to nail home the superiority of the Eastern Empire, residents of Constantinople, although most of them were born and bred in the areas around the Black Sea, were now even calling themselves Romans.

Christianity had been legalised by Constantine at the time when the eastwards move took place. It was a far cry from the days of the Emperor Nero when blame for the Great Fire of Rome moved on from Nero and eventually, without proof, settled on the followers of Christ.

As the new Eastern Empire settled into a regular routine of money-making security, officialdom inevitably began to stretch its claws. The official language of the Empire was changed to Greek, the Western stayed with Latin.

Language was only one difference between the empires of the east and the west. The Eastern Empire was far more intent on trade than its western counterpart but, as with any body or organisation dependent on merchants and traders, it still retained a vital, energetic and efficient army. If for nothing else the army offered protection.

It was not all easy going for the Eastern Empire. Assassinations, wars, invasions, defeats and victories were the lot of the Byzantine people of the East just as they were in the West. It was, put simply, a difficult time for both sections of the Roman Empire. The difference was that the Eastern Empire had the people and the money to withstand the difficulties that undoubtedly came its way. That was clearly not the case in the west.

By the middle of the sixth century, the Western Empire was paying huge subsidies to the Persian Empire – just to stay alive! The Lombards had already invaded Italy and the Empire which had reached its zenith under Hadrian in the second century CE was already on a fast downward spiral.

From a military standpoint, Constantinople, unlike Rome, was in the ideal situation to defend the Danube and all of the rich lands around the mighty river. The huge walls around Constantinople, begun by Constantine, were evidence that the rulers of the Byzantine Empire meant business. It was truly a 'second Rome.'

War against the Persians and effective methods of restricting the Lombard advance down the long leg of Italy seemed, now, to be resting solely in the hands of the Eastern Empire. There were many in Constantinople who were more than a little averse to helping anyone. Look after your own seemed to be the message of many, particularly those who sat in their counting houses and the bazaars, watching while their stocks of leisure goods passed into the hands of eager buyers.

This was in complete contrast to the Western Empire which was increasingly under threat, both real and imagined, and seemingly always lurching from one crisis to the next. It was not that long after the division that the richest provinces of the Western Empire, Egypt and Syria, were conquered by the Arabs and lost to the western world for many years.

The decline and eventual end of the Western Empire can be clearly seen in a request made in 476 CE by the senators of Rome to Emperor Zeno. It was a prophetic request:

'The tough barbarian soldier Odovacer, having become effective master of Italy through a series of battles, forced the latest boy emperor, Romulus Augustulus, to abdicate and retire to his family's estates in Campania ... The Roman senators begged Zeno to assume rule over the whole empire and to recognise Odovacer as administrator of Italy.'[1]

The shackles, chains and final kicks of an empire that was now little more than a leaderless melee of past glories was not what Zeno needed. The Western Empire was filled with dead men walking and he had no intention of sending his own kingdom down the same route. The request, as might be expected, was ignored.

Both the Eastern and Western Empires were faced by tangible threats in these years. In particular they were threatened by invasion from external forces and by internal civil wars amongst themselves. The economy of the Western Empire in particular was in tatters and that had knock-on effects for the Romans or Byzantines in the east. Troubles in the Empire? Blame the leaders.

The late 400s were a particularly difficult time for the rulers of the Eastern Empire. Emperor Leo I died in 474, succeeded by his grandson, also called Leo, with his father Zeno as co-emperor. The second Leo did not survive long, with the result that Zeno became sole emperor. Confusion, plot and counter plot quickly followed in one of the most troubled reigns in the history of Rome and Constantinople.

Things were not made any easier by the good old Roman tradition of killing off opponents or likely ones. Assassination was not confined to the city of Rome and the Western Empire. At least seven Byzantine emperors were assassinated in the 900 years that the Eastern Empire existed, along with somewhere around eighteen significant others. Some of the murders were to have a profound effect on the last days of the ancient world.

Illus and Leontius

By 484 CE General Flavius Illus was unhappy and disillusioned with what he clearly viewed as the ineffective efforts of Emperor Zeno. Consequently, he split from the ruling party and left the Emperor's side. He fled from

Byzantium/Constantinople and drew up his forces in a direct challenge to his previous commander.

Zeno sent General Leontius, commander of the Imperial army in Thrace, to confront Illus but, after discussions and secret dealings between Illus and Leontius Zeno's general and commander changed sides and joined Illus.

Realising that he, like Zeno, was hugely unpopular with the people of Constantinople - they were both from Isaurian stock and therefore considered barbarians by many of the city population - Illus decided he would use Leontius as a 'front man.' He, Illus, would be the power behind the throne.

Leontius was duly acclaimed Emperor, being crowned in great style at Tarsus on 19th July 484. Illus and his acolyte even found time to appoint court officials and to mint coins showing the head of Leontius, all done before Zeno really understood that his two previous comrades were now mounting a serious challenge to his position. It meant that, for a short period at least, the Eastern Empire had two separate emperors.

Leontius, the usurping monarch, was acclaimed in Antioch and several other centres but on 8th August, just outside Antioch, his forces came face to face with Zeno's reformed army. Zeno had at last realised his danger and his army was now made up of experienced and well trained Romans and Ostrogoths.

Leontius and Illus were soundly defeated by Zeno and forced to take refuge in the fortress at Papurius. For almost four years they held out. It was an amazing defence but the two rebels were finally betrayed and the fortress fell.

Illus and Verine, who had joined them in the fort, were killed in the attack but Leontius was captured. After a period of punishment in prison, Leontius was finally assassinated on the orders of Emperor Zeno back in Constantinople. The deed was quickly done and the severed head of Leontius was sent as a gift to Emperor Zeno. If there was a moral in the episode it was simply not to trust those in power who would do anything to retain their positions.

The Emperor Basiliscus and Illus, again

Flavius Illus had led a somewhat chequered life and career without really gaining a great deal of credit or esteem for his efforts. An experienced soldier, he had originally supported Basiliscus, brother of dowager queen Verine, when he rebelled against Zeno. Verine was the widow of Leo, the previous emperor, and a woman with ambitions of her own.

In an attempt to dethrone the unpopular Emperor Zeno, Basiliscus marched on Constantinople. His revolt was successful and in 475 Zeno sought exile abroad.

Verine now began to scheme and plot in an attempt to put her lover Patricius on the throne. At first Basiliscus seemed to be supportive of his sister's plans but he, too, was not above changing his mind. He managed to convince the Senate that he should be made emperor rather than Patricius.

Much against their better judgement, the Senate proclaimed him Emperor of the Eastern Empire. Their opinion of him was never high, even to begin with, but soon they were viewing Basiliscus as a self-centred usurper.

The people of the Empire also shared the Senate's view, complaining about high taxes and the autocratic approach of their new ruler. As might be expected, Basiliscus set about removing enemies wherever they might be found. These ranged from Senators to Verine's lover Patricius who was quickly assassinated.

The complaints and grumbles increased. The Senate could do little about it, however, their decision having placed Basiliscus on the Imperial throne. It had been the perfect coup d'état but it was not the end of the game.

Yet again, internal discord set in motion betrayal and changes of heart. This was seen when Illus and his brother suddenly declared for Zeno. It was a dangerous switch.

The brothers were defeated in battle in July 476 and forced to seek refuge in hastily erected forts high on a hill that was, ironically, named Constantinople.

A siege began, the two brothers bolstered by constant messages from the Constantinople Senate, urging them to fight on in the name of Zeno. Eventually they slipped away, marching to Nicaea where they confronted Basiliscus and defeated him. It had been yet another change of heart by the duplicitous Illus.

Basiliscus had never been a great general. Early in his career, during the reign of Leo I, he had been defeated by invading Vandals. He thought he had secured a peace treaty and a financial deal which involved paying 130,000 pounds of gold to the Vandal king. The Vandals promptly used the money to construct a fleet of fire ships for use against Constantinople.

Now Basiliscus was forsaken by his troops and left to roam around the countryside before he was found and taken prisoner. Apparently he hid in a church and refused to come out unless the enemy promised not to kill him. The promise was given but it was, of course, worthless.

The end was only to be expected. Zeno returned to Constantinople in August 476, yet another betrayal, this time by the defending general Flavius Armatus, enabling him to enter the city with relative ease. His first step was to rid the Empire of Basiliscus.

Taken from his prison cell and exiled to Cappadocia, it was only a matter of time before the assassins got to work.

Basiliscus and his family were thrown into in an old, dried up cistern where they all eventually died. It was now 477 CE. Some say the cause of Basiliscus's death was down to starvation, others by the assassins knives. The choice is yours.

Leontius, Emperor 695 to 698

Same name but different person! This second Leontius came to prominence as a soldier during the reign of Emperor Justinian in the seventh century.

Successful in war, at least to begin with, Leontius was eventually defeated at the Battle of Sebastopolis in 692 CE. His reward for the defeat was not compassion or comfort but to be slung into prison for three years.

He recommenced his military career when he was released in 695 but, as might be expected, his anger and resentment towards Justinian had not dissipated. In fact it was huge. Rebellion was inevitable and Leontius duly became Emperor in place of his tormentor.

He reigned for just three years before being overthrown by Apsimanus who took the name Tiberius. The subsequent treatment of Leontius was nothing short of barbaric.

Tiberius had the nose and tongue of Leontius cut off and then imprisoned him in the monastery of Dalmatou. He remained there until 761 CE when Justinian defeated Tiberius and recovered his throne. If Leontius was hoping for relief and acceptance back into the fold he was gravely mistaken.

Justinian's actions were almost as merciless as those of Tiberius. Both Leontius and Tiberius were dragged by their heels to the Hippodrome where they were officially assassinated. Their heads were cut off and their bodies thrown into the sea like so much discarded rubbish.

The Emperor Maurice

Maurice was the ruler of Rome's Eastern Empire between 582 and 602 CE. He was nominated by the Emperor Tiberius on his death bed after his joint nominee Germanicus refused the title on grounds of diplomacy and humility.

The last of the Justinian Dynasty, Maurice ruled an Empire that, during his period in power, was almost constantly at war. Unlike previous emperors from Constantinople, he felt it was right to assist the Western Empire whenever he was able, something that was appreciated by the Romans but was hugely expensive and draining on funds.

Maurice managed the various wars he fought in a reasonably good style or technique, bringing a long-running conflict with Sasanian Persia to a successful and victorious conclusion. For the first time in many years the Roman Empire did not pay the Persians their annual tribute of thousands of pounds in gold.

Extensive campaigning in the Balkans resulted in the Pannonian Avars being pushed back over the Danube. It was an enormously significant achievement, ending the Avar occupation and, importantly, the annual levy of 80,000 pounds of gold which had been paid from the Empire to the Avars for several years was finally stopped.

In 584 Maurice established the Exarchate of Italy in order to halt the advance of the Lombards. He became the first Roman Emperor for two centuries to campaign in the lands beyond the Danube. The Exarchate of Africa, founded by Maurice sometime later, solidified the power of Constantinople and Maurice's Empire in the Western Mediterranean.

However, the constant campaigning, in particular the long conflict with Sasanian Persia, had drained much of the Empire's resources and finances. Constantinople and the Eastern Empire were, as a consequence, gravely weakened, almost exhausted.

It was a problem that also afflicted Maurice's enemies, the Persians, who had invested huge sums of money and manpower in a war that could not be easily won. The result of this constant draining of resources - on both sides – was virtual devastation and a restricted willingness to fight on. It brought an inevitable unhappiness and discontent to the two major empires of the Mediterranean zone.

More importantly, their inevitable exhaustion led directly to the rise of the Islamic Empire. As their input fell away, there grew a gap in the balance of power, one that the Islamic nations eagerly stepped forward to fill. After 630 CE Islam became, increasingly, the dominant force in the area, a growth in power that led, in the years ahead, to the wars between Christian Europe and the Muslim warriors of the east.

And Emperor Maurice? For him there was no happy ending. By the end of 600 CE he had alienated the public and, more importantly, the army as well. There was grumbling and talk of rebellion. At first it was just talk but then came the gravest mistake of his life, one which ensured discontent would quickly change to open rebellion.

Tradition in the Eastern Empire had dictated that the Legions should withdraw south of the River Danube and encamp below the river for the winter months. But in 602 Maurice overrode this policy and declared that in future the army would remain north of the river. Not only that, he insisted on a new campaign to be fought during the winter, something that had not been done before. The result was mutiny.

Maurice should have seen it coming. He was a man of insight and courage but for some reason his abilities left him in the face of the troubles he encountered in 602. His decision in ordering the Legions to stay north of the Danube rather than head for warm quarters and then embark on a winter campaign for which they were not equipped or trained, was nothing short of foolhardy:

> 'His fault was too much faith in his own excellent judgement without regard to the unpopularity which he provoked ... He was a better judge of policy than of men.'[2]

The Legions followed up the mutiny by turning to Phocas, an unhappy and disillusioned officer from within their ranks, and elevating him to be their leader in place of Maurice. Almost at once, Phocas headed south and entered Constantinople in November 602 where he was immediately crowned Emperor.

On hearing of the mutiny there were riots in support of the soldiers amongst the people of Constantinople. Maurice and his family left on a warship, hoping to find security in one of the provinces. When told that Phocas had entered Constantinople, he turned around and headed back. He was arrested the moment he stepped on shore.

Maurice was assassinated in the harbour at Eutropius where he had landed. It was not just Maurice who was meant to die. He faced the horror of watching as his six sons were executed before him. Then the assassins turned to him. He was beheaded on 27th November 602.

The assassination of the Emperor Maurice was, in itself, neither unusual nor particularly significant. It was just another Emperor meeting his fate, as many had done before and many more would do in the years to come. The Eastern Empire of Rome lasted for another eight hundred years before it followed the Western Empire into the dust of history, something that gave plenty of opportunity for assassins to strike.

What made the assassination notable was the series of events leading up to the actual killing. They were something that Maurice had inherited when he became Emperor in 582 and remained with him. He had inherited war and he kept fighting a whole variety of other wars for the rest of his life. Some were defensive in nature, others being aggressive wars of conquest.

While Maurice did what he thought was best for his country, it is interesting to speculate on what would have happened if there had been no wars. Similarly, if there had been no assassination, could he have stabilised his Empire? Or was the Byzantine power in southern Europe truly finished for ever?

There can be no doubt that the perpetual series of conflicts during the reign of Emperor Maurice effectively bankrupted Rome's Eastern Empire. Maurice found himself in the classic Catch Twenty-two situation. He could not ignore so many of the conflicts and could not afford to deal with any of them. It was the classic decline and fall.

The fact that Maurice's major enemy, the Persians, suffered the same fate meant that by the beginning of the seventh century the gaping hole that was facing the various powers in the Middle East had become a canyon.

Neither the Persian nor the Roman empires could effectively fill the gap and for the first time in its history Constantinople began to fade and die as a successful military power. Its end was some time in coming, the decline of the Byzantine Empire being mirrored by the gradual rise in the power of the Ottomans.

Osman Khan was the first of the Ottoman Sultans, his kingdom eventually stretching for some 16,000 square kilometres. The Ottoman dynasty went on to become the longest lasting dynasty in the world, ruling for 641 years.

The Muslim nations of the east witnessed with glee the demise of the Byzantine Empire. Their growth and significance were gradual but over a period of several hundred years they rose to become the greatest threat the Christian world had ever seen.

Inching slowly westwards, by the end of the Middle Ages there were few countries that had not been threatened and terrified in some way by the wielders of the Koran.

The Ottomans, in particular, knew that they could fill the hole left by a weakened Constantinople and Persia. And, of course, they did their best to achieve exactly that.

The killing of kings was an essential but somewhat ignoble element in the world of change. And if ever there was an assassination that changed the course of history, the execution of Emperor Maurice was it.

Chapter Fourteen

The Dark Ages

It is difficult to know when the so-called culture of the ancient world ended and the infamous Dark Ages began. The immediate question to ask yourself is 'Does it really matter?' Perhaps not, at least as far as pure historical accounts are concerned, but as a means of structuring interest and gaining knowledge the two eras do require some attention. That, after all, is why they were called into common parlance in the first place.

To some extent both terms are misnomers, nothing more than descriptions or definitions given to two conjoined but distinctively different periods in history in order to make analysis and understanding of them easier. And, of course, like any divinely gifted appellation, everyone has a different interpretation, altering or allocating exact dates and events to fit in with their own purposes and requirements.

Yet, however and why-ever it is used, the term 'Dark Ages' remains something of a wrong or false turning. So much so that the phrase is now rarely used by academics and historians. Even so, we need to look briefly at the origin of the description and the period in history it was meant to cover.

Like so much of the post-Roman period, exact definition and identification of dates and events are hard to fix. The writer Petrarch was one scholar who defined the centuries following the collapse of Rome's Western Empire as 'dark.' They were, he declared, dark years as opposed to the 'light' ones that symbolised the classical age of antiquities.

Petrarch defined his Dark Ages as a period covering some 900 years, from the fall of Rome in 476 to the rise of the Renaissance and the rediscovery of culture in the fourteenth and fifteenth centuries. He was writing a considerable number of years after the events he was describing, when hindsight had affected many of the actual facts. Even at the time of writing, many historians and readers disagreed with his views and with his belief in the Dark Ages lasting for an exceptionally long length of time.

To Petrarch and to historians over the following years the phrase Dark Ages symbolised a cultural and economic waste land. It was, they believed, a time of death and disease, when writing, research and academic achievement reached an all-time low. It was, many thought, accompanied by an urban decline, when people turned in upon themselves. Warfare was constant and was symbolised by the dissolution of Rome's Western Empire.

The period undoubtedly did see considerable bloodshed and warfare but the old idea of a barbarian free-for-all is far from accurate. It was a time of migration, certainly, when tribes and nations like the Franks, Huns and Goths moved into what had been land dominated by the Roman Empire. They came not just to destroy and despoil but to find new living space, new markets and new ways of bolstering their economy.

And urban decline? Not quite. The era saw the creation of many new communities based on trade and specific industries such as shipping, brewing and ceramics. The warm period between 850 and 1000 saw an increase in the population of many countries across Europe and Asia. These people had to live somewhere and the development of towns was an obvious answer.

That brings us to religion and to education, the two being inextricably linked. The rapid growth of the Christian religion offered two distinct services – one, the provision of spiritual assistance and two - and more subliminally - the growth of temporal support.

Education was central to the development of Christianity, something that was needed in order to offer an intellectual understanding of the faith and its many mysteries. The Dark Ages may have witnessed the end of the Roman educational system but there were alternatives.

The writings of Boethius, director of civil education for the Ostrogoths, and Cassiodorus were consciously aimed at educating the public. In the seventh and eighth centuries education of the laity grew to be very important, the Christian Bible becoming the main source of moral education and life.

Ireland created centres of learning in places like Armagh and Kildare while, in Britain, flourishing schools of theology were founded in centres such as Canterbury and in the monasteries of the north. In Wales the college of St Illtyd in Llantwit Major saw as many as 2000 students attending lectures at any one time. The college in the Vale of Glamorgan was, for many years, a highly significant centre of learning, counting people like St Patrick and St David amongst its students.

Agriculture and rural living also witnessed progress in this period. Prosaic as it may seem, inventions such as the heavy plough and the horse collar, along with seemingly innocuous developments like metal horse shoes and the use of horses rather than oxen or man power for field work were factors that revolutionised agricultural labour.

At the end of the food chain, on the market stalls and in early forms of town shops, urban existence was also greatly improved by the provision of better and more readily available food stuffs.

Meanwhile, literature and art continued to thrive, albeit mainly in the monasteries, outposts that were out of reach for the ordinary man and woman. For monks and the more educated upper classes the works of literature were readily available.

What was missing amongst all that was on offer during the Dark Ages were detailed records of what was done and when events took place.

When such recording did occur it was either retained in the monasteries or, more usually, appeared in the fictional and inaccurate accounts written by people like Geoffrey of Monmouth. Geoffrey, like many other early scribes, offered fictional accounts posing as facts. Legends of King Arthur, Morgan la Fey and others date from this period.

Add in the coming of the Little Ice Age with the accompanying famines and then the advent of plague in the fourteenth century and it is relatively easy to see why the concept of a 'dark age' should take hold of public imagination. Yes, it was dark; yes, it was brutal. But the post-Roman period was an important end to the ancient world.

For the requirements of this book, the term Dark Ages has been retained. That might well upset some of the purists out there but as a marker for the end of the ancient world the Dark Ages is a period that needs to be included. All too often it is overlooked when studying various aspects of the ancient world. That is a mistake. The period is best defined as a bridge between one era and the next, illuminating and, at the finish, useful or even necessary.

If you like, view the Dark Ages as the last five minutes of a rugby or soccer game, a time when many winning tries and goals are scored. Ignore it and we miss the opportunity of putting the final full stop beneath the assassinations of the ancient world.

Right or wrong, I have taken the Dark Ages as the period in time between the fall of Rome in 476 and the year 1000. Fixing dates is a potential minefield but for the sake of brevity and clarity it sometimes has to be done.

Weird and Dangerous Papal Deaths

The growth of Christianity was never likely to be a straightforward or gentle process. In fact it took place over a time of great turmoil with violence not confined simply to the secular world.

It has been estimated that approximately twenty-five Popes met their deaths in unnatural circumstances during this period. Arguably that death toll began with St Peter, the rock on which Christ intended that his church should be built.

Peter's crucifixion in 64 CE, upside down to increase the pain and duration of suffering – his choice, not the Romans - was linked to the supposed Christian involvement in the Great Fire of Rome. Having fled Rome, Peter decided to return and let events take their course as, in his mind, God had intended. His death is, therefore, regarded as martyrdom rather than outright assassination.

Several other Popes, beginning with Pontian in 235, were martyred for their beliefs. One of the most unusual was St Clement I who, in 99 CE, went to his death tied firmly to an anchor and then hurled into the sea.

Others like St Marcellus were lucky. He was simply banished by the Emperor Maxentius in January 309. Another 'lucky' Pope was John XII who died in 964. He was a notorious womaniser, so much so that during his time as Pope, the Papal Palace was described as The Brothel. He managed to avoid the assassins blade, however, dying a relatively peaceful death.

John II was Pope from July 561 until 574. He found himself faced by the Lombard invasion of northern Italy with Rome regularly enduring siege and attack from the invaders. In desperation, John travelled south to Naples to plead with the immensely unpopular Governor Narses, then hiding in the city, asking him to return to the capital and lead the fight against the Lombards.

Narses agreed to return but this was so unpopular with the people that much of the hatred normally directed at him was transferred to Pope John. The rationale was simple. John had asked Narses to return in the first place, without permission from the populace. And that was enough to turn the mobs of Rome against him, despite the constant threat from the Lombards.

The hatred became so great that John was forced to abandon the Papal Palace and take up residence in the Catacombs along the Via Appia two miles outside Rome. He even consecrated Bishops from his hidden quarters.

John died of natural causes on 13th July 574 but he was lucky. If the Roman crowds could have caught him he would have been another Pope to suffer death at the hands of others.

The line between assassination and martyrdom becomes somewhat blurred when dealing with religious figures. People like St Peter or St Clement went willingly enough to their deaths believing that this ending was what had always been intended for them.

Lay victims like Julius Caesar and Philip of Macedon may not have courted death quite so willingly but they knew it was a possibility, an option they would have to face in carrying out their duties. The aims of the assassins were basically the same – to remove opposition figures who held different views and were fuelled by different beliefs.

It is equally difficult to confine religious beliefs and problems to the spiritual world. The Dark Age activities of significant figures like Popes very often merged into the world of political wheeling and dealing. They held powerful and influential positions, something which meant that they were vulnerable to attack from secular sources, not for their religious beliefs but for purely political issues.

Pope Benedict VI, for example, was assassinated in 974, having been Bishop of Rome for just over a year.

Unpopular with the people who felt that he had been imposed on them by the Holy Roman Emperor, he was also hated by many of Rome's nobility, particularly the powerful Crescenti family. In their eyes he was nothing more than a puppet of Otto I, the newly appointed Holy Roman Emperor.

Grumbling and moaning soon changed to action when the death of Otto, shortly after Benedict was made Pope, gave the nobles the opportunity they were desperately looking for.

In the vacuum between Otto I's death and the succession of Otto II there was a fair degree of confusion. It was the perfect time to strike. Benedict was apprehended and taken as a prisoner to Castel Saint Angelo. There he was strangled by a priest named Stephen. There was not a religious motive or reason behind his death, not in any shape or form, but it was a crucial step in the political manoeuvring of the time.

Following Benedict's death, his body was stripped and dragged through Rome. When the corpse was eventually abandoned it lay in the street where it was trampled on by the crowd and stabbed many times by spears and lances. The Crescenti's quickly appointed their nominee as the new Pope, shouldering the Holy Roman Empire out of the picture.[1]

John XIII is now acknowledged as the first Pope to suffer death by assassination as opposed to martyrdom, dying on 16th December 882. He had been in office for ten years. A very able man, he was elected Bishop of Rome and Ruler of the Papal States in 872 and spent most of his time in office as Pope trying to halt the advance of various Muslim powers in their march on Rome and down the spine of Italy.

He strengthened the defences of the capital but failed to make peace with the Franks and Byzantines. Similarly, he could not bring the Carolingians into an alliance with him against the incomers and, annoyingly, failed to prevent regular Saracen raids.

Forced to pay for the defence of Rome out of Papal funds, Pope John's activities exhausted the Treasury and caused the Papal delegates and officers to consider ridding themselves of a man in whom they had lost confidence.

One of John's relatives was persuaded to slip him poison in his drink but the process was too slow. Illness and an upset stomach were all it produced. It meant that more drastic action was needed and Pope John was then clubbed to death by his own clerics.

The final years of the Dark Ages was a period of numerous Papal assassinations. The killing of so many Popes reflected the political uncertainty of Europe, particularly of Italy, at this time. In many cases the victims seem to have brought disaster on themselves. The demise of Stephen VI is a classic case in point.

In January 897 Stephen, after being Pope for less than a year, ordered the exhumation of the body of his predecessor Formosus in order to put his remains on trial. This disturbing procedure was against all the beliefs and principles of most supporters of the church but Stephen carried on regardless of what was clear dissent from the people of Rome.

Known as the Cadaver Synod or the Cadaver Trial, the whole affair caused considerable disquiet amongst the Romans who watched the proceedings with brooding malice and growing anger.

Accused, amongst other things, of perjury, illegally ascending to the Papacy and presiding over several diocese at the same time, Formosus was found guilty. His body was stripped of its vestments and three fingers of his right hand – which he had used to give blessings – were cut off. His body was then buried in the graveyard designed for foreigners but was soon dug up again and thrown into the Tiber.

Disquiet turned to vicious anger, particularly when the broken body of Formosus washed up on the river bank. Riots broke out and Stephen was promptly deposed as Pope.

The ex-Pope was incarcerated in prison where he rotted away for several months. Eventually he was strangled to death. Yet another Pope whose death was politically motivated rather than theological.

It remains hard to know if the Papal deaths and bizarre behaviour around their demise hindered or helped in the growth of Christianity.

In most cases the deaths of the Popes showed discipline and belief in the Christian concepts. The victims would hardly have seen it that way but, ultimately, their assassinations and misguided treatment probably did help the Christian religion to grow and develop.

Discontent and disorder were not just reserved for the Christian world. The Muslim states did not escape repeated outbreaks of assassination during these years, either.

Three successive Rashidun caliphs – Umar, Uthman ibn Affan and Ali ibn Abi Talib – all met their deaths at the hands of assassins, one after the other in regular succession. No fewer than seven Persian kings of the Achaemenid Dynasty had been assassinated in the one hundred and eighty years between 550 BCE and 370 BCE. Clearly assassination knew no bounds or limits.

Charlemagne, Holy Roman Emperor

Charlemagne ruled as King of the Franks from 768 CE. In addition, he became King of the Lombards in 774 and Holy Roman Emperor in 800. He continued in those roles until his death in 814, the first 'Emperor' to rule western Europe in the three hundred years following the fall of Rome in the fifth century.

The Western Empire had endured considerable upheaval in the years after 476, various Germanic tribes seizing control of northern Italy for most of the sixth and seventh centuries. Then, from the middle of the eighth century came the Carolingians under Charles Martel. They offered a fierce but loose leadership which clearly needed revision and reorganisation. Under Charlemagne that is exactly what they were given.

Coming from the warlike Carolingian Dynasty, Charlemagne was a natural warrior. He greatly expanded his first kingdom which, within a few years, had grown to include territories like modern day France, northern Italy, Germany and the Low Countries.

His time as a monarch was a time of almost continual warfare. That was understandable given the decline and death of Rome's Western Empire. Already King of the Franks and of the Lombards – the very people who had been battling for years against Rome – on Christmas Day 800 Charlemagne was crowned as Holy Roman Emperor.

Three years earlier Constantine V, the Emperor of the Eastern Roman Empire, had been removed from the throne by his mother who declared that she would now rule in his place. The Latin Church only recognised male emperors and so a search was begun to find the most appropriate man to become Emperor of Christendom. Charlemagne was quickly identified as the most natural candidate.

He was duly crowned Holy Roman Emperor by Pope Leo, although the title was not used until the thirteenth century. During his lifetime Charlemagne's domains were referred to as the Roman Empire or the Christian Empire. Whatever it might have been called, from 962 until the twelfth century the Empire created by Charlemagne was the strongest monarchy in Europe.

After Charlemagne's death in 814 the Empire was involved with considerable in-fighting and trying to work with the Byzantine Empire of the East. The title Holy Roman Emperor lapsed in 924 before being revived in 962 when Otto I was crowned.

From that point onwards the Holy Roman Empire continued to be a force to be reckoned with, only finally being dissolved in 1806 during the Napoleonic Wars.

Aethelbald of Mercia

Aethelbald was a nobleman of Mercia in Britain. He was assassinated in 747, having risen to be king of the region or territory of Mercia. In doing so he brought Mercia back to its previous position of supreme power in the post-Roman land of Britannia.

More importantly, it was during his reign as King of Mercia that people began referring to themselves as English. The term originated with Aethelbald who called himself King of the Gens Anglorum – the name Anglorum being adopted instead of the previously used names of Saxons and Angles.

His life was dramatic, filled with success and failure. Originally forced out of Mercia by Ceolred, a rival cousin, Aethelbald eventually succeeded Ceolred and returned to Mercia.

On his return, he immediately began a policy of 'take over,' conquering significant parts of Wessex, and modern day Berkshire. By 730 CE he had become so powerful that he was ruling all of England south of the Humber.[2]

Although claiming to be a Christian, Aethelbald was not a great supporter of the church. Despite influencing and being involved in the selection of at least three Archbishops of Canterbury, he constantly used church funds for his own purposes. He ravaged his way across England and in the year 740 burned York and its cathedral along with much of present-day Northumberland.

So great were his abuses that Aethelbald eventually received a letter from Bishop, later Saint, Boniface, supported by seven other Bishops, warning him that he should change his behaviour before it was too late.

In particular Boniface was referring to Aethelbald's regular theft of church funds, his practice of imposing forced labour on members of the clergy and his regular fornicating with nuns. The message was simple. Stop now or else a terrible death awaits you.

Aethelbald, of course, ignored the rebuke. But a terrible death was exactly what did await him. According to the Venerable Bede, in 747 at Seckington in Warwickshire he was surprised at night and assassinated by his supposedly loyal bodyguards.[3]

Bede does not give a reason for the killing of Aethelbald, an omission which might just indicate that the church, somehow, was involved in the assassination. It remains supposition.

There appears to be some evidence that Aethelbald was beginning to change his ways in the last year of his life. He presided over a Council which condemned the more outlandish behaviour of the clergy and insisted there should be 'distance' between the clergy and the laity. Perhaps the warnings of Boniface had hit home after all?

Saint Boniface

Regarded now as one of the men who established and developed the Latin Church in Europe, Boniface was born in 675 CE. During his lifetime he established many churches and monasteries across England and consolidated the Christian faith in Germany.

He left England for the continent in 716, feeling that this was where he was most needed. He was appointed Bishop of Mainz by Emperor Gregory III and thereafter spent the rest of his life working in Europe. He is renowned for chopping down the Donar Oak, a landmark and symbol for the Germanic people. A fierce wind blew in across the fallen tree but

Boniface was unharmed and the pagans immediately threw themselves on his mercy.

In 754 CE Boniface decided that he would attempt to convert the pagan Frisians. It was a dangerous and, as it turned out, fatal move. Boniface, along with 52 others, was killed by a mob of pagans who had no desire to convert to Christianity.

Wenceslas – Duke of Bohemia, Posthumous King of Bohemia, Christmas Carol Hero

The name Wenceslas will be forever associated with the famous Christmas Carol *Good King Wenceslas*. Part fable, part Christian ideology, the story we are given in the carol is really a long way from the truth. Never a king in his lifetime, Wenceslas was posthumously declared monarch after his death. That death came in 935 when he was assassinated by a group of Bohemian nobles.

Wenceslas came from a family and a country that were well used to the art of assassination, much of it designed and carried out by family members on other family members. Most often these were individuals who were interested in power and good living rather than in family ties.

His grandmother Ludmila of Bohemia was the victim of just such an assassination plot, organised and directed by her daughter Drahomira, the mother of Wenceslas.

Drahomira had become hugely jealous of Ludmila, her position and power, and, in particular, of the influence she exerted over her son Wenceslas.

Drahomira employed two noblemen, Tunna and Gorama, to murder her mother. On 15th September 921 they apparently killed Ludmila by strangling her with her own veil. After her death Ludmila was canonised and venerated as the Patroness of Bohemia.

Drahomira hoped to benefit in several ways from her mother's death. She came from a peasant family of pagan stock, albeit supposedly converted into Christianity. It was a belief that was barely skin deep and, with Ludmila dead, she immediately embraced her paganism again. She also began to eliminate Christianity from Bohemia.

Ludmila and her husband Borivoj had been the first Christian nobles of the country, so the Christian faith was not yet deeply ingrained and Drahomira took advantage of that, hoping to make an easy and painless return to paganism. She assumed the title of Regent and ruled briefly before being overthrown by Christian nobles and exiled.

Wenceslas took control of the Bohemian government after his mother's departure, bringing in German priests to help advance the Christian faith. Not every member of the Bohemian nobility was supportive of his actions and policies, however.

Boleslav, younger brother of Wenceslas, was one of the disgruntled nobles. He gathered together a group of like-minded individuals and, working silently together, they drew up a plan to assassinate the Duke.

Boleslav invited his brother to a feast celebrating St Cosmas and Damian. There Wenceslas was attacked and knifed by Boleslav's three companions, noblemen by the names of Tira, Cesta and Hnevsa. As he fell to the floor Wenceslas was run through with a lance, wielded by Boleslav.

Almost as soon as he died a cult grew up around Wenceslas, particularly in England and Bohemia. Holy Roman Emperor Otto I conferred the title of King upon him but the famous Christmas Carol, with lyrics by Czech poet Valais Alois Svoboda, did not appear until 1853. It remains the lasting tribute for the man who had now become Good King Wenceslas.

Edmund, King of the English

Edmund, grandson of Alfred the Great, ruled as King of England from 939 until his death on 26th May 946. He was killed while he was attending a St Augustine's Day Mass in the church at Pucklechurch in Gloucestershire. The post-conquest chronicler John of Worcester recorded his death briefly and succinctly:

> 'While the glorious Edmund, King of the English, was at the royal township called Pucklechurch in England, in seeking to rescue his steward from Leofa, a most wicked thief, least he be killed, was himself killed by the same man on the Feast of St Augustine.'[4]

The fracas between Edmund's servant and the outlaw seems a reasonable enough story. The uninvited Leofa was, perhaps, after a free drink and food and the steward was possibly trying to get the unwelcome guest out of the room.

When Edmund decided to intervene, he grabbed Leofa by the hair, pulling him backwards. That dragged the outlaw away from the steward but left the King's belly and chest wide open. For a warrior like Edmund it was a foolish mistake.

One blow with Leofa's knife and Edmund was dead before he hit the floor. On the face of it, a brawl, not an assassination. Or was it?

The outlaw Leofa was certainly in the crowd during the Mass and then appeared in the King's hunting lodge where the royal family had gone to relax and dine after the service. Wine and ale flowed copiously, a fact which might reinforce the idea of the outlaw looking for refreshment.

Leofa had no right or business to be in the hunting lodge or, for that matter, in the church. He had been recently convicted of various crimes and in consequence of this he had been sentenced and sent away from England to suffer six years of exile.

Leofa had, so the original story went, decided to return. No reason was given but if the man was of dubious and aggressive character then he might have made his decision to return to England. That alone seems highly unlikely and it is now believed that Leofa had been directly employed or brought back in order to kill the King:

> 'Characterisation of Edmund's killer as a thief was fabricated by later chroniclers to counter rumours that the King had been the victim of a political assassination.'[5]

If it was assassination there are several questions to be asked. The most important is who paid Leofa to carry out the killing. That remains unknown but there are several candidates.

The first, and perhaps most likely one, is Eadred, Edmund's brother, who was clearly jealous of Edmund's standing. The King's achievements fighting against the Vikings, along with expelling them from York, would have pleased the populace in general but not necessarily all members of the court. A jealous brother would have been a dangerous weapon.

It may not have been just the glory that Eadred resented. Edmund had spent long periods away fighting in the north, leaving Eadred to take care of things at home. So, angry and bitter? Possibly.

In the wake of Edmund's death Eadred ruled the country as Regent until the oldest of Edmund's sons came of age in 955. For Eadred, whether or not he had planned it, the assassination had certainly proved its worth.

Then there were the Vikings. They had ruled England, either portions of the country or all of it, for many years. Edmund, for good or bad, changed that.

Edmund's recent wars had set the borders of Wessex at Watling Street, the Viking influence remaining in the north. Watling Street was not too far from Pucklechurch and what you cannot achieve in battle might well be obtained with the old tradition of assassination.

Another possible cause was that Edmund's marriage to Aelfigu, at least in the eyes of the religious faction, was not strictly legal. As a result there were already concerns being expressed about the rights of their two sons to succeed to the throne.

Edgar and Eadwig, the sons, were too young to have planned such a killing but some unknown noble or cleric might have decided to rid the country of such an irreligious figure as Edmund.

The tenth century had seen a monastical revival in the country, making it possible that the motive behind the killing was religious rather than secular. And then, with concerns about the right of Edgar and Eadwig to succeed to the throne, brother Eadred comes into the picture once again.

The one person who might have been prevailed upon to declare the truth was Leofa. Unfortunately, he was dead, literally ripped to pieces by the furious crowd and was not able to give any account of why he had assassinated the King.

Chapter Fifteen

Mass Assassination

Mass assassination in the ancient world was not exactly common but it did occur, probably more often than we think. It was all too easy to disguise the killing of hundreds, maybe even thousands, of victims as the result of a battle or an act of war so that many examples have probably slipped by without undue notice.

Unlike the assassination of individuals, mass executions were invariably carried out by soldiers or officers of the government. The General or the Emperor gave the order, the rank and file carried out the execution. Simple but effective.

Now, with distance, it is sometimes difficult to separate fact from fiction. The enormity of the mass assassinations has proved to be a magnet for writers and artists, ancient and modern alike. But, as with many oft-told stories, facts have often been changed according to the need of the artist and the purpose behind the creation

It is not often remarked upon but the Bible is full of mass assassinations. Moses, for example, massacred all those who worshipped the golden calf and then went on to deal with King Og and the Bashan. Those episodes are rarely written or spoken about, just like Moses's extermination of the Midianites.

Like most Biblical tales we are left wondering what is fact, what is fiction, and there are many more stories that are referenced by a variety of sources. So, for the moment, we will leave Moses out of the picture.

However, the massacre of innocent children by King Herod the Great is one Biblical example that probably has a basis of truth but which has been extended and magnified many times.

The Massacre of the Innocents

The account of King Herod's massacre of the children of Bethlehem has become an essential element in the Nativity story. It is both chilling and heart-rending.

Herod learns from a prophesy that a new king has been born somewhere in his kingdom. A new king? What sort of new king? Where does he lie, what is his purpose? But he is the King of Judea, he tells himself, there can be no other while he is alive. Can there?

With the prophesy ringing and rolling around in his brain, an angry King Herod finds himself clutching at straws. He has placed his trust in three wandering Magi who have come to his palace. He wines them and dines them and sends them off with the request that they will return with evidence of the new king's birth and, more importantly, his location. He will then, Herod declares, travel to the place of birth in order to worship the new monarch.

The Magi, also searching for the newly born baby, are warned in a dream of Herod's real intentions – put simply, to kill the baby. They decide on taking another way home, missing Herod's palace altogether. That leaves an obsessed and increasingly psychotic Herod to fume and fret. This new king might be a challenge to his position, might raise an army when he grows up, might. … It is all too much to consider. There is only one thing to do.

In order to 'make assurance double sure' Herod orders his soldiers to kill all of the male children in Bethlehem and its immediate surroundings. A degree of realism creeps into the tale when he limits the assassinations to children under the age of two. Anyone older than two is outside the range and distance of the prophesy.

The story is told in the Bible, *Matthew, chapter two, verses 16 to 18*: - 'He [Herod] was furious, and he gave orders to kill all the boys in Bethlehem.'[1]

Most Biblical scholars have now dismissed the story of the Massacre of the Innocents as a myth or legend. For many years, however, it was an accepted fact that the massacre had taken place. And the assassination of the children was not just recorded in the Christian Bible.

The Greek liturgy tells of 14,000 Holy Innocents being put to the sword while the Syrian List of Saints records the number as 64,000. Coptic sources tell of a massive 144,000 victims and even gives the date of the massacre as 29th December.

However, *The Catholic Encyclopaedia* was clear that Bethlehem and its environs were too small to provide such massive numbers and reduced the figure to between 6 and 26 in the town, 12 or so from the surrounding area. The figure has now been taken as a much more realistic total, remaining as a Biblical example of mass assassination.[2]

Regardless of numbers, large or small, the massacre has become a record of innocent martyrs for the Christian church. It has retained the ability to terrify, transcending the barriers of country and time, particularly in the field of art. The massacre has featured on many paintings, notably by the Bruegels, Elder and Younger alike, who transferred the scene of the massacre to their native Flemish homelands:

> 'Bruegel has set the biblical story in his own time and country. Soldiers are forcing their way into the houses of a snowbound village, tearing the children from the arms of their mothers – wintry stillness on the one hand, murder and manslaughter on the other.'[3]

It is that frightening picture of brutality and heart-break amidst the cold of northern Europe that has kept the story of the Massacre of the Innocents at the forefront of people's imaginations. It is one that has reappeared several times, artists using the Biblical story to make significant comments about injustices in their own time.

The *Book of Exodus* told of a similar attempt by the Egyptian Pharaoh to kill the children of Israel. Moses – appearing again - is warned of the killings in a dream. He leads the Israelites to safety. Sound familiar? Fact or fiction, such massacres provided artists and writers with material strong enough to survive the passage of time.

The Sack of Carthage

The Roman sacking of the city of Carthage on the northern coast of Africa was the signature event of the Third Punic War between Carthage and Rome. The three wars, fought between the two major trading powers of the Mediterranean, are most famous for the story of Hannibal leading his elephants across the Alps, However, the Third Punic War, fought between 149 and 146 BCE, was the most lethal and most tragic conflict of them all.

In 149 BCE a Roman army landed at Utica and soon appeared outside the walls of Carthage, demanding that the city should surrender. The Carthaginians refused. They would give up hostages and even pay tribute money but they would not surrender.

As the Romans prepared their besieging equipment, the men of Carthage strengthened the city walls and their fortifications. The siege of Carthage lasted for two years, numerous assaults being beaten back by the defenders.

A middle ranking officer by the name of Scipio Aemilianus had distinguished himself in the various attacks and was eventually promoted to the position of commander of the African forces. Previous commanders had been woefully inadequate and the appointment of Scipio was a decisive move.

Amongst other tactics, Scipio built a large mole in the city harbour in order to prevent blockade runners bringing in supplies. Not long afterwards, the Carthaginian navy was defeated. Now, only the city remained.

When the final assault was made in the Spring of 146 BCE, somewhere between 400,000 and 500,000 people were sheltering in the city. Most of these were not soldiers, just ordinary citizens of Carthage.

It took Scipio and his men six days to breach the walls, to then push back the defenders and work their way through the residential areas of Carthage, killing indiscriminately and setting fire to buildings as they went. The Carthaginians defended furiously, making the Romans fight and die for every inch of territory.

Once inside the city walls, however, no matter how desperately the defenders might fight, the result was inevitable. At the end of the affair, the entire population of Carthage was dead, apart from 50,000 prisoners taken on the final day. They were sold into slavery

The city was flattened, burned to the ground, its people deliberately killed in one of the largest mass assassinations in ancient history. The city and the state of Carthage literally disappeared, including 900 Roman deserters who had gone over to the Carthaginians and held out as long as they could. It is believed that somewhere in the region of 400,000 Carthaginian casualties were reported.

Rome made a mighty contribution to the history of the ancient world but the destruction of an entire state – not a takeover, a total destruction – cannot help but show the brutality of their regime. It also indicates the effectiveness of mass assassination.

The Death of the Druids

Rome perpetrated another mass assassination in the year 60 CE. This time it took place in the recently conquered territory of Britain, more specifically on the Isle of Anglesey – the Island of Mona as it was known by the Romans.

Anglesey or Mona was the home of the Druids, almost a last bastion, the final pagan corner of Britain. The Romans had first encountered the Druids in 55 BCE when their rites and practices had filled the so-called civilised Romans with horror.

Druidic worship of pagan gods was just the tip of the iceberg. Dependence on the seasons of the year, worship of nature and of the natural world, were harmless enough. But it was reported that the Druids practiced human sacrifice and that was considered the ultimate horror.

It seems now that the Romans greatly exaggerated the extent of such practices but at the time of the massacre, the Roman soldiers believed implicitly that the Druids regularly put people to death for the benefit of their gods. It frightened the soldiers, an interesting fact given that the Romans' own propensity for brutality, both in the Circus Maximus and in society in general, was so vast.

In 54 CE, almost a hundred years after Rome's first contact with the Druids - the name deriving from the Irish word Doire, meaning 'oak tree' - the Emperor Claudius had declared all Druidic practices to be illegal.

By that time Britain, or Britannicus as the Romans knew it, was in the final throes of being 'Romanised.' Most southern parts of the country had been conquered, apart from isolated outposts like Anglesey. And it was on Anglesey that the last of the Druids had created their sacred home.

Tribes such as the Ordovices, pushed back into the hills by the Legions, continued to conduct regular guerilla attacks on Roman territories and settlements. These became so troublesome that by 60 CE the Provisional Governor of Britain, Suetonius Paulinus, realised that action was needed.

He prepared carefully. Then, sweeping past Chester he and his Legions pushed along the Welsh coast until they came to the Menai Straits.

And there on the far shore, barely two miles away, stood the Druids and wild Ordovice tribesmen. The Roman historian and writer Tacitus, although not present himself, later described the scene:

> 'On the shore stood the forces of the enemy, a dense array of arms and men, with women dashing through the ranks like furies. The Druids pouring forth dire implications with their hands up lifted towards the heavens, struck terror into the soldiers.'[4]

The women, wild haired and bearing lighted torches, were particularly frightening and for a while it seemed as if Suetonius Paulinus and his army had come to the end of the road. It took stern words from the Centurions and dire implications of what would happen if they did not move forward, but eventually the soldiers conquered their fear:

> 'The cavalry swam their horses across the Straits while the infantry made the crossing in small, flat bottomed boats. And when they reached the Anglesey side their blood lust knew no bounds.'[5]

The boats were built by the soldiers themselves, something that must have taken time. However long it took, the Romans managed to put their fears behind them and concentrate on what they would do when they came ashore. What happened was an orgy of destruction. Men, women and children were slaughtered, their bodies then flung into the fires that the Druids themselves had lit.

After the initial massacre Suetonius and his Legions roamed across the island, destroying the sacred oak groves of the Druids, burning their temples and altars, killing anyone they encountered, regardless of who they were.

Only the rising of Boudica of the Iceni people in the eastern provinces brought the slaughter to an end, Suetonius immediately departing for East Anglia and leaving Anglesey to its own devices. It was sixteen years before the Roman Legions under Agricola returned to finish the conquest.

In that time the few remaining Druids had either fled to the hills or taken refuge in Ireland. It was the end of a whole way of life, not just for the tribes but for the Druids themselves. Their power had been broken.

Edward Gibbon in his *Decline and Fall* was clear that this ending was no accident or mere happenstance. It was a deliberate action on behalf of Rome:

> 'Under the specious pretext of abolishing human sacrifice, the emperors Tiberius and Claudius suppressed the dangerous power of the Druids; but the priests themselves, their gods and their altars, subsisted in peaceful obscurity until the final destruction.'[6]

It was an accurate summing up although 'peaceful obscurity' was hardly the way most Romans saw the power and influence of the Druids. The number of Druids killed on the shores of the Menai Straits was never made public but it was yet another example of mass assassination.

The Legend of Masada

The siege and eventual conquest of Masada took place on top of the mountain fortress overlooking the Dead Sea between 72 and 73 BCE. The only primary source concerning the events leading to the fall of the fortress was provided by the writer Flavius Josephus, a Jewish rebel captured by the Romans who went on to become one of Rome's greatest writers. He was also an historian of note.

Originally a fortress and palace built by Herod the Great, Masada was in a magnificent position, seemingly miles from anywhere. Part royal palace, part fortress, Masada spread itself across the top of the mountain with splendid views in all directions.

At first glance the fortress appeared unconquerable. Standing 1500 feet above the desert and the Dead Sea, there was only one way up the mountain, a single track pathway known as the Snake that was too narrow to take two men walking abreast. The flat mountain top was encircled by a high stone wall, complete with watch towers situated at regular intervals around the defensive perimeter.

In 72 BCE Masada was occupied by a group of Jewish extremists called the Sicari, a breakaway sect of the Jewish Zealot faction. Led by Eleazar ben Ya'r, the Sicari – a ruthless murder and outlaw sect – had run rampant through Jerusalem for several years, killing and robbing anyone who did not fit in with their belief of a totally free and independent Judea.

They did not limit their activities to Jerusalem but, according to Flavius Josephus, operated as bandits, raiding farms and villages in the surrounding countryside. Nobody was safe, it seemed. Even the High Priest Jonathan was assassinated by the Sicari as he made his way to the Temple:

> 'It was the most significant public murder yet carried out by the crime family ... This was a time when all of Judea was filled with the effects of their madness.' [7]

Eventually, the Sicari had been expelled from Jerusalem and had moved south to take refuge on Masada. From there they raided local farms and villages, almost at will.

With the war between Rome and the Jews still raging, Lucius Flavius Silva, governor of Judea, assembled a force of 15,000 Legionaries and Auxiliaries to take Masada. At that time the Sicari force inside the fortress consisted of 950 men, women and children.

Preparing himself for a long siege, Flavius Silva built several camps and a large wall around the bottom of the mountain, its purpose being to prevent any of the Sicari escaping. Escape was the last thing on the minds of the defending Sicari soldiers.

The siege ground on, the Romans building a steep assault ramp up the side of Masada, wide enough to take a large siege engine and several ranks of archers. The ramp was completed early in 73 BCE and the siege engine wheeled up its huge length with bowmen loosing off wave after wave of arrows into the fortress

The defensive wall at the top of the mountain was breached on 16th April. There was no reaction from the defenders and for some reason the Romans, rather than pour in through the gap, retired to their camps for the night. The following morning, on the orders of Flavius Silva, they prepared to attack again.

Inside the walls the Romans found, not lines of desperate defenders, but a citadel of death. According to Josephus and Judean legend, the Sicari had drawn lots to decide on ten killers. Each family headman had been given the choice to kill their charges or not. If they chose not to, then The Ten would do it for them. When that was done they would assassinate the rest of the garrison, men, women and children alike. Finally, The Ten would then die themselves. The last man was granted forgiveness for committing the sin of suicide:

> 'The work had to be done. The fathers, blank-eyed, their duty finished, lay down in the blood of their families and put loving arms around the bodies and offered their own necks to those deputed for the work. These knelt to the work, then turned up their own chins.'[8]

The story of the massacre on Masada became an essential part of Israeli history once the new country was established in 1948. It symbolised the determination of the people to never give in, never to allow themselves to become slaves, the motto 'Masada will not fall again' being defiantly presented on walls, on posters and on T Shirts.

And yet, the question remains, did it ever actually happen, at least like the story we are told? Very few bodies were ever found in the fortress, leaving historians and archaeologists bemused.

Three options remain as possible solutions. One, there was a mutually agreed mass suicide; two, the Romans killed the entire garrison; three, the Sicari escaped down the side of the mountain on the last night. Any one of those options could be the answer but the lack of bodies remains a total mystery:

> 'Only a handful of skeletons have ever been found on the mountain; first, a small family group of three in one of the palaces where Josephus says all of the killings took place. Then, a larger party of twenty-five bodies was discovered in a cave on the southern edge of the plateau.'[9]

Modern archaeological digs have failed to come up with an answer. Israeli sources stick defiantly to the suicide story, sceptics sniff and shake their heads. Nobody really knows what happened. Suicide or the killing of over 900 defenders on the mountain, if either of those two options are genuine, the massacre on Masada has to qualify as yet another mass assassination.

Assassination in Thessalonica

The assassination of what was virtually an entire town of some 7000 men, women and children was perpetrated by Roman soldiers in approximately 390 CE. Thessalonica was located in Macedonia, Greece, and by the end of the fourth century was a well-developed Roman city state.

The exact date of the mass assassination is unclear as there were no contemporary reports of the events. We have only fifth century religious or church accounts that tell the story. They are, in part, contradictory and therefore leave the historian unclear as to what is fact and what is fiction. It is generally believed, however, that the massacre did actually take place.

And the story we have been given runs like this. Early in the year a popular local charioteer was arrested and imprisoned for sexual assault. The people objected but Butheric, the garrison commander of Illyricum, which included Thessalonica, refused to change his mind. The man must be punished. Unfortunately for him, the crowd's anger swelled to major proportions. Butheric was apprehended by the mob and promptly lynched.

Protests and minor riots continued for some weeks but in April 390, when most of the population of Thessalonica was gathered in the town Hippodrome, the Roman soldiers were let loose. The result was a blood bath of assassination and murder, men and women, even children, perishing on the swords of the Legionaries.

That year was a bad time for the Roman Empire with food prices high, starvation of the poor common and regular raids from the Germanic tribes bringing uncertainty and fear to the populace. Emperor Theodosius had inherited the situation when he succeeded to the Imperial throne in 379 and, strong individual as he was, took steps to improve the situation. The assassination of nearly 7000 citizens of Rome, however, was not on his original agenda.

Whether Theodosius unleashed his troops on the citizens or the Legionaries simply got out of control is not known but the delay between Butheric's murder and the massacre would seem to show that it was a considered action by those in charge, Theodosius included. He was intent on re-uniting what appeared to be a divided Empire and probably felt that he needed to show a strong hand.

Ambrose, Bishop of Milan and advisor to the Emperor, was not present at the time of the massacre. However, when he heard what had gone on he immediately sent a letter to Theodosius, reproving him for what had occurred.

In his letter, Bishop Ambrose was clear that the Emperor must express his repentance for the massacre. He would be denied the Eucharist until he had done so. Emperor Theodosius, naturally enough, chose to comply.

It was perhaps the first time that the church had shown its authority over the secular leaders of the Empire. And, despite the many deaths in the Hippodrome, that was a significant moment in the history of the Ancient world.

Muhammad and the Massacre of Banu Qurayza

The massacre of Banu Qurayza took place in January 627 CE. It was part of the prophet Muhammad's invasion of territory occupied by the Banu Qurayza people following his victory in the Battle of the Trenches. The Banu Qurayza tribe were of Jewish origin and were once allied to the Muslims. They even loaned the Muslims digging equipment for use in the Battle of the Trenches.

However, the Banu Qurayza refused to take part in the battle as they were unhappy with the treatment of the Jewish people at the hands of Muhammad. As a result the 'treaty' was torn up and Muhammad invaded their territory. The tribesmen retreated into their defensive fort and a siege lasting for twenty-five days was begun.

The siege ended in a Muslim victory and despite pleas for leniency, Muhammad decided that one man from the Banu Aws tribe should pass judgement on the tribe, deciding what punishment was to be meted out. The Banu Aws tribe was one of several Jewish tribes that had become followers of Muhammad and Sa'd ibn Muadh was the chosen man. He had been severely wounded in the recent battle and was probably consumed by pain.

Pain or not, his decision was swift and final. All male members of the tribe, those who had reached puberty, should be executed, their property divided and the women and children sold into slavery.

Muhammad agreed with the decision, declaring that it was God's judgement. Between 600 and 900 members of the Ban Qurayza tribe were duly assassinated. [10]

Charlemagne and the Massacre of Verden

Charlemagne, the first Holy Roman Emperor, followed happily in the footsteps of Suetonius Paulinus and other deadly Roman officials. Except that he went one better. In October 782 he ordered the killing of 4500 Germanic tribesmen, not over any protracted period of time but in one single day!

The reasons for such an event remain a little unclear. There are several options to choose from. Charlemagne's period in power was one of continual warfare and the cause or causes of the mass assassination probably rest somewhere in the mire of the Saxon Wars which flared up intermittently during his reign.

In 782 the Saxon chieftain Widukind managed to persuade a group of warriors who had previously submitted to Charlemagne to change their affinity and rebel against him. They won a great victory over Charlemagne's supporters at the Battle of Suntel and had seemingly freed the Saxon tribes from Frankish overlordship.

The Emperor Charlemagne was not the sort of man to stand for that, however. He rapidly gathered together his army, invaded Saxony and demolished Widukind's forces. The campaign was arduous, many of

Charlemagne's friends and colleagues falling either at Suntel or in Charlemagne's follow up campaign.

Revenge for the deaths of these men might well have been behind the assassinations. Charlemagne certainly had the temper to inflict such punishment. But there are other options.

Charlemagne had always compared himself to the Israelite King David and wanted to behave like him in the Biblical stories. He was a fierce proponent of the Christian faith and while he might respect pagan traditions, he saw his Empire as a successor to the glory that was Rome – with him at the head. Punishment for the treachery of Widukind and his followers was inevitable.

Charlemagne ordered all of the Saxon tribes to gather at Verden in Lower Saxony, at the junction of the Aller and the Weser Rivers. Once the Saxons were before him, Charlemagne issued an order. The Saxons could convert to Christianity or they would be assassinated.

Nearly 4500 took the assassination route, being beheaded by the Frankish warriors. Widukind was not amongst the victims as he had earlier fled to join the Northmen.

The executions were brutal. Prisoners, helpless and terrified, were laid out on the ground and asked if they would convert to Christianity. Those who refused were beheaded there and then. It was estimated that two out of every three Saxons were assassinated.

The mass assassination was something of a stain on the reputation of Charlemagne, a man who prided himself on his honour and ability to hear all sides of an argument. This was cold blooded murder, in the tradition of the original Roman Emperors.

In the late nineteenth and early twentieth centuries the mass assassination of the Saxon tribesmen at Verden became something of a talisman for the German nationalists. Charlemagne was reframed as an enemy of traditional German culture.

When the Nazi Party came to power in 1933 Adolph Hitler ordered the building of a memorial on the site of the assassinations at Verden in order to commemorate the victims. Known as the Sachsen Hain Memorial it was completed in 1935, a total of 4500 standing stones being erected on the site.

Chinese Mass Assassinations

The Chinese were well versed in the art of assassination, numerous mass assassinations taking place in China during the ancient period. They helped formulate the western world notion that China was a barbaric and dangerous environment in which to live.

There is the additional fact that, for their part, the Chinese held the opposite view, regarding westerners as barbarians, a people not to be trusted. Put those two together and the recipe for disaster is clearly seen.

The most significant of the assassinations are shown below. There is no doubt that they took place but the figures and number of deaths reported have to be questioned.

The Yongjia Massacre took place in 311 CE during the Jin Dynasty when the forces of Xiong captured and then sacked the city of Luoyang. They went on to put the inhabitants of the city to the sword, a reported figure of 30,000 civilians supposedly meeting their deaths in what was clearly a mass assassination. Included in the casualties was the Jin Crown Prince.

The Jie Genocide took place in northern China between 350 and 352 CE. The victims – 200,000 of them according to the records – were mostly merchants and other 'barbarians' as the Chinese dubbed them.

The killings took place over a two year period, hence the epithet genocide rather than assassination. Given the length of time that the killings took place, the figure of 200,00 is not an unlikely total. Why the traders and merchants did not simply run for their lives remains a mystery.

Another massacre of traders and merchants, the Yangzhou Merchants Massacre, occurred in 760 CE. The merchants were mostly Arabs and Persians but no numbers are available. Given the propensity of the various Chinese groups to target merchants, it remains astounding that people still came east to trade. The power of gold and the desire to 'make it rich' clearly knew no bounds.

The Massacre of the Uyghur Manicheans is one of the few mass assassinations in ancient China to be fixed to an exact date, in this case 13th February 843. The death toll is both frightening and accurate.

General Shi Xiong of the Tang Dynasty slaughtered 10,000 Uyghur Manicheans and then went on to lead what is known as the Hucheng Persecution. A number of other, smaller massacres took place during this persecution.[5]

Mass assassination knows no rules or regulations. However, it is generally a premeditated and deliberate act by a significant number of people. The name 'mass assassination' tells you that the victims are also present in considerable numbers.

Similar in many respects to single-person assassination, killing en masse is different in one major respect. Prompted by issues such as political and military grievances or ambitions, mass assassinations knowingly destroy the innocent as well as the guilty.

The assassins 'take out' the disinterested as well as the main players. People suffer, many of them simply because they have been found in the wrong place at the wrong moment in time.

Lack of conscience or the need to achieve maximum discord tends to overrule issues of right and wrong as far as mass assassinations are concerned. Personal gain rarely comes into the picture. That is reserved for the organisers, the powers that lurk behind the sword or lance.

The actual assassins are usually comprised of groups of subservient soldiers or assistants who are merely doing their job – an old cliché that, admittedly, did not help the Nazi defendants at Nuremburg. Yet they are obeying orders and in the ancient world that was something which was an essential requirement for any soldier.

In the twentieth century the US Congress defined mass murder or mass assassination as the killing of three or more people in one event. Compared to some of the mass murders of the ancient world, that figure of three appears amazingly low but one death is still one death too many. It puts the ancient mas assassinations into some sort of perspective.

Significantly, the US Congress decided, there was no 'cooling off' period in instances of mass assassination, no fallow periods as you would usually find with serial killers who might leave days or even weeks between one murder and the next.

Mass assassination, except in cases like the Jie Genocide in Ancient China which covered several years, tend to conform to that American definition. The killing spree, particularly in the ancient world, was usually over in a few hours,

What is true now, in modern society, was equally as true and as relevant in the ancient world. For mass assassination to be successful, the requirements were simple. A single location, a short period of time, a swift and sudden death – then on to the next problem.

Chapter Sixteen

A Conclusion (of sorts)

The assassinations referred to in this book are just the tip of the iceberg. There were dozens more, hundreds probably, all of which deserve identification and investigation. Not yet, not here. At some stage in the future, perhaps?

All of the assassinations included in this book had a dramatic effect on the history of the ancient world, sometimes directly, sometimes after a further chain of events. The assassination of Julius Caesar is a classic example, an event that led to civil war and several false starts but eventually resulted in the creation of the Roman Empire.

Organised and carried out by Marcus Brutus and numerous others with the intention of preventing single person rule in Rome, the assassination eventually led to exactly what the Republicans did not want, single person rule and the destruction of the Republic that was so important to Brutus and his colleagues.

The killing of over 4000 Germanic and Saxon tribesmen by the forces of Holy Roman Emperor Charlemagne in the year 782 might have been an act of revenge but it was also instrumental in establishing the Holy Roman Empire as the most powerful kingdom in, first, the Ancient World and then the Dark Ages. It was an Empire that, give or take a few hiccups, lasted until the beginning of the nineteenth century.

And so on. The instigators of the various assassinations rarely had such long term aims and ambitions in mind. But that remains one of the fascinating aspects of assassination as a process.

Without trying to be too fey or bizarre, some of the assassinations included here are intriguing. Phalaris, roasted inside his own brass bull and Bagoas, forced to drink his own poison, are just two of the more unusual deaths. Then there are examples that simply have no motive, no rationale – Amenemhat who was killed in bed by his palace guards, no reason given, then or now. There are so many more in what has become a fascinating slice of history.

A Conclusion (of sorts)

Assassins earned praise and criticism, according to their motives. In the play *Julius Caesar* Shakespeare makes Mark Antony clearly express himself about the motives of Cassius and most of the other conspirators in the assassination plot. To Antony they were filled with jealousy and envy. For Brutus, however, he has only praise:

> 'Nature might stand up
> And say to all the world
> This was a man!'[1]

Where assassins can be identified, the perpetrators rarely went on to live full, active and successful lives. The list of hapless killers is vast, from the executioners of Tiye and Pentawere in Egypt to Emperor Philip of Macedonia and Phalaris of the old Persian Empire. There is no point listing them all, just read the book and see for yourselves.

Notes/References

Introduction

1. General Sun Tzu '*The Art of War*,' translated by Lionel Giles.
2. Birnbaum, Aiton '*Political Assassination in Biblical Israel*,' article in 'Semantics Scholar,' Page 191

Chapter One

1. https://enwikipedia.org/wiki.History-of-assassination
2. https://listverse.com/2018/09/06-notable-poisonings-from-the-ancient-world
3. Masters, John '*The Deceivers*,' Page 16
4. Carradice, Phil '*Masada*,' Pen and Sword, Page 30-33
5. Ibid, listverse.com/2018/09/06/10
6. Campbell, Colin '*Poisons in Ancient History*,' article in 'The Collector'
7. Shakespeare '*Julius Caesar*,' Act III, Scene II
8. Ibid
9. Gibbon, Edward '*Selections from Decline and Fall of the Roman Empire*,' Page 105
10. Baker, Kenneth '*On Assassination*,' Unicorn, Page 8-9

Chapter Two

1. Withington, John '*Assassins Feeds*,' Reaktion Books, Page 13
2. Ibid, Page 14
3. www.//en.wikipedia/org/wiki/Userkare
4. Bryce, Trevor quoted in https://en.wikipedia.org/Sea-Peoples
5. Withington, John, Ibid, Page 14

Chapter Three

1. Byron, Lord George Gordon *'The Destruction of Sennacherib,'* Cassell Anthology, Page 243
2. Cowley, Robert (editor) *'What If,'* Page 17-18
3. https://ancient-origins-net.historic.assassinations

Chapter Four

1. https://en.wikipedia.org/wiki/Emperor-Anko
2. https://www.sciencenews.org/article/massacre-sacred-ridge
3. https://en.wikipedia.org/wiki/The-Emperor-and-the- assassin

Chapter Five

1. Cowley, Ibid *'What If,'* Page 49
2. https://www.bing.com/philip-of-macedon
3. Article by Sara Pruitt *'Death of Alexander the Great,'* on https://www.history.com/news
4. Quoted in https://simple-to-remember-Aristotle

Chapter Six

1. Lewis, Bernard *'The Assassins,'* Folio, Page 134
2. Carradice, Phil (adaptor) *'The Ottomans,'* Osmanli Press, Page 24-25
3. Book of Judges, Chapter Five, Verse 20
4. Ibid, Verses 28-30

Chapter Seven

1. Jewish Bible Quarterly, Vol 13, No 3, Page 193-194
2. Book of Kings, I, verses 12-18
3. Ibid, Jewish Bible Quarterly, Page 194
4. Book of Judges, Chapter 3, Verses 12-30
5. Book of Chronicles, Chapter 2, Verse 18
6. https://www.bing.com//search?q-Joash
7. Ibid, Cowley *'What If,'* Page 105
8. Book of Samuel 2, Verses 8-10

9. Ibid, Verses 15-17
10. Dryden, John *'Absalom and Achitophel,'* Page 1
11. Book of Samuel, 2, Verses 18-33

Chapter Eight

1. Book of Judges, Chapter 9, Verses 53-54
2. sbwatkinseditor@gmail.com

Chapter Nine

1. Article by Tom Holland *'Peace at the Point of a Sword,'* in BBC History Magazine, Aug 2023
2. Edward Gibbon, Ibid, Page 25-26
3. Withington, John, Ibid, Page 35
4. Shakespeare, *'Julius Caesar,'* Ibid, Act I, Scene II

Chapter Ten

1. https://www.bing.com/search?q-cleopatra
2. Shakespeare *'Antony and Cleopatra,'* Act 1V, Scene XIV
3. Baer, Robert *'A Perfect Kill,'* W&N, Page XXI
4. Carey, John (editor) *'The Faber Book of Reportage,'* Page 10-11
5. Plato *'Phaedo,'* Translated by HN Fowler, pub by Loeb, New York
6. Cicero, quoted in https://wikipedia/writings-of-Cicero
7. Ibid
8. https://www.natulgeographic.co.uk/history-and-civilisation
9. AE Houseman *'A Shropshire Lad'*

Chapter Eleven

1. https://www.bing.com/search?q/tiberius+gracchus+death
2. Quoted in https://wikipedia.org/wiki/Tiberius
3. Tacitus *'Annals,'* Book 6, Page 50
4. Ibid
5. Withington, John, Ibid, Page53
6. Cassius Dio *'Roman History'* LV III, Page 5
7. Suetonius *'The Lives of Twelve Caesars: The Life of Caligula'*

Notes/References

Chapter Twelve

1. https://en.wikipedia.org/wiki/Caligula
2. Tacitus *'The Annals of Imperial Rome,'* translated by Cynthia Damon, Penguin
3. Tacitus, Ibid, *'The Murder of Agrippina the Younger.'* Book 14, Page V

Chapter Thirteen

1. Patrick Ryes, Review in *'Bryn Mawr Classical Review,'* 2001
2. CW Previte-Orton *'The Shorter Cambridge Medieval History,'* Cambridge University Press, Page 203

Chapter Fourteen

1. https://www.britannica/biography/Benedict-V1
2. The Venerable Bede, *'Ecclesiastical History of the English People,'* Page 324
3. Ibid, Page 324
4. Quoted in https://en.wikipedia.org/wiki/Edmund-1
5. Ibid

Chapter Fifteen

1. Book of Matthew, Chapter Two, Verses 16-18
2. The Catholic Encyclopaedia, March 1907
3. Hagen, Rose-Marie &Rainer *'Bruegel,'* Taschen, Page 10
4. Tacitus, *'Annals'*, Ibid
5. Carradice. Phil 'BBC Wales History Blog *'Death of the Druids'*
6. Edward Gibbon, Ibid, Page 40
7. Flavius Josephus *'The Jewish War,'* Book 2, Chapter 22
8. Kossoff, David *'The Voices of Masada,* Collins, Page 219
9. Carradice, Phil *'Masada,'* Pen & Sword, Page 98
10. https://en.wikipedia.org/wiki/imvasion-of-Banu/Quayza

Chapter Sixteen – Conclusion

1. Shakespeare *'Julius Caesar,'* Act V

Bibliography

Primary Sources

Bede, the Venerable 'Ecclesiastical History of the English people,' translated by Bertram Colgrave, Judith McClure and Roger Collins, Oxford World's Classics, Oxford, 2008
Cassius Dio 'The History of Rome,' Loeb Classical Library (Harvard University Press)
Joseph, Flavius 'The Jewish War,' (66 to 67 CE), translated by GA Williamson, Penguin, London, 1959
Plato 'Phaedo,' Loeb Classical Library (Harvard University Press)
Suetonius, Gaius 'The Lives of Twelve Caesars,' translated by Robert Graves, Penguin, London, 1957
Sun Tzu, General 'The Art of War,' translated by Peter Harris, Everyman's Library, London, 2018
Tacitus 'Annals,' translated by Cynthia Damon, Penguin, London, 2012

Secondary Sources

Books

Aldhouse-Green, Miranda and Howell, Ray 'Celtic Wales,' University of Wales Press, Cardiff, 2017
Baer, Robert 'The Perfect Kill,' Weidenfeld and Nicolson, London, 2015
Baker, Kenneth 'On Assassinations,' Unicorn, London, 2023
Carradice, Phil 'Masada,' Pen & Sword, Barnsley, 2019
            'The Ottomans,' (as adaptor) Osmanli, Istanbul, 1982
Carey, John (editor) 'The Faber Book of Reportage,' Faber, London, 1987
Dryden, John 'Absalom and Achitophel,' Barnes and Noble, London, 2017

Bibliography

Cowley, Robert (editor) 'What If,' Pan, London, 2001
Gibbon, Edward 'Selections from Decline and Fall of the Roman Empire,' edited by JW Saunders, Harrap & Co, London, 1949
Graves, Robert, 'I, Claudius,' Penguin, London, 1976
Gregory, Donald 'Wales Before 1066,' Gwasg Carreg Gwalch, Llanrwst, 1989
Hagen, Rose-Marie and Rainer 'Bruegel,' Taschen, English Edition, undated
Kafarakis, Kosta 'The Siege of Masada,' Amazon, undated
Kossoff, David 'The Voices of Masada,' Fontana, London, 1973
Lewis, Bernard 'The Assassins,' Folio, London, 2005
Masters, John 'The Deceivers,' Penguin, 1953
 'Night-runners of Bengal,' Penguin, 1951
Previte-Orton, CW. 'The Shorter Cambridge Medieval History,' Cambridge University Press, Cambridge, 1975
Shakespeare, William 'Antony and Cleopatra, Nelson Doubleday, New York, 1968
'Julius Caesar,' Nelson Doubleday, New York, 1968
Spignesi, Stephen 'In the Crosshairs,' Skyhorse Publishing, New York, 2016
Withington, John 'Assassins' Deeds,' Reaktion Books, London, 2020

Poetry

'Cassell's Anthology of English Poetry,' London, 1938
AE Houseman 'A Shropshire Lad'

Magazines/Newspapers

BBC History Magazine, August 2003
History Today, March 2003
The Bryn Mawr Classical Review, 2001
The Catholic Encyclopaedia, March 1907
The Collector, 2019
The Jewish Bible Quarterly, various dates
Semantics Scholar, 2015

Blogs

Phil Carradice 'BBC Wales History Blogs,' various dates, 2010 to 2013

Biblical Books

Chronicles 2
Exodus
Judges
Judith
Kings 1
Samuel 2

Web Sites and Pages

https://en.wikipedia.or/wiki/History-of-assassination
https://listverse.com/2018/09/06-notable-poisonings-from-the-ancient-world
www.en.wikipedia/org/wiki/Userkare
https://en.wikipedia.org/Sea-Peoples
https://en.wikipedia.org/wiki/Emperor-Anka
https://wikipedia.org/wiki/The-Emperor-and-the-Assassin
https://www.bing.com/philip-of-macedonia
https://simple-to-remember-Aristotle
https://en.wikipedia.org/wiki/invasion-of-Banu-Quayza
https://en.wikipedia.org/wiki/Edmund-1
https://www.britannica/biography/Benedict-VI
https://en.wikipedia.org/wiki/Caligula
https://wikipedia.org/eiki/Tiberius
https://www.bing.com/search?q/Tiberius+gracchus+death
https://natulgeographic.co.uk/history-and-civilisation
https://wikipedia/writings-of-Cicero
https://www.bing.comsearch?q-cleopatra
sdwatkinseditor@gmail.com
https://www.bing.com/search?q-Joash
https://www.history.com.news

Index

A
Absalom 2, 85–88
Achithophel 86–87
Alexander the Great 52–57
Amnon 84–85
Aeschylus 40
Art of War, The (book) 44
Augustus, Emperor 13, 14

B
Bagoas 38–39
Berenice III 27–28
Bathsheba 83–84
Brihadratha 42–43
Brutus 3, 100–105

C
Caesar, Julius 96, 99–109
Cain and Able 212, 217
Cassius 105–107, 183
Cicero 114–117
Cleopatra, Queen 109–111
Commodus, Emperor 143–144

D
Darius 111 38–50
David, King 80–83
Deborah 68–70
Delilah 95–96
Diadochi, War of 60–62

E
Eglon, King 78–79
Ehud 78–79

F
Four Emperors, The Year of 141–143

G
Germanicus One and Two 121–123
Guang of Wu 44–45

H
Holofernes, King 92–93

I
Ish-Bosheth 82–83

J
Jabin, King 2, 87
Jael 68–70
Jezebel 89–91
Jing Ke 49–51

L
Li Si 70

M
Mark Antony 11–12, 109–112
Mithridates 66–67

N
Nero, Emperor 136–139, 141–142

O
Octavian (see Augustus)

P
Phalaris 32–37
Philip of Macedon 52–55
Pompey the Great 115–116, 98–102

Q
Qingji, Prince 47–48

R
Ramesses II 21
Ramesses III 21–24

S
Sacred Ridge Massacre 48–49
Samson 95–96

Sennacherib 30–31
Sulla 101–103

T
Thebes, The Band of 2
Teti (Pharoah) 56–57
Thebes 56–57
Tiger Women, The 73

V
Valarian, Emperor 67

X
Xerxes I 33–35, 36
Xerxes II 37–38

Y
Yao Li (assassin) 47–48

Z
Zealots, The 9
Zhuang Zhu 45
Zhu, Empress 70–71